THE
EVERYTHING®
CANNING & PRESERVING BOOK

Dear Reader,

My love affair with preserving began when I tried to come up with new gift ideas for the holidays. Making kitchen baskets with dried herbs, soup bases, and seasoned rubs had been a huge hit, but I wanted to make a greater, more customized variety. I found inspiration in my memories—my mother making freezer jelly and my grandmother canning and drying all manner of things. Ah-ha! I was on to something.

Being a frugal person, the best way to get myself really inspired was to invest in basic equipment. The very first thing I created after shopping was pink grapefruit jelly, and from that point forward our whole family was hooked. The fresh flavors, the ability to decrease waste, the financial savings, and the ease of the process combined to form something perfectly suited to our home—and yours.

I have been a hearthside gourmet for many years, and this book is a dream come true for me. Thank you for sharing in it and sitting at my virtual table for a while. To adapt an old Irish saying a bit, may you always have tea beside the fire, laughter to cheer you, those you love near you, and a full pantry ready to be shared.

Trish Telesco

Welcome to the EVERYTHING® Series!

These handy, accessible books give you all you need to tackle a difficult project, gain a new hobby, comprehend a fascinating topic, prepare for an exam, or even brush up on something you learned back in school but have since forgotten.

You can choose to read an *Everything*® book from cover to cover or just pick out the information you want from our four useful boxes: e-questions, e-facts, e-alerts, and e-ssentials.

We give you everything you need to know on the subject, but throw in a lot of fun stuff along the way, too.

We now have more than 400 *Everything*® books in print, spanning such wide-ranging categories as weddings, pregnancy, cooking, music instruction, foreign language, crafts, pets, New Age, and so much more. When you're done reading them all, you can finally say you know *Everything*®!

E-QUESTION
Answers to common questions

 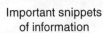

FACTS
Important snippets of information

ALERTS!
Urgent warnings

Quick handy tips

PUBLISHER Karen Cooper

DIRECTOR OF ACQUISITIONS AND INNOVATION Paula Munier

MANAGING EDITOR, EVERYTHING SERIES Lisa Laing

COPY CHIEF Casey Ebert

ACQUISITIONS EDITOR Katie McDonough

ASSOCIATE DEVELOPMENT EDITOR Elizabeth Kassab

EDITORIAL ASSISTANT Hillary Thompson

Visit the entire Everything® series at *www.everything.com*

THE
EVERYTHING®
CANNING &
PRESERVING
BOOK

All you need to know to enjoy
natural, healthy foods year round

Patricia Telesco
with Jeanne P. Maack, Founder of Creative Canning Cuisine

Avon, Massachusetts

*This book is dedicated to Tradition. Whether we carry on our
ancestors' traditions or create new ones of our own, may we all
celebrate, commemorate, and facilitate wonderful culinary moments
worth remembering for many years to come.*

An Everything® Series Book.
Everything® and everything.com® are registered trademarks of F+W Media, Inc.

Published by Adams Media, a division of F+W Media, Inc.
57 Littlefield Street, Avon, MA 02322 U.S.A.
www.adamsmedia.com

ISBN 10: 1-59869-987-3
ISBN 13: 978-1-59869-987-6

Printed in the United States of America.

J I H G F E D C B A

Library of Congress Cataloging-in-Publication Data
is available from the publisher.

*This book is available at quantity discounts for bulk purchases.
For information, please call 1-800-289-0963.*

Contents

Acknowledgments

There are several people to thank for their help with this book. First, my gratitude goes to everyone at Adams Media (and especially Katie) for being so enthusiastic and helpful. Without your ongoing insights there would be no book.

Second, to Jeanne, who trusted a complete stranger with her knowledge and wonderful canning skills. You have been a pleasure to work with from day one.

Next, Dianne and Bobbi, both of whom have come to my rescue when things looked gloomiest and kept me going. Everyone should have friends as thoughtful as you both. I am doubly blessed.

Fourth, I'm very grateful for Food Network personalities like Mario Batali, Alton Brown, Duff Goldman, and Anthony Bourdain, who reinforce several important ideas to viewers. First, the wonder of gourmet cooking need not be lost in a drive-through society. Second, gourmet doesn't have to mean difficult (it really is okay to play with your food). Lastly, truly anyone can learn to make great meals, especially when they cook from the heart.

Finally, my sincere thanks goes to my family, who have sat through all my experiments as taste testers without grumbling. Not everything came out perfect, but we have had great fun getting there, and truly, it's all about the journey.

Introduction

▶ HAVE YOU EVER pried open the lid of a store-bought can of soup, fruit, or vegetables and wished it contained the fresh flavors you wanted? More importantly, wouldn't it be nice to know what's really in your food without needing a dictionary? *The Everything® Canning & Preserving Book* gives you both of these things, without eating up all your free time. By applying the instructions in this book, anyone can create interesting, unique, preserved edibles at home that are spiced just right and created with loving care.

As you might suspect, this is not your run-of-the-mill recipe collection. From gourmet jam flavors and luscious mustards to mouthwatering marinades and pleasing pickles, you're going to find refreshingly creative recipes to add to your repertoire. Perhaps they'll even become new traditions. After entering the world of preserving, families will discover important budgetary advantages and the wonders of a full pantry that appeals to everyone's taste buds. Children will love helping out, and single readers will find that these methods can help with the not-wanting-to-cook-for-one-person blues. Now singles can preserve perfectly sized portions of a favorite creation and take out a single serving whenever the craving strikes.

It's true that the arts of canning and preserving fell out of fashion for a while. After all, the supermarket had nearly anything you wanted at a reasonable cost. Today, things are different. What happened to inspire a renaissance? Many things. There's the move toward getting away from chemically treated food, and organic gardens have sprouted up in many backyards. This book is meant for anyone who wants to know what they put in their mouth is safe. It's also written for the large number of television viewers who have caught the cooking bug from various shows. Perhaps most important, more families are trying to find ways to protect valued histories, including recipes, and the art of preserving is one way of achieving that goal.

Beyond those three reasons, home preserving saves you money and fits in superbly with healthy living choices. With these methods, you can give your family the food they love, prepared the way you like it and neatly personalized for allergies or dietary restrictions! Better still, the endeavor isn't a one-shot deal; you end up with several months worth of stock to enjoy. And you won't be alone in your efforts: Nearly 30 percent of Americans are rediscovering the natural goodness that canning and preserving offer.

If you're wondering whether you have the time or money for another hobby, don't worry. Canning and preserving doesn't require you rework your kitchen to look like a magazine ad, and the cost of the basic components is more than covered by the savings in your grocery budget. It isn't even necessary to gather all the equipment for all preserving methods immediately. Instead, focus on one method and begin watching for bargains.

The Everything® Canning & Preserving Book offers your kitchen tried-and-true methods for canning, freezing, drying, and pickling so you can pick what you like best. Additionally, throughout this book you'll find time-saving hints so you can really enjoy your projects. Food should be fun! Preserving is an alchemical art, and playing with your food is encouraged. While there are some guidelines you need to follow, there's still plenty of room for creativity. With that in mind, this book has one central underlying theme: Food changes life, life changes food, and preserving allows us to remember and celebrate this every day.

Are you ready to give it a try? Let's get cooking!

Chapter 1

Canning and Preserving Fundamentals

Over the last ten years, the preserving bug has hit many an unsuspecting home. People who were once quite content to run to the local twenty-four hour store for canned goods are now making their own. Why? Well, perhaps a friend or family member brought over a luscious homemade jelly, sauce, or soup. The taste was so good, so fresh, and so tantalizing that it inspired someone to try canning or preserving. This chapter offers some background and basic guidelines for setting up your kitchen for canning and preserving at home.

What Is Canning and Preserving?

The basic idea behind preserving is handling and keeping food in such a way that the food maintains quality flavors, textures, and colors while avoiding the spoilage and bacterial growth that cause illness. Throughout history, humankind has been rather creative at discovering ways of doing this. For example, the ancient tribes could use the surface of a frozen lake to keep meat cold. Other methods for preserving include cooking, freezing, salting, drying, pickling, curing, smoking, and placing the food in alcohol or sugar syrup.

Each of the aforementioned approaches provides similar results in terms of avoiding bacteria or mold, but they use far different processes and yield dramatically different products. For example, freezing and drying both cause a reduction in water, which deters spoiling. However, the textural result of freezing versus drying is vastly different. Likewise, heating food kills many organisms, as does soaking food in alcohol. Again, the resulting taste of the food is very dissimilar. In many cases, the choice of preservation method is highly personal, subject to personal tastes. For example, some people may enjoy the ease of dried fruit while others prefer the fresher taste that freezing offers. The only time there really aren't options is when food safety comes into question.

E-QUESTION

How popular has home canning and preserving become?
The Spanish writer Jose Bergamin once said that tradition means we "continue what is worth continuing." It seems people around the world agree that preserving is worth continuing—if you type canning or preserving into your favorite search engine, you'll get more than 20 million results!

Throughout this book, you'll find numerous tips for maintaining your old family recipes in their original forms without giving up any measure of safety. Please read and apply those tips carefully for the best, healthiest results.

The following sections offer a brief overview of the various preserving methods you'll learn about in this book.

Canning

Canning begins with good food and sterile jars. It's very important that the storage containers used in canning are properly cleaned to kill bacteria. Additionally, canning includes hot-water baths (for high-acid items) and pressure-cooking (for low-acid items) to create a vacuum and kill off any lingering, potentially harmful microbes, specifically botulism, which has no odor or taste and is potentially deadly.

Drying

Drying is a very effective way of preserving many foods because it decreases water, therefore thwarting or slowing any unhealthy organism's growth. Drying is best suited to meats, fruits, and grains.

Freezing

Freezing is among the most utilized preserving processes. Items have a very long shelf life when properly packed and wrapped.

E-QUESTION

What causes freezer burn?
Freezer burn is caused by dehydration in foods that aren't properly wrapped and packaged. The food often looks lighter in color and the flavor or texture is likely to have been altered slightly. Experts recommend using vacuum sealing and other moisture-resistant packing methods. You should also eat the items that have been in your freezer the longest first.

Jellying

There are a variety of items that create a jelly-type base for preserving, including fruit pectin, gelatin, and arrowroot flour. After jellying, the resulting food is often canned for increased longevity.

Pickling

Pickling preserves food by the use of brine (a liquid with high salt content) mixed with vinegar, alcohol, or oil. Pickling usually applies heat somewhere along the way so the food accepts the brine until the point of saturation. This also improves flavor! Nearly all vegetables are well suited to pickling.

Salt Curing

Similar to drying, salt draws out the water in meats. Some salt curing processes add sugar for the same effect.

Smoking

Smoking offers a two-fold benefit: It preserves food using heat and smoke, which also gives it extra flavor. Many people who grill enjoy using a variety of wood for smoking to achieve different tastes and aromas. Meat, poultry, and fish are the three most predominantly smoked items. Some nuts are also commonly smoked.

ALERT!

If you're planning on making your jams, jellies, and other preserved products into a sideline business, do your research. You may need a food permit or a totally separate kitchen for preparation to comply with state laws. Check your local ordinances regarding zoning, and don't forget things like state tax permits and insurance.

Sugaring

Most commonly seen in the preservation of fruit, sugar may be combined with water to create syrup or alcohol. Additionally, sugar may be crystallized on a fruit or spice to create a protective coating, as in candied ginger.

A Little History

The minute an animal dies or a vegetable leaves the soil, it begins to decompose. Our ancestors looked to nature for insights into keeping things from spoiling. Nearly every modern idea or method about preserving came from the careful observations of our ancestors. They may never have understood the science behind why some things lasted or why others made them ill, but they paid attention to the big picture and taught what they learned to the next generation. In colder regions, people froze food on the ice. In hot regions, people looked to the sun or fire to dry foods.

Drying: A Time-Honored Method

Drying is perhaps the oldest of all methods. There is evidence ancient peoples dried food as long ago as 12,000 B.C.E., especially in the Middle East. Trade routes would help spread the use of this method along with a healthy bit of folklore, especially regarding dried herbs. By the time of the Roman Empire, buildings were created for drying herbs, fruits, and vegetables. When sun was lacking, fire was used instead.

FACT

The ancient Peruvians had a primitive but effective method for freeze-drying food: They would take their crops high into Machu Picchu and store them there. At that altitude, the air pressure began to vaporize the water, and the cold neatly kept the food frozen.

Fermenting Records

Most historians consider the discovery of fermentation an accidental wonder. There's no question that the art of brewing was known to the ancient Sumerians by around 10,000 B.C.E., more than likely because a bit of bread was left in water too long. The first fermented beverages were venerated as divine in origin, especially after people found that this brew was often healthier than drinking water. Over time, people moved beyond fermenting beverages and began fermenting foods as well. Studies indicate that foods can develop more vitamins as they ferment, creating a healthier end product.

Various cultures buried foods as a type of fermenting method. Examples include eggs in China, shark in Iceland, kimchi in Korea, and rice bran pickles in Japan. Fermenting can take a toxic item like raw cassava root and make it consumable.

Pickling in the Past

Pickling has been popular for at least 4,000 years. Pickles as we know them began in India and Babylon around 2000 B.C.E. and quickly spread to other parts of the world. Once this tasty sensation hit Rome there was no stopping it. Romans even used the brine from pickles for fish sauce because they didn't want to waste it. The first containers for pickling were made of stoneware so the acid content in the brine wouldn't dissolve a less hearty clay pot.

FACT

Many famous people in history were fans of pickles. Cleopatra considered pickles essential for beauty, Caesar and Napoleon both fed them to their troops, and the Roman Emperor Tiberius ate them daily. Christopher Columbus, Queen Elizabeth I, and George Washington were also known to indulge.

The Saga of Smoking

It's difficult to pinpoint exactly when people began to smoke food in order to keep it longer. We do know that the Roman world loved sausage, which was likely smoked for longevity. Smoking was also wildly popular in the Middle Ages, especially for fish such as cod and herring. Typically, these fish were smoked for about three weeks before they were ready for transport to various markets away from the coast. On the other side of the world, Native Americans were cutting, seasoning, and smoking various meats for storage.

Curious about Freezing?

The first documented ice cellars appear in China around 1000 B.C.E., and the Greeks and Romans used a similar method to preserve their food. However, it wasn't until the 1800s that refrigeration as we know it came into popular use.

The Greeks and Romans preserved foods with sugar and honey. One favorite method was to press the fruit into jars with the chosen sweetener, but meats could be preserved with honey and sugar as well. The Romans also used various spices such as coriander to preserve foods.

Canning and Curing

The 1800s also saw the development of canning and curing. Curing had a little bit of a head start; some of our ancestors used salt to keep food for longer periods. Canning began at the turn of the century when a confectioner named Nicolas Appert applied heat to sealed glass bottles for the French navy. Canning tins came about in 1810, and in 1864 the renowned scientist Louis Pasteur explained why these preservation processes helped prevent illness.

While canning tins were available in the early 1800s, can openers were not; they weren't invented until 1858! Ezra Warner of Waterbury, Connecticut, came up with this wonderful invention so people no longer had to hammer their tins open.

Why Do People Do This?

When people hear about canning projects, their first reaction is commonly surprise that someone would undertake such a daunting task. But people who preserve their own food want healthy, tasty meals where each ingredient is chosen personally and blended according to individual tastes. While the initial process takes a little while, the end result lasts for months and requires no tinkering to perfect! Devoting a few hours on a weekend to making tomato sauce yields several jars, which means it's one less thing to pick up at the grocery store. In addition to the convenience of having tomato sauce at your fingertips whenever you need it, making your own sauce will probably save you money.

Fresh and Healthy

There is also a freshness factor to preserving. If you have a garden, you will find this a particularly delightful way to enjoy the fruits of your labor year-round, long after the garden has gone brown or become covered in snow. For example, the gardener with gently tended organic grapes can harvest and can them into jelly or jam on the same day and retain that treasured fresh flavor. If you grow tomatoes, you can take the fruit at the height of its growth, when it has greater concentrations of vitamin C, and create all manner of rich salsas and sauces. Nothing in the commercial market comes close.

ALERT!

If you're looking for high amounts of vitamin C, trust in broccoli, red and yellow sweet peppers, kohlrabi, kiwi, mango, papaya, and tomato. A whole mango, for example, provides more than 180 mg of vitamin C.

Home canning gives you a healthier option as well. Commercially preserved goods often include chemicals that aren't remotely part of an average person's working vocabulary. They also include added salt, sugar, and preserving agents, some of which cause allergic reactions. These additives are potentially harmful to people with serious health issues. Sulfates may trigger hives and aggravate asthma in people with sensitivity to this chemical. In high amounts, salt is considered a contributor to strokes and heart disease. Home preserving gives you the power to decide what to put in your body. Rather than risk eating a preprepared item to which you might have a bad reaction, you can make something at home that you know will be tasty and healthy.

You should always review the basic costs before you begin. Include the recipe ingredients, the tools and equipment you need to buy, and the gas or electricity needed to process the item. Even if it turns out that your home-made products cost you a little more, it's well worth the effort to have fresh and healthy food on your table.

Keeping Tradition Alive

Another reason many people preserve is because it continues a family tradition. At various times of the year, children and adults alike would help prepare whatever was about to be put up for the season. Family stories were retold and Mom's best-kept secrets were shared in the hopes of safe-guarding recipes for future generations. It's only since World War II that such warm, communal scenes began to disappear from our homes. The disconnect between a family and its history, the lessened communication, and the loss of all manner of customs represents just the tip of the proverbial iceberg. Many modern preservers are often looking to reconnect with that lost sense of wholeness and revive old traditions with modern safety precautions.

In addition, people who can always know how well stocked the home is. It's best to be prepared in case disaster strikes. The well-stocked pantry is a blessing, as is the ability to remain self-reliant.

E-QUESTION

What do victory gardens have to do with canning?
Victory vegetable gardens sprouted up during World War II. The goal was to decrease the amount of food a household needed to buy so that commercially canned edibles, which were rationed, could go to the troops. About 40 percent of household consumable fruits and vegetables were preserved from these gardens until the late 1940s.

Finally, and probably most fulfilling on an individual level, there is a personal pleasure and pride that comes from making your own food. When people come to visit, you can offer them samplings from your stores and share the stories that go with each dish. This is how other people get inspired to preserve and how recipes get passed along from family to family and generation to generation.

Guidelines for Beginners

These guidelines are generalized toward all preserving efforts, especially for people who are new to the art. Even if you have been preserving for a while, though, take a peek to jog your memory. Sometimes we get into bad habits or forget some of the basics that are so important to positive results. Touchstones like this will help.

FACT

Canned goods require a cool, dark, and dry place for storage. The recommended temperature is between 50°F and 70°F. Under these conditions, your canned goods will last about a year. Temperatures greater than 90°F and exposure to direct sunlight dramatically decrease safe storage time.

The following are some strategies for successful preserving:

- **Learn one method first.** Pick out one preserving method that really appeals to you and get a good handle on it before launching into another one. This yields better results than if you split your attention and budget.
- **Have a game plan for your projects.** Why are you preserving? How much do you need to preserve to keep up with your household or gift-giving demands? How much is feasible based on your schedule? Set dates based on your demands and time constraints.
- **Set a reasonable goal with a specific focus.** For example, make one or two types of jelly in one weekend. Focus on sauce another weekend.
- **Start out small.** Small batches of everything tend to work better in preserving. You don't need to learn everything overnight. Take your time and really gain expertise.
- **Start clean and end clean.**

- **Have a functional sitting/working area.** If it's going to be a long round of peeling or chopping, you'll really want that chair!
- **Keep measurements tight and recipes come out right!** Some preserving recipes require very specific components to work correctly.
- **Adhere to the processing times provided in recipes.** These are necessary to deter microbe growth. If you're not sure, check that information against the USDA guidelines.
- **Know your audience.** If you're preserving for other people, make sure you're aware of their personal tastes and allergies. When people ask for the same thing twice, those are your winners!
- **Write it down!** When you adapt a recipe and it works right, document your process and keep it in a safe place for future reference.
- **Label and date everything.** This provides you with a visual gauge for shelf life and distinguishes a red, sweet gooey thingy from a red, hot spicy thingy.
- **Keep track of your stock.** Keep a running list of what you have in your storage pantry so you can plan meals and future preservation efforts. Remember, you only want to store enough for about a year's consumption from a safety perspective.
- **Have the right tools for the job and follow the manufacturer's instructions for those tools.** Each section in this book will provide you with necessary and fun tools so you can budget accordingly.
- **Use the highest quality ingredients your budget will allow.** Investing a little more in your components will result in far more pleasing items.
- **Create adequate space for your preserving projects.** You need enough space for your tools, components, and the resulting products. Get creative. For example, an old wooden crate can transform into perfect shelving for a cellar!
- **When in doubt, throw it out!** Never take chances with your health. If something seems off, it probably is!

Finally, seek out others in your area or on the Internet who share your passion. Exchange ideas. Talk about those utter failures and amazing successes so everyone benefits. Share recipes and have product parties where everyone gets to taste test and offer feedback! This is a wonderful way to make new friends and improve your skills at the same time.

Chapter 2

Canning

Canning used to be thought of as something Granny did, but not anymore. Many people have rediscovered this lost art and appreciate the fact that it saves money and creates healthier food choices in the home. If you're nervous about canning food, the processes used today are very safe when you follow the directions carefully. This chapter familiarizes you with the types of canning and the implements you'll need.

Hot Water Bath or Pressure Canner?

The most important piece of equipment in your canning adventures is the canner itself, but a lot of people don't know what type of canner to get or when to use pressure canning versus a hot-water bath. The simple rule of thumb is that all high-acid foods go into a hot-water-bath canner and everything else must be processed in a pressure canner. High-acid foods are all fruit products (jams, jellies, preserves, conserves, fruit butters, and marmalades) and anything pickled with vinegar like pickles, relishes, and vinegar-based sauces. The hot-water bath increases the temperature in the canning jar enough to kill bacteria and it also pushes out air bubbles as the content expands. As the jars cool, the air pressure creates the seal that makes the lid pop.

FACT

A can of corn originally made more than forty years ago was recently discovered in a California home. When the can was opened, the corn looked and smelled like freshly canned corn, and it even tested safe from contaminants!

Low-acid foods are all nonpickled vegetables, meat, fish, poultry, and dried beans. The pressure cooker gets much hotter than a bath canner (250°F), and it maintains that heat throughout processing to kill microbes.

Notice there's no mention of tomatoes here. That's because tomatoes (which are fruits) can either be water-bath processed or pressure processed. In either case, lemon juice must be added to bring up the acidity level.

Buying Guide

Hot-water-bath canners are made of aluminum or porcelain-covered steel. They have removable perforated racks and fitted lids. The canner must be deep enough so that at least 1" of briskly boiling water will be over the tops of jars during processing. Some boiling-water canners do not have flat bottoms, which are essential for use on an electric range. Either a flat or ridged bottom can be used on a gas burner. To ensure uniform processing of all jars with an electric range, the diameter of the canner should be no more than 4 inches wider than the element on which it is heated.

You need a hot water canner that is deep enough to submerge the jars you're using. Look for one that has a rack for the jars so they don't clank together during boiling. Some home preservers use a large stockpot and homemade rack system, but department stores offer very affordable hot-water bath canning kits starting at around $30.

ALERT!

Do not use a saucepan for home canning. It will easily boil over and may not cover your jars effectively. Also, don't shop for a canner in a second-hand store. The older canners may not have good gaskets and are often missing parts that may be impossible to replace.

By comparison, home-use pressure canners have been extensively redesigned in recent years. Models made before the 1970s were heavy-walled kettles with clamp-on or turn-on lids. They were fitted with a dial gauge, a vent port in the form of a petcock or counterweight, and a safety fuse. Modern pressure canners are lightweight, thin-walled kettles; most have turn-on lids. They have a jar rack, a gasket, a dial or weighted gauge, an automatic vent/cover lock, a vent port (steam vent) to be closed with a counterweight or weighted gauge, and a safety fuse.

A pressure canner runs about $100 for a 10–16 quart size. However, a pressure canner easily becomes a hot water canner just by leaving the lid off. It can also be used for other culinary efforts, such as tenderizing cheap cuts of meat. If you're planning to do a lot of canning or more than jam and pickles, get a pressure canner; it offers more options.

Tools of the Trade

The following is a list of the basic canning equipment a home canner will need to operate. Now is the time to take an inventory of your canning supplies and equipment and start gathering screwbands, lids, and jars. If your pressure canner uses a rubber gasket, get a pair of them. If a gasket blows in the middle of a canning project, you'll need the replacement right at your fingertips.

Check out your local thrift shops and see if you can get a supply of Mason jars cheap. You may have to ask because they don't always put out jars. Also post a note on your local Freecycle network (*www.freecycle.org*); sometimes you can get canning equipment, and all it costs is the gas to go pick it up.

FACT

Until the mid-1800s, canning jars included tin lids and sealing wax. Then John Mason created a jar with a threaded lid that was reusable. This innovation was followed by the Lightning jars of Henry Putnam (with easily sealed lid clamps), Ball Jars, and Kerr jars (self-sealing jars with wide mouth). The Kerr system with sealing lids is the one used today.

Basic Canning Equipment

- One or more canning books with recipes (This makes one!)
- Water-bath canner (You can use a large stockpot with a lid. Any pot used as a water-bath canner must have a rack to keep the jars off the bottom.)
- Pressure canner if you intend to put up vegetables, meats, and nonacidic products
- Canning jars—pints, quarts, and jelly Mason jars
- Lids and rings
- Large spoons for mixing and stirring
- Metal soup ladles
- Sharp paring knives
- Veggie peelers
- Canning funnel
- Colander and/or large strainer
- Large slotted spoons
- Measuring cups and spoons
- Squeezer or juicer
- Food mill, food processor, and/or blender

- Canning-jar lifter and lid wand
- Stirrer for getting air bubbles out of jars
- Kitchen timer
- Cheesecloth for making spice balls or large tea balls
- Pickling or canning salt, Fruit-Fresh, powdered and liquid pectin, and ClearJel A
- Kitchen towels
- Aprons
- Disposable rubber gloves
- Long-handled jar scrubber
- Kitchen scale (optional)
- Jelly bags (optional)
- Zester, mandolin, melon baller, apple peeler, or cherry pitter (optional)

Jars, Lids, and Screwbands

Only Mason jars are safe for canning. Commercial jars like those used for mayonnaise and peanut butter were designed for one-time use only. They may crack or shatter in either a water bath or a pressure canner. While the old bail-wire jars look pretty, they are no longer recommended for canning. Save the antique jars for storage purposes.

Use canning jars in sizes suitable for the product and your family's needs. Canning jars generally are sold in half-pint, pint, and quart sizes with wide and regular mouths. Wide-mouth jars are convenient for packing such foods as whole tomatoes and peach halves. Quart jars are convenient for vegetables and fruits if your family has four or more members.

Canning as a preserving process gained its first foothold in nineteenth-century France. Napoleon was advancing, and the government offered a generous reward for someone to improve the way foods were preserved to feed the armies. Nicolas Appert won the prize by coming up with a way of cooking and sealing food in bottles fitted with corks, finished in a hot water bath.

Some commercial pasta sauces are packaged in Mason jars. Note, however, that they are not a full quart. Also, make absolutely certain that the screwband fits it perfectly, as some threading on these jars does not match that of the commercially available screwbands.

If you have extra unused lids, store them protected in a dry, cool place. A Rubbermaid storage box with a tight-fitting lid works quite well for storage of extra lids and screwbands. The U.S. Department of Agriculture does not recommend reusing lids because there is a chance they may not seal properly. Before storing used screwbands, wash them in hot soapy water, dry them well, and put them into your storage container.

Preparation

Before you start canning, read your recipe at least twice and get your ingredients together. Organize the supplies and equipment you will need to complete your project. Learning you are out of a certain ingredient in the middle of a canning session is not fun!

Also remember: Canning projects require your uninterrupted attention from start to finish.

Next, prepare your workspace. Arrange the kitchen counters so you have ample space to work. You need counter space for preparing your foods as well as space for filling your jars once the food is prepared.

Determine how many jars your recipe calls for. Examine these carefully, making certain there are no cracks or chips. You may put them through a sterilizing cycle in a dishwasher if you have one. Otherwise, use a bottle brush to scrub them inside and out, rinse them in hot water, and sterilize them in a stockpot or water-bath canner. Meanwhile, your lids should be placed in a bowl of hot water to soften the rubber sealing compound.

ALERT!

When filling jars, place an old terrycloth bath towel folded in half or two terrycloth kitchen towels on your counter. Never put jars on an uncovered countertop. Putting a jar on it uncovered and then filling with hot food and/or liquid may cause the jar or countertop to crack or shatter.

Remember to leave the proper amount of headspace—¼ inch for jams, jellies, preserves, and most other water-bath processed foods and 1 inch for pressure-processed foods. Each recipe will specify the amount of headspace. Too little headspace may cause liquid to seep out. Too much headspace and food at the top of the jar may dry out.

Finally, remove air bubbles from the jar. This can be accomplished by gently stirring the contents of the jar with a plastic stirrer (a wide, plastic soda straw works great). Use a damp kitchen towel to wipe the outer rims, then put on a lid and screw the band firmly. Do not overtighten screwbands. Doing so may cause lids to buckle in the canner.

Processing

In a water bath, jars are placed on a rack and covered 1–2 inches with boiling water. Put a lid on the bath and begin timing when water is boiling. Remove jars with a jar lifter and place them on a towel-covered counter to cool. Leave undisturbed for 12–24 hours. Check the seals and remove the screwbands.

The old computer saying "GIGO" (Garbage In = Garbage Out) applies to home canning as well. Your finished product is only as good as the ingredients you begin with. The sooner you jar freshly picked fruits and vegetables, the better. Canning will not improve stale foodstuffs.

In a pressure canner, jars are placed on a rack and boiling water is added according to the manufacturers' instructions, usually several inches. Lock the lid securely into place. Leave weight off the vent pipe or open petcock and exhaust steam for 10 minutes. Place weight back onto vent pipe or close petcock. Canner should start to pressurize in 5–10 minutes. Once the canner has reached the required amount of pressure, start the timer. Allow canner to come down to zero pounds on its own. Do not try to speed up this process by removing weight or opening the petcock, as it may cause jars to crack and/or lose liquid. Do not put the canner into cold water to hasten the process. Let jars sit in the canner for 5–10 minutes to allow them to cool down. Remove jars with a jar lifter and place them on a towel-covered counter to cool. Leave undisturbed for 12–24 hours. Check the seals and remove the screwbands.

To check the seals on cooled jars, press your thumb in the middle of the lid. If the lid seems to give and come back up, the jar isn't sealed. If you're not sure, tap the lid with a knife in the same place. It should sound like a bell; a muffled sound means the jar isn't sealed right. Finally, there's the visual; the surface of the lid should be concave.

What happens if your jar doesn't seal properly? All is not lost! You have several options here. One is to put the jar in the refrigerator and use it soon. Second is to try reprocessing the jar within twenty-four hours of the original effort. If you're going to do this, open the jar, make sure the lid has a clean surface, try changing out the lid, and put everything back in your canner. Your third and fourth options are using other preservation methods covered in this book, namely freezing or drying, if practicable.

After Processing

Wash off all of your sealed jars, label them with the date of canning, and move them into a suitable storage place. To prevent spoiling, keep your jars away from places that are too hot or damp, and don't expose them to bright light. Use your canned goods within one year unless otherwise specified by the recipe. Write expiration dates on your jars to remind you how long they will remain good.

Ever wonder how much to can for one person to use in a year? Begin with about 140 quarts of fruits and vegetables, 36 pints of meat, 18 quarts of soup, 20 pints of spreads, 5 pints of relish, and 26 pints of various types of pickles!

When you use your canned goods, always check for signs of spoilage. The most obvious sign is the loss of a vacuum seal on the jar and mold growing inside. Other indicators include gas bubbles, odd coloring, and foul smells. Never test suspect food—throw it out!

Safe Temperatures for Canning

At sea level, water boils at 212°F. This is the processing temperature for all high-acid and pickled foods. It is the temperature at which molds, yeasts, and some bacteria are destroyed.

Low-acid, nonpickled foods are processed in a pressure canner at 250°F. It is the temperature at which bacterial spores (botulinum) are destroyed. Botulism is odorless, colorless, and tasteless. In the case of an otherwise healthy adult, it mimics flu symptoms. In the case of a small child, an elderly adult, or a person with an impaired immune system, it may be fatal.

E-QUESTION

What is botulism?
Botulism is a rare but serious paralytic illness caused by a nerve toxin that is produced by the bacterium *Clostridium botulinum*. Food-borne botulism is caused by eating foods that contain the botulism toxin. Contracting botulism is a potentially fatal medical emergency.

The classic symptoms of botulism include double vision, blurred vision, drooping eyelids, slurred speech, difficulty swallowing, dry mouth, and muscle weakness. Infants with botulism appear lethargic, feed poorly, are constipated, and have a weak cry and poor muscle tone. These are all symptoms of the muscle paralysis caused by the bacterial toxin. If untreated, these symptoms may progress to cause paralysis of the arms, legs, trunk, and respiratory muscles. In food-borne botulism, symptoms generally begin eighteen to thirty-six hours after eating a contaminated food, but they can occur in as soon as six hours or as late as ten days.

Botulism can be prevented. Food-borne botulism has often been contracted from home-canned foods with low acid content, such as asparagus, green beans, beets, and corn. You should follow strict hygienic procedures to reduce the risk of contamination. Oils infused with garlic or herbs should be refrigerated. Potatoes that have been baked while wrapped in aluminum foil should be kept hot until served or refrigerated.

Also pay close attention to the canning instructions given in this or any canning guide. Extensive instructions on safe home canning can be obtained from county extension services or from the USDA (*www.usda.gov*).

E-QUESTION

How common is botulism?
In the United States, an average of 110 cases of botulism are reported each year. Of these, approximately 25 percent are food-borne, 72 percent are infant botulism, and the rest are wound botulism. Outbreaks of food-borne botulism involving two or more persons occur in most years and are usually caused by eating contaminated home-canned foods.

The Importance of Altitude

Do you know how high you are above sea level? You'll need to find out for canning. Water boils at different temperatures depending on your altitude. The higher you live, the lower the boiling point. This means that processing time has to be increased to offset the lower temperature or you'll have to opt for a pressure canner. Recipes throughout this book are set for altitudes under 1,000 feet. For levels over 1,000, use the following charts.

ALTITUDE CHART	
Boiling-Water Canner	
Feet Above Sea Level	*Increase Processing Time By*
1,001–3,000	5 minutes
3,001–6,000	10 minutes
6,001–8,000	15 minutes
8,001–10,000	20 minutes

ALTITUDE CHART		
Pressure Canner		
Feet Above Sea Level	*Weighted Gauge*	*Dial Gauge*
0–1,000	10 pounds	11 pounds
1,001–2,000	15 pounds	11 pounds
2,001–3,000	15 pounds	12 pounds
3,001–6,000	15 pounds	13 pounds
6,001–8,000	15 pounds	14 pounds
8,001–10,000	15 pounds	15 pounds

What Not to Can

Anything with pasta, rice, and barley cannot be canned safely. These low-acid ingredients common to soups, stews, and other convenience meals need to be pressure processed at length. During this time they break down and may, in fact, make the foodstuff too dense for the heat to safely kill the botulism spores.

Second, any dairy products like eggs, milk, cream, cheese, and butter are not safe to can. You can make pickled eggs and refrigerate them, but they need to be used within two weeks. Oils also aren't good candidates. While flavored oils can be made for short-term use, oils generally get rancid very quickly.

FACT

In 1901, Frank Gerber joined his father's canning company. When his baby fell ill in 1928, Frank set out to make his own baby food, consisting of puréed and strained fruits and vegetables. These became so popular locally that an entire business was born. The first canned baby foods sold by Gerber were priced at 15 cents a jar.

Anything heavy in fats doesn't can well. Excess fat should be removed from meat and ground beef should be sautéed and drained of excess fat. Allow soups and stocks to cool, skim the fat off, and then reheat and process them. Like oils, fat tends to go rancid.

Last but not least, don't can anything thickened with flour, cornstarch, arrowroot, or breadcrumbs. ClearJel A, which is a modified cornstarch, may be used for safely canning pie fillings, but is not safe for thickening sauces or gravies.

Equipment and Methods Not Recommended for Home Canning

Processing freshly filled jars in conventional ovens, microwave ovens, and dishwashers is not recommended because these practices do not prevent all risks of spoilage. The following list details other methods of canning and preserving to avoid.

- **Steam canners.** Processing times for use with current models have not been adequately researched. Steam canners may not heat foods in the same manner as boiling water canners, so this could require changing processing times. Without certainty, food spoilage may result.
- **Pressure processes that are in excess of 15 PSI, especially when using new pressure canning equipment.** Most manufacturers also do not recommend operating their pressure canners above 15 PSI.
- **Canning powders.** These are not preservatives. You still need to properly process your canned goods.
- **Jars with wire bails and glass caps.** While these make attractive antiques or storage containers for dry food ingredients, they're not recommended for use in canning.
- **Using old lids (even unused ones).** The longer a lid sits, the more likely it is that it won't seal right. Don't purchase more lids than you anticipate using in a year.

Finally, one-piece zinc porcelain-lined caps are no longer recommended. Both glass and zinc caps use flat rubber rings for sealing jars, but too often they fail to seal properly.

Help and Hints

All steps of any canning project should be carried through as rapidly as possible. Follow the slogan, "Two hours from harvest to container." Work quickly with small amounts of food at a time, especially vegetables with high starch content that lose their quality rapidly, such as corn and peas. Any delay will result in loss of flavor and nutritive value. Additionally, following these simple rules will make your efforts more successful and satisfying:

- Use prime products; discard any parts with defects.
- Keep same-sized items together in jars for even processing.
- Wash tools and ingredients thoroughly. Be fastidious!
- Always use a rack on the bottom of your canner to set jars on to avoid breakage and ensure water circulation. Do not use a folded towel; this is not safe.
- Follow up-to-date recommendations for detailed procedures in canning, available in USDA or Extension publications. Check for updates and new recommendations regularly.

Finally, have fun! While the rules sound like drudgery, they're really not difficult. With just a little practice you'll find the preparations and mechanisms come quite naturally—and you'll have a plethora of wonderful canned goods to enjoy.

Chapter 3

Freezing

Freezing and refrigeration are the most common types of preserving in homes around the world today. Where refrigeration slows bacterial action, freezing comes close to totally stopping microbes' development. This happens because the water in frozen food turns to ice, in which bacteria cannot continue to grow. Enzyme activity, on the other hand, isn't completely deterred by freezing, which is why many vegetables are blanched before being packaged. Once an item is defrosted completely, however, any microbes still within will begin to grow again. This chapter will introduce you to freezing fundamentals for your home.

What Can Be Frozen?

Except for eggs in the shell, nearly all foods can be frozen raw, after blanching and/or cooking. So the real question here is what foods don't take well to freezing. The following list includes the foods you generally cannot freeze:

- Cream sauces separate even when warmed completely after being frozen.
- Mayonnaise, cream cheese, and cottage cheese don't hold up well, often losing textural quality.
- Milk seems to be a 50-50 proposition. While it can be frozen quite safely, it sometimes separates after being frozen. If remixed, this milk is an option for cooking and baking.
- Precooked meat can be frozen, but it doesn't have as much moisture as raw and will often dry out further if left frozen more than four weeks.
- Cured meats don't last long in the freezer and should be used in less than four weeks.

If you're ever in doubt about how to best prepare an item for freezing (or even if you should), the National Center for Home Preserving (*www.uga .edu/nchfp*) is a great online resource. It offers tips on how to freeze various items ranging from pie and prepared food to oysters and artichokes.

FACT

The ideal temperature for keeping foods frozen for the longest time without losing textural or taste quality is 0°F (18°C). Before buying a freezer, check to see that it achieves that temperature, if not colder.

Frosty Facts

In freezing, zero is your magic number. At 0°F, microbes become dormant. The food won't spoil, and any germs therein will not breed until you defrost the food. Bear in mind, though, that the longer the food remains frozen the more it tends to lose certain qualities such as vivid flavor and texture. Always try to freeze things when they're at their peak, and remember that cooking your defrosted food as soon as it's thawed will also stop microbial growth.

E-QUESTION

How do you keep icy crystals from forming in frozen foods?
The faster food freezes, the fewer ice crystals will form. This is especially important for meat, which loses juiciness and tenderness as a result of freezing. If your freezer has a quick-freeze cycle, use that to help deter ice crystal formation. Otherwise, just wrap and seal your foods properly and put them in the coldest part of your freezer.

The first step in freezing is keeping those items cold until you're ready to prepare them. This is very important with meat, but it also makes a difference in how fruits and vegetables come out of the freezer.

Equipment

Once you're ready to begin, assemble all the items you need. For example, if you're freezing fruit, you'll want a clean cutting board, a sharp knife, and your choice of storage containers. If you're doing any preparation on the fruit before freezing it, you'll also need cooking pans. Stainless steel is highly recommended; galvanized pans may give off zinc when fruit is left in them because of the fruit's acid content. Additionally, there's nothing like stainless steel for easy cleanup.

If it's in your budget, a vacuum sealer is another great piece of equipment to consider. Vacuum sealers come in a variety of sizes with a similar variety of bags that are perfect for preservers who like freezing and drying methods. They're fairly cost effective when compared to freezer bags or plastic containers, and they eliminate the excess air that contributes to ice crystals.

A third item that you shouldn't be without is a freezer-proof label system. If you double-wrap your frozen items, put a label on each layer. If one gets knocked off, the other remains.

Help and Hints

Freezing, like any other method of preservation, requires some observation and annotation to achieve success. As you're working with recipes, remember that practice really does make perfect. For example, you may follow a recipe for frozen butter pickles exactly, but you find you'd like the cucumbers sliced more thinly for greater flavor. Make a note of that and change it next time.

As you note changes you'd like to make, also consider if that means getting different types of equipment for your kitchen. In the case of the cucumbers and other thinly sliced vegetables, a mandolin might be the perfect fix. Put it on a wish list. Being prepared saves a lot of last-minute headaches, and having the right tools is always a great boon.

Vegetables

Vegetables should be chosen for crispness and freshness. Home gardeners should pick their items a few hours before packing them for the ultimate in organic goodness. The next step for vegetables is blanching, which will improve the lifespan of your frozen goods.

Blanching has several benefits. It stops enzyme action that decreases vegetables' textural quality, flavor, and color and it cleans off any lingering dirt. To blanch vegetables, fill a pan with water and bring it to a rolling boil. Add the vegetables and make sure they're immersed. Follow the blanching time recommended in the recipe and then turn the vegetables in to a bowl of ice. This retains the vegetable's vitamins and firmness.

If there's no specific blanching time provided in your preserving recipe, here's a brief overview to get you started (see facing page). Remember to move your vegetables into an ice bath immediately after blanching until they're totally cooled.

Timing and Techniques for Blanching Vegetables

- **Asparagus.** Remove the tough ends from the asparagus. Depending on the storage container, you may need to cut the stems in half. If your stalks are thin, they'll only need 2 minutes of blanching; thick stalks require twice as much.
- **Beans (green or wax).** Remove any tips. Leave the beans whole and blanch them for 3 minutes.
- **Brussels sprouts.** Clean off outer leaves, then soak the sprouts in cold salt water for 30 minutes. Drain and blanch for 4 minutes.
- **Cabbage.** Remove the outer leaves. Shred the cabbage and blanch for just over 1 minute and leave in the water for another 30 seconds before icing.
- **Carrots.** Clean the skins, then slice into ¼" pieces. Blanch for 3 minutes. Whole baby carrots need 5 minutes of blanching.
- **Cauliflower and broccoli.** Break off the pieces from the central core and clean well (a spray nozzle at the sink works very well). Soak in a gallon of salt water (3–4 teaspoons salt) for 30 minutes. Pour off the salt water. Rinse and blanch for 3 minutes.
- **Corn.** Rinse, remove from the cob, and blanch for 5 minutes.
- **Mushrooms (small).** These can be frozen whole. Toss with a little fresh lemon juice and blanch for 4 minutes.
- **Greens (including spinach).** Rinse. Remove any leaves that have spots or other damage. Blanch for 3 minutes.
- **Peas.** Blanch out of the husk for 90 seconds.
- **Peas in the pod.** Trim the ends and remove strings. Blanch for 1–2 minutes, depending on the size of the pod.
- **Peppers.** Slice open and remove the seeds. Cut into desired size and blanch for 2 minutes.
- **Potatoes.** Wash and scrub thoroughly. Remove the peel and blanch for 4 minutes.
- **Tomatoes.** To easily peel the skins, use a straining spoon and dip the tomatoes in boiling water for 30 seconds. Peel and remove the core. These can be stored whole or diced to desired size.
- **Zucchini and squash.** Peel. Cut into ½-inch slices and blanch for 3 minutes.

Fruit

Do small batches of fruit so it doesn't brown while you're packing. Fruit need not be packed in syrup, but many people do prefer the texture and taste that sugar or sugar syrup adds to frozen fruit. Some folks use sugar substitutes for dietary reasons. In any case, small fruits such as berries take well to a simple sprinkling. Larger chunks such as peaches do well in syrup. The average ratio is ½ cup of syrup to every pint of fruit. Some preservers like to use ascorbic acid to improve the quality of frozen fruit. Adding about ½ teaspoon of this per pint is sufficient; just mix it into the syrup or a little water.

Packaging

Since 95 percent of American homes freeze some of their food regularly, it's not surprising to find people have a lot of questions on the best type of storage containers to use and how to prepare food for the table after it's been frozen. Plastic bags are the most common receptacles, followed by plastic containers. While some people have been known to use glass, this is a bit risky since the glass may crack and break when the food inside expands in the freezing process. Additionally, slippery glass jars coming out of the freezer are easily dropped.

FACT

A woman in England has a 1931 Electrolux cooler that's still running after seventy-seven years of use. She, her husband, children, and grandchildren have all used it. The only thing that ever had to be replaced were the refrigerator's seals.

Overall, it's always a good idea to use bags and containers that are rated for freezing. Avoid using waxed cartons; they don't retain the food's quality very well and defrosted food often becomes limp and unstable for handling. Your packaging materials should also be leak and oil resistant, and all packing materials should be able to withstand freezing.

Size Counts

Another consideration with your containers is size. Think about how many people you plan to serve and choose freezing containers accordingly. If you're going to put several servings in one large container, separate them with a piece of aluminum foil or plastic wrap so you can take out one at a time fairly easily.

Space Constraints

When you're packing food into a container, always leave a little room for expansion. Let the food reach room temperature before you freeze it (right out of the ice bath is a perfect time with vegetables). Putting warm or hot food in the freezer creates a temperature variance for all the food inside the freezer.

Most importantly, remember to label and date everything. This will help you gauge what should be eaten first so it retains the greatest quality.

Wrap It Up

Many preservers wrap meat with aluminum foil or freezer wrap, then transfer it into another freezer bag or container. This decreases the chance that water crystals will form and protects the foil from being accidentally torn. Note, however, that waxed paper isn't a good choice for freezing because it doesn't resist moisture.

E-QUESTION

How do I keep fruit from getting soft or turning brown after freezing?
Fruit has a lot of water, meaning the faster you freeze it, the less mushy it will be when you defrost it. If your freezer goes to −10°F, that's an ideal temperature for freezing fresh fruit. As for browning, preservers often use lemon juice, citric acid, and ascorbic acid to deter it. Lightly steaming the fruit before freezing also prevents browning.

Stews and Leftovers

If you know in advance that you'd like to set aside some of what you're cooking for the freezer, it's a good idea to leave it a little undercooked. Freeze the goods as soon as they reach room temperature. When you warm it up, you will finish the cooking process and can also doctor the flavor a bit at that time. Your frozen foods need not be defrosted before you start cooking them. Just remember to get all the packing materials off the item first—you would not be the first person to forget this step and find unpleasant paper or wrapping in a meat serving!

Always read USDA labels on meat. This label provides valuable information about freezing and cooking for safety. For example, some poultry products require that you cook them from the frozen state, while others can be defrosted. An educated consumer is a strong advocate for family health.

Safe Storage Times

Frozen food can be kept nearly indefinitely at 0°F or colder. Nonetheless, the longer the food stays frozen, the more nutrients you lose and the greater the likelihood that ice crystals will form and decrease the overall color, taste, or textural quality of the product. One great way to deter this is by simple rotation. Diligently arrange your freezer shelves so that the oldest item is in front and newly preserved items are in the back. Keep in mind that the amount of time foods can be safely kept frozen decreases with temperature fluctuation in your freezer, including the variations caused by opening the door to put food in or take it out. The longer you leave the door open, the greater the temperature will change and the more it will affect the food stored inside.

Here's a quick overview of suggested storage times on various common pantry items (see the facing page). More information about storage will typically be noted in the recipes you're using for freezing. Longer lists are also available online at many preserving websites.

FREEZER TIMES	
Food	Time
Bacon and sausage	1–2 months
Banana (peeled and dipped in lemon juice)	4–6 months
Bread, pastries, and cakes	3 months
Butter	1 year
Casseroles	2–3 months
Cheese, aged/hard	6–8 months
Cherries, grapes, melons, and berries	8–12 months
Cookies (baked)	up to 1 year
Egg whites (unshelled)	1 year
Fish, cooked	4–6 months
Fish, fatty fillet	2–3 months
Fish, lean fillet	4–6 months
Frozen dinners	3 months
Gravy	2 months
Ham	6 weeks
Hot dogs	6 weeks
Leftovers of spaghetti, chili, rice, beans, etc.	about 4 months
Lunch meat	6 weeks
Meat, cooked	3 months
Meat, ground	3 months
Meat, uncooked	4–12 months
Poultry, cooked	4 months
Poultry, cut	9 months
Poultry, whole	1 year
Shrimp	6–12 months
Soups	2–3 months
Tofu	5 months
Vegetables	8–12 months
Wild game, uncooked	8–12 months

Defrosting

Many people have questions about how to safely defrost food. The first rule of defrosting is don't leave anything at room temperature for hours at a time. Instead, there are three tried-and-true ways to safely defrost your food.

- **Leave the food in your refrigerator.** This takes a while, and it's wise to put some paper towels down or a platter underneath the item to catch any water or juices that run out during defrosting.
- **Put the food in a cold-water bath.** keep the item in the wrapper or container, and if need be put it in an additional resealable bag for protection. It's recommended that you refresh the water every 30 minutes until the item is defrosted.
- **Use the defrost setting on your microwave.** Microwave powers vary greatly from machine to machine, so watch carefully to make sure your food isn't being partially cooked because that can give your food a rubbery texture. As with the refrigerator, you will want something to gather any liquid that's released during the process for faster cleanup.

Of these three options, using the refrigerator is the recommended approach to best protect the overall quality of the food. Note that about 1 pound of food takes about a day to defrost this way, so plan accordingly.

E-QUESTION

Is it okay to keep tea in my freezer?
Tea lovers will tell you that they never freeze tea leaves. The moisture in a freezer damages the leaves, and aromas can cause the scent of the tea to change. Instead, keep your tea in a sealed container in a dark area.

Refreezing

The beauty of thawing food in your refrigerator is that you can refreeze it quite safely, as long as it's kept properly cold. You might lose a little moisture with meat and bread products, texture with vegetables, and flavor with juices, but there's no issue with microbial growth because the average refrigerator keeps food at 30–48°F (30–40°F is ideal). Similarly, if you cook an item that was previously frozen, you can freeze any leftovers safely. Note, however, that some experts feel it's a good precaution to cook completely thawed meat before refreezing.

Partially defrosted food is a little different. If there are still ice crystals in the pack and the food has not been left at room temperature, it's relatively safe—just make sure there's no discoloration or odd odor. Any food that's been completely thawed to warm or room temperature should not be refrozen, and should be discarded if it's been out longer than two hours.

E-QUESTION

How long will my food stay frozen if there's a power outage?
If you leave your freezer closed, and it is in a cool part of the house (like your basement), food stays frozen up to four days in a well-stocked freezer. When the freezer is half full or less, food will start to thaw in twenty-four hours.

Choosing a Freezer

There are many advantages to having a freezer. When stores have sales you can buy in bulk and extend your grocery savings over several months. From this basic stock, you could also choose to do marathon cooking and fill your freezer. This saves you time in the months ahead, which is especially nice when you just don't feel like standing over the stove. A third advantage comes from the element of surprise. You will always have extra when family or friends stop over unexpectedly. With all that in mind, how do you choose a good freezer?

Cost Factors

This isn't going to be a minor purchase. While you can get good comparative prices on basic freezers, there are a lot of other things to consider, including energy use, internal space, the product's warranty, and special features such as a quick-freeze cycle. Don't rush your choice. Most freezers will last ten to twelve years, so think about your future needs as well as your present ones.

Hot water actually freezes faster than cold water. If you put a cup of hot water in your freezer next to a cup of cold, the hot water will form ice more quickly, but the cold water will still reach the solid state before the hot water.

Location and Space

Consider your space constraints. Where are you going to put the freezer? Does that space have a suitable electrical outlet? Many new appliances require a 220 line for them to run effectively. Placing the freezer in a cooler area of your home will help keep the cost of operating your freezer down. Once you've found a spot, measure it. That measurement will tell you pretty quickly if you can get an upright or chest cooler. Bear in mind that an upright freezer usually has far more features.

Upright or Chest Freezer

An upright is very easy to access, especially if someone in your family has back problems. When you open the door, a fast visual survey will tell you what's inside. Uprights also typically offer conveniences like auto defrost and ice makers. Chest freezers, by comparison, hold a little more. They allow you to store oddly shaped items inside, and the internal temperature varies less than an upright. On the down side, you may forget what's at the bottom, and you'll have to manually defrost these foods. While you're looking at features, see if there's a defrosting hose. This makes cleaning and upkeep much easier.

How Big?

By now you're probably starting to narrow your choices; don't forget to consider the size of the machines. You know the space you've got, but that doesn't mean you have to buy a freezer that will fill that entire space. Most people get a larger freezer than they need, and unfortunately, that means a loss of energy. Consider how much food you would freeze and use in a six- to eight-week period, then buy a freezer based on that volume. Alternatively, figure 1.5 cubic feet per person in the house, then allow extra space beyond that for the volume of your preserving efforts.

ALERT!

Frost-free freezers save people time, but they dry out foods more quickly. Without that feature, you must regularly thaw and clean your freezer and circulate stock. While you do so, make an inventory, including the date each item was frozen. Keep that list handy when you go shopping so you can really begin to enjoy those savings!

Energy Savings

Besides the size, check out the bright yellow Energy Guide tag. The lower the number on that tag, the better. This is like looking at the miles per gallon a car gets. You want to save money with your freezer, not spend it all on electricity. Note that frost-free freezers use more energy than regular ones, and upright freezers are less energy efficient than chest coolers.

Chapter 4

Drying

Drying was one of the first preserving methods ever used, probably because of its simplicity. While you can get commercial equipment designed for drying, there are items in your home right now that will fit the bill nicely. An additional advantage to drying is that food has a long shelf life when it's dried properly. Without water content, food doesn't spoil, and it packs very neatly onto cupboard shelves. This chapter will familiarize you with the various types of dry preserving and what foods they're best suited for.

4

Drying Methods

Unlike canning, drying is a little more alchemical because of all the things that affect it. For example, temperature variations and humidity will both affect the drying process, specifically how long it will take. Pay attention to these things so that you can adjust your drying method accordingly. There are a variety of different ways to dry food.

ALERT!

When considering which drying method is best for you, don't forget to look at your environment. To sun-dry food, for example, you'll need about five days of low humidity and high temperatures (95°F being ideal). While someone in Arizona might use this method with no difficulty, it's not likely to be practical for, say, someone in New York in January.

Air

Herbs and flowers are the most common air-dried foods. If you grow your own, harvest herbs and flowers before 10 A.M. to retain the greatest amount of essential oil for aroma and flavor. The later hours in the day cause the oils to retreat into the plant stem (or dry) from the heat of the sun.

If you're hanging the plants, don't bundle too many together; about six stems is good. Hang them upside down from a string in a dry, warm spot with a paper lunch bag draped loosely over the bundle to keep it free from dust and to protect the bundle against sunlight. Use a toothpick to make holes in the bag to allow air to circulate. The plant matter should be dry in fourteen days.

An alternative method of drying is to remove the flower petals or herb leaves from the stem and lay them on a screen. It's very important that the screening material be clean and that the plant pieces don't touch each other. Place a piece of cheese cloth (or a large paper bag with pinholes in it) over the top of the screens. Again, this protects the flowers and herbs from airborne dust and dirt. Keep the trays out of the sunlight and in a cool, dry area. As with hanging, it will take about two weeks to thoroughly dry the plant matter.

Sun Drying

Sun drying is not always practicable due to geography. You need several days of 90°F–100°F temperatures and low humidity for successful, even preserving. Additionally, great caution is required to keep the items safe from bugs, dirt, wandering animals, and other hazards. Sun drying is not recommended in areas with high levels of air pollution.

E-QUESTION

What kinds of food can be dried?
There's a wide variety of food that can be dried, including fish, fruit, edible flowers, meat, vegetables, and herbs. The taste and texture of dried food is different than fresh or frozen, so make small batches at first to see how well you like the results. Keep a list of items that you like best and return to those recipes to make larger batches later.

If you live in a region with consistent hot, dry weather, you can look into commercial sun dryers that use screening to protect the foods. If the weather changes unexpectedly, it's best to bring the items inside and finish the drying using your oven.

Pressing

Pressing as a preserving method is most commonly seen with flowers. While some people use pressed flowers and herb parts for decoration, they can also be stored for culinary purposes as long as the flowers were grown organically. Similar to herbs, flowers should be gathered early in the morning as soon as they're open a bit. This makes cleaning them off easier. Gently run the flowers under cool water to remove any debris. Leave the plant parts on a paper towel while you set up your pressing method. Your layering materials include cardboard (8" × 11"), newspaper, paper towels, and a heavy book (8" × 11").

Begin by putting the cardboard on a flat surface. On top of that, put three sheets of newspaper, followed by three sheets of paper towels. Lay the flowers or herbs on the top sheet, leaving space between them. Over the top of this, place three more paper towels, three more sheets of newspaper, and another piece of cardboard. You can keep going for two or three more layers, topping everything with the heavy book; good-sized stones or bricks also work very well. Your plant matter will press dry in about a month.

Many flowers are edible and a great source of vitamins, especially vitamins A and C. Wondering what petals you can eat? There's quite a list, including angelica, apple blossom, borage, carnation, chrysanthemum, dandelion, jasmine, lavender, lilac, marigold, nasturtium, rose, and squash flowers!

Sand Drying

Sand drying isn't recommended for culinary purposes, but it's an excellent way to make beautiful gifts and decorative garnishes. About the only flowers that don't seem to preserve well by sand drying are short-lived varieties such as daylilies. Beyond that limitation, the visual results of sand drying are quite stunning.

Unlike other preserving methods, you'll want to harvest the intended blossoms when they're fully open but before they start showing any sign of wilting. Once cut, gently push a thin piece of wire into the flower's stem to mount it. This wire helps keep the flower upright in the sand. It can also be used later for flexibility in dried flower arrangements.

Next you'll need a bag of white sand and a box deep enough to cover the flowers and wide enough that they don't touch each other. Pour 2 inches of sand in the bottom and place the wired flowers in. Fill the box with sand up to the base of the petals, then slowly sprinkle sand below and above each petal. Be careful here; you want to preserve the natural shape of the flower, and adding too much sand too quickly crushes the petals.

Once covered, it takes twenty to thirty days for the flowers to dry completely. Don't peek! They need to remain covered for the best results. Use gardening tags to mark where your flowers are in the box. This is helpful when you unearth them.

Finally, reach down into the sand below a flower and hold the wire. With your other hand, begin brushing away the sand around it with a small paintbrush. In this final form, the flowers have a good shelf life. If you plan on using them more than once, preservers suggest using clear varnish for improved strength. Otherwise, put them in a padded container for storage.

For longer lasting floral decorations, treat the flower petals with glue. Use a small paint brush and mix the glue with a little water. Paint this on the base of each petal where it attaches to the stem. Let the glue dry completely before moving the flower into the sand-drying container.

Microwave Drying

Microwave ovens vary in their overall power, which makes providing tried-and-true instructions for their use difficult. Overall, herbs are the items best suited to this preservation method, but you have to be careful.

Take some fresh herb leaves or flowers and put them on a paper plate. If your microwave has a power setting, go to 50 percent power and dry the herbs in 30-second intervals. Each time you check the herbs, turn them over. If your microwave platform doesn't rotate, you'll also need to rotate the herbs on the plate. Most herbs dry in 2 minutes using this method, but they may not be well suited to cooking because the microwave evaporates many oils that make herbs flavorful and aromatic.

FACT

In 1946, Dr. Percy Spenser was trying to make a vacuum tube when he stumbled onto the basics of microwave technology. Commercial micro-waves were marketed in 1947, and the first countertop microwave oven hit stores in 1967. By 1975, microwave sales surpassed sales of gas ranges.

Oven Drying

Using the microwave makes things faster; using your oven for drying may be costly. Because you're leaving food on low heat for many hours, the bottom line on your electric or gas bill may price this method right out of your comfort zone.

On the other hand, oven drying is very simple. Get out oven trays, pre-heat your oven to 140°F, and pre-prepare your food according to instructions. Most oven trays hold up to 2 pounds of food. Unless you have a very large oven, it's suggested that you dry no more than three trays at a time, shifting their position and turning the food every 30 minutes for best results. Finally, try to keep the door of the oven open about 2 inches throughout this time. This improves air circulation and decreases the amount of heat you lose when you circulate the drying items.

If you have any stainless steel screens, put these on your oven racks to elevate the food. This will give all sides of the item more air exposure and improve even drying. Aluminum screens are not recommended for this purpose because they can impart an odd flavor.

Food Dehydrator

Using a commercial electric dehydrator takes half the time as drying in an oven, making it perfect for the energy-conscious consumer. An additional benefit is that these devices are created specifically to maintain air circulation, sustain even heating, and safeguard nutritional value. Fruits, herbs, and meats are good candidates for the dehydrator.

The market for dehydrators has grown, which means you can find some great optional features—for a price. You can pay more than $300 for a stainless steel dehumidifier with 16 cubic square feet of interior space, but most home preservers don't need anything quite so impressive. If you plan to spend between $60 and $75, you'll usually get a good quality machine.

Watch for machine features that will make your life easier. For example, a temperature gauge lets you adjust the heat to specific food groups, allowing you to produce a higher quality dried item. Additionally, you want a dehydrator that fits in your kitchen comfortably, has enough trays to make several layers of dried goods, a timer to keep things from overcooking, and a good warranty. Last but not least, dishwasher-safe parts save you a lot of time.

ALERT!

There are two basic types of dehydrators on the market. One dries the food using a fan and heat from the side; the other dries food from the bottom of the machine. Drying from the side produces better results when you want to preserve a variety of items at one time because it doesn't allow the flavors to mix.

For Drying Success: Freshness, Attentiveness, and Airflow

In drying, "fresh is best" is your mantra. The sooner you begin drying items after they've been harvested, the happier you'll be with the results. This is also one of the few times in cooking when you'll hear "faster is better." When you carefully and quickly dry goods, it helps create a continuity of texture and ensures that the center of the item doesn't retain moisture. Nonetheless, most drying techniques do take a little while, so allow for the time in your schedule. If you have to stop in the middle of drying something, you're opening the door for microbial growth.

You don't have to over-moderate the drying process if you're following the temperature and time guidelines provided for the chosen method. It's suggested, however, that you keep an eye on the food in the last hour. Fruit, vegetables, and even meats can contain very different amounts of liquid. You don't want to burn your efforts, and due diligence during the last hour helps you avoid that.

Drying doesn't require a lot of fancy equipment, but some items come in handy. A countertop scale helps you measure out portions for recipes, and a range thermometer allows you to adjust the temperature for even drying in the oven. If money is tight, put these on the wish list for another day.

Finally—and this cannot be stressed enough—good air circulation is your best ally in successfully drying products, no matter what process you're using. To get the best benefit from that circulation, also remember to rotate and stir the drying items periodically. This exposes each side to the air to improve continuity in your dried food.

Drying Fruit

Bargains are great, but you don't want items that are overripe or damaged. Pick out a piece of fruit that you'd put out that day for someone to enjoy. When you get the fruit home, the sooner you can begin the drying process, the better. If something deters you, store the fruit in a cool area until you can prepare it for your chosen drying method.

Cleaning and Slicing

All fruit requires a good washing before you begin. With items like peaches or apples, you'll need to get rid of the inedible core or pit. Peel the fruit before slicing it thinly. If you're drying something like grapes, treat the skins to a swim in boiling water. Use a strainer to dunk them in a bowl of cold water, then lay them aside to dry. This method is called cracking, and it lets air into the fruit for better drying.

Battling Browning

Once sliced, fruit begins to brown fairly quickly. You want to keep the browning to a minimum because it does impact the overall quality of dried fruit. The popular method for offsetting oxidation is adding ascorbic acid to the fruit once it's cut (1 teaspoon dissolved in 1 cup of water for 5 quarts of soft fruit like peaches; 2 teaspoons for hard fruit like apples).

E-QUESTION

What's better for keeping fruit from browning?
Sulfuring preserves fruits' colors for the longest amount of time and helps them retain vitamins A and C. By comparison, ascorbic acid is about half as effective and lemon juice is a third as effective. However, some people have sulfur allergies that make lemon juice or ascorbic acid appealing.

If you find yourself unhappy with the results obtained by ascorbic acid, try a solution of sulfite instead. You need 1 tablespoon of food-grade sodium bisulfite (available in drug stores) in ½ gallon of water. Soak the fruit for about 7 minutes; leave light-colored fruit for a full 10 minutes. Afterwards, drain and dry. Soaking lengthens the drying process, so factor in extra time.

Budget about six to twelve hours to completely dry fruit pieces. Smaller slices or pieces dry the fastest. Always cut open a piece and check the interior to make sure the process is complete.

Drying Vegetables

Not all vegetables take well to drying. When you start thinking about drying vegetables, consider which ones have the shortest shelf life and which of those might be better suited to freezing. For example, the texture of asparagus doesn't translate well with drying and dehydration, so this is one short shelf life vegetable you may want to freeze instead.

Your vegetables should be fully grown and in peak condition. If you can harvest them from your garden, that's fantastic. However, don't buy or harvest more than you want for drying in one batch. This keeps your kitchen space more manageable. Thoroughly clean and cut the vegetables to the desired size, remembering that the larger the piece, the longer the drying time. Most vegetables require a fast blanching to stop enzymes from continuing to break down the plant matter. The exceptions to this rule include okra, onions, carrots, mushrooms, and peppers.

ALERT!

When a drying recipe calls for you to blanch a vegetable, don't throw that water away! It's rich in flavor and vitamins. Instead, reduce it down over a low flame, adding whatever spices you like, and freeze it for future soups, gravies, and stews.

Some vegetable parts, such as celery leaf, dry quickly; other parts will take as long as comparable fruit pieces. Dried vegetables are hard and crunchy. It's recommended that you store each type of vegetable separately in airtight, carefully labeled containers. Keep them away from sunlight or heat for the greatest longevity.

Drying Herbs

There's an old saying among herbalists: Don't grow mint unless you want a lot of it. Members of the mint family have a reputation for being overly hearty, which also makes them an excellent candidate for drying since you'll have an abundance to share. And mint is only one of the many herbs you can dry. In ancient times, dried herbs were commonly sold along trade routes, and merchants used legends about their healing powers to boost prices. Drying was the easiest way to retain flavor, a necessity when traveling through different environmental conditions. For modern preservers, drying is a good way to get organic spices in a relatively short timeframe.

Choosing and Cleaning Herbs

The fresher-is-better mantra also applies to herbs. If you're growing herbs at home, new growth bears better flavors than larger, older parts. It's also a good idea to harvest these early in the morning to conserve as much natural oil as possible. Once you've purchased or harvested the plants, make sure there are no dark leaves or any pieces that look withered. Remove those pieces along with the stalk. Put the herbs in a colander to rinse and drip dry. The herbs are now ready to be dried using whatever method you prefer.

ALERT!

If there's little or no aroma when you open a container of dried herbs, that means the plant has lost its remaining aromatic oils, which also give the herb flavor. Toss the dried herb into your compost heap; it's no longer useful for cooking.

Timing Is Everything

Oven drying will take an average of three hours. In the microwave, sandwich the herbs between pieces of paper towels and use a low setting for

30-second intervals until the herbs are crunchy dry. Store the herbs in an airtight container. Label it and place it in a cool dark area of the house. In this form, herbs have a shelf life of one year for the best culinary results.

Drying Meat, Poultry, and Fish

Drying is one of the oldest and most traditional forms of preserving meat. Not only does dried meat last a long time, it travels well and doesn't weigh as much once it's dehydrated. Many people associate dried meat with meat jerky. Making jerky at home is really cost effective. A pound of turkey jerky, for example, can cost upward of $6 depending on where you live. A pound of ground turkey and jerky spices costs about $2.50. Even after running a dehydrator, you're still saving money and you know exactly what's in your snack!

Preparation Process

Choose very lean cuts of meat or fish and immediately get rid of excess fat, which can go rancid even after drying. Cutting with the grain, slice the meat into ⅛"-thick pieces about 1" wide. You'll want a good, sharp knife. Dry the meat as it is or add salt, pepper, or other spices as desired. Cover the meat and let it sit in the refrigerator for 8–12 hours before drying it.

Freeze your meat halfway so that cutting it is a piece of cake! If you're drying game meat, freezing it completely for several weeks will kill parasites. When you're ready to dry it, defrost it only partially for cutting.

Dry Aging

Dry-aging beef can be done at home if you're exceedingly careful. Always begin with USDA Prime or Choice cuts from a trusted butcher. Rinse and dry the roast, then cover it with three sheets of cheesecloth or with an absolutely clean, new cotton towel. You can also rest the roast on a rack inside a plastic food container that you've poked full of holes to allow air in. Place the wrapped or sealed roast on a rack in the lowest part of your refrigerator.

Dry-aging experts usually like to age their meat for 10–21 days. However, the home preserver is safest aging the meat for 3–7 days. On each of those days, you will need to replace the cheesecloth or towel with a fresh one. Make sure there is nothing in your refrigerator with a strong aroma, and make sure nothing can leak onto your roast. After 7 days, the roast will shrink about 8–10 percent and gain a distinctively rich flavor.

ALERT!

If you're going to dry-age beef, it's essential to get an accurate thermometer for your refrigerator. In order to keep the meat safe from spoiling, the temperature inside the refrigerator should remain consistently below 35°F.

Finally, unwrap the roast, carefully cutting off any exterior dried meat or fat. Cook this as it is or slice it into steaks. This meat may be frozen for future use. It has a shelf life of about 4 months.

Chapter 5

Pickling

Pickling was among the most popular preserving methods for sailors, both because it was safe and because folks genuinely liked the flavors pickling produces. Basically, pickling preserves food in brine consisting of salt and water (1.5 tablespoons salt to 1 quart water), vinegar and water (1:3 ratio), sugar and water (1 cup salt and sugar per gallon), and additional spices to create distinctive tastes. Some items require only salt for pickling because they have high water contents, kimchi being one example.

Pickling 101

There are four basic types of pickles. The first is fresh pack, which is like the refrigerator pickles covered later in this chapter. It is blissfully simple to prepare. Second is fruit pickles that are prepared with a sugar-vinegar syrup. Third is chutney and relish, such as the recipes provided in Chapter 6. Finally, the most popular is salt-cured or brined pickles. No matter what type of pickle you intend to preserve, always start with firm fruits or vegetables, fresh spices, and clean water. If you're harvesting your own fruits and vegetables, do so early in the morning and refrigerate them immediately before preparing all your pickling equipment. This is also true of store-bought items. Heat makes pickled items softer.

FACT

Kimchi has been around for more than 3,000 years. In its earliest form, it was simply cabbage salted and aged to create the pickling effect. Later, herbs (hot pepper, scallions, garlic) and sometimes other vegetables (cucumber and radish) were added to the blend to customize the dish.

Basic Equipment

One of the great beauties of pickling is that it doesn't require a lot of fancy equipment. Stainless steel and glass are ideal for pickling projects. Aluminum, enamel, and iron pots or tools aren't recommended because of brine's natural acidity; when the acid reacts with those bases it changes the flavor of the resulting food items. The following list includes some of the items you'll want for pickling:

- Paring knife
- Vegetable peeler
- Stone jar or crockery for fermenting (Note: You will need a plate or other cover that fits inside your fermenting jar. This holds the pickles beneath the brine. Kitchen plates work well.)
- Large bowl, plastic zip lock bag, or plastic food container (These may substitute for the stone jar or crockery as a fermenting vessel.)

- Pots large enough for simmering the brine and spices
- Ladle
- Funnel
- Measuring tools
- Storage jars or containers
- Hot water canner (if you're planning to put up the pickles)

Finally, a timer is a nice addition to any preserver's kitchen, but it's not required.

E-QUESTION

What are sea cucumbers?
Sea cucumbers are an invertebrate similar to starfish. First appearing in fossil records some 400 million years ago, there are more than 1,000 species of them throughout the world. They've been used by humans in both pharmaceutical and culinary preparations, including appetizers, soups, and pickled fare.

Embracing Brine

Brining has become a very popular method in cooking, not just for pickling but also for marinade. For example, some people who love deep-fried turkey swear by herb-laced brine as one method for making a truly flavorful bird. The longer an item remains in brine, the more the base changes the taste and texture of the food.

Brining is very easy and very popular for meat because the salt helps keep it moist during the cooking process. To the foundation of salt and water, many cooks now add other flavorings to transport taste to every part of the meat (rather than just the exterior, as sometimes happens with a marinade). Meats that benefit from brining include lean poultry, pork, and seafood.

When using brine for meat, it's very important to soak it in the refrigerator at about 40°F. Before the meat goes in, both the brine and meat should already be at the correct temperature. This avoids bacteria. Smaller meat cuts accept brine easily within about 4 hours. Note that brined meat cooks in about two-thirds the time of nonbrined meat.

The same concept holds true for vegetables, fruits, and flowers. Whatever spices you add to fermenting or pickling brine are transported with the salt into the vegetable. This typically results in a unique texture that not everyone likes, so start your brining efforts small until you find a process that's pleasing.

Salt by Any Name

Table salt and sea salt are the most common ones used in brining, and some folks like a gourmet touch like fleur de sel and Hawaiian salt—but these get costly. Recipes will usually specify which salt they recommend. If you're going to substitute, 1 cup of table salt becomes 1½ cups of kosher salt.

Brine Containers

Food storage containers, large cooking bowls, and stainless steel stockpots all work very well as brine receptacles. Alternatively, if you're doing a large amount of brining, try a clean cooler (this needs to be sterilized). Remember that you'll need enough brine to completely cover the food. If you can't guess, put the food in the container and cover it with plain water. Measure that water and add your salt accordingly. Note that no matter how much you might like a blend, you should never reuse brine.

FACT

In the 1600s, a fish brine from China called *ketsiap* traveled via spice routes to numerous countries. As the soy-like substance reached different regions, the various cultures put personal spins on the basic recipe. In 1711, the word *ketchup* was born, and 100 years later the first tomato ketchup recipe was printed in the United States.

Hotter . . . Colder . . . Hotter

Some cooks adjust their meat brine according to the temperature at which they plan to cook it. Slow and low cooked meat receives more sugar and salt compared to high-heat (grilling or broiling) meat. Generally, the slow cooked brine takes ¼ cup of kosher salt and sugar to 1 pint of water. For high heat cooking, use 1 quart water, 1 tablespoon sugar, and ⅛ cup of kosher salt. In terms of brining time, about 1 hour per pound is a good measure.

Pickle Brining

Pickle brine includes vinegar for curing along with the traditional salt and/or sugar. Cucumbers are far and away the most popular vegetable for pickling. They are best purchased or harvested unwaxed, when they're small and very firm. Brining waxed cucumbers won't work because the salt cannot penetrate the skin. The basic brine for pickling is 1 quart water to ½ cup salt. It's important that the vegetables remain under the brine throughout the fermenting period. It takes about a month for a whole pickle to be completely fermented. The best test is to cut one open and look for uniform color.

ALERT!

Always use the amount of vinegar or salt suggested in a recipe. If you find the blend is too harsh for you, add a pinch of sugar to balance out the tartness. Both vinegar and salt are important to safeguard against bacterial growth.

Now you can rinse the pickle mixture and move it into 3 parts of good quality vinegar (5 percent acidity) with one part filtered water and any additional flavorings. Cider and malt vinegar are mild and work well in sweet pickle recipes, while white vinegar is the most commonly used because it doesn't discolor the vegetables. You can certainly substitute one type of vinegar for another in your recipes, as long as the vinegar has the 5 percent acidity necessary for pickling.

If a recipe calls for sugar, you could try substituting honey if white sugar isn't in your diet. Use about ¾ cup honey for every 1 cup of sugar. Be aware this changes the flavor of the end product. At this juncture, you can store the pickles in the fridge for snacking or can them. However, pickles fermented in this way will lose some crispness to canning.

Salt Preserving/Pickling

Salt pickling is really just another name for brining, with one exception—dry salting, most commonly used with meat and fish. This method goes back to ancient Egypt, if not earlier, and it can be used with vegetables to create a pickle-like item. For example, cabbage, radishes, cucumbers, and even greens can be fast pickled by cleaning them off, dusting them evenly in salt, and then putting them in a bowl with pickling seasonings. In this case, a heavy plate needs to go on top of the pickles to press them (try filling a 2 liter bottle of water and put that on top). Twenty-four hours later, after a quick rinse and chill, your salt pickles are ready. Note that the shelf life for these is only 2 days in the refrigerator.

E-QUESTION

Where does the phrase "beneath the salt" originate?
During the Middle Ages, salt was a highly valued commodity that was traditionally utilized only by the wealthy. When people ate together, those of high birth would sit at a high table or the head of the table where an ornamental salt server had been placed for their use. Everyone else would sit at a Low Table—literally beneath the salt, indicating their place in society.

Refrigerator Pickling

Refrigerator pickling (also known as quick pickling) is fast and easy and you can use it to treat any vegetable or fruit that you like to pickle. It won't preserve your food nearly as long as other processes, but it's tasty and time effective. The following directions explain how to pickle cucumbers, which are among the most popular vegetables for refrigerator pickling because they take exceedingly well to the process. Other good options include cauliflower, baby onions, and sliced carrots.

1. Find the freshest, crispest produce that has no signs of being past its prime. You'll need about 6 cucumbers approximately 4" long for a quart jar. Carefully wash the cucumbers and slice them into bite-sized pieces.

2. Sterilize your jars. If you have a sterilizing cycle on your dishwasher, you can prepare the jars while you're cutting! Otherwise, fill a large stockpot with water, add your jars and lids, and bring them to a full boil.

3. Mix together and heat 6 cups water, 2 cups white vinegar, ½ cup sugar (if you want sweet pickles), ½ cup canning salt, and 1 teaspoon of each of your desired spices. Dill and garlic are both great flavors, as are sliced onion, mustard seed, and celery seed. You may also want to add ½ teaspoon of alum for crispness.

4. While the brine heats, pack the cucumbers into the jars, leaving about ¼ inch at the top.

5. Pour the hot mixture over the cucumbers; cover. Let sit at room temperature for 24 hours. Chill and enjoy.

E-QUESTION

How long will refrigerator pickles keep?
Let your refrigerator pickles age for about 7–10 weeks to let the flavors soak in before consuming them. These last for about 2 months in the refrigerator (if you can keep people from eating them). If the solution ever starts looking cloudy, that's a good signal to toss them.

Pickling Olives

According to Greek mythology, olive trees are associated with Athena, the goddess of wisdom. The gods devised a contest to decide whether Athena or Poseidon, god of the sea, would have the honor of being the patron of Attica. Each would make a gift to the people, and their fellow immortals would name the winner. Athena presented the citizens of Attica with an olive tree, which symbolized peace and provided shade, food, and medicine. She triumphed over Poseidon, whose gift was a horse—practical but also a symbol of war. The people of Attica built a city to their new patroness and named it Athens.

Historically, olives and olive oil were important items throughout Asia Minor, where they have been cultivated for thousands of years. Olives are long-lived evergreens that can reach a height of more than twenty feet and begin to yield fruit by the time they are about five years of age. The fruit of the trees has many uses, but they cannot be consumed raw. They have to be brined or otherwise processed, meaning that the idea of pickled olives is really a twice-pickling method.

ALERT!

Olive oil can only be labeled virgin if it's extracted from the olives physically instead of chemically. Extra-virgin olive oil comes from the first pressing of olives and cannot contain any refined oil, whereas pure olive oil is typically a blend of refined olive oil with either of the two virgin oils.

For success in pickling olives, select ones that are firm, and don't attempt to mix different types of olives together. Since you'll probably get olives that are already brined the first time, it's acceptable and even preferable to mix one type of olives with garlic, onions, or other items for pickling. To keep the olives as firm as possible, do not cook them in brine. Instead, mix them with other chosen ingredients and pour the brine over the top. In this form, the pickled olive mix can be refrigerated or canned but not frozen. The pickled olives last about 3 months in the refrigerator; canned olives should be used in 1 year.

Troubleshooting Pickling Problems

What's a cook to do when the pickles turn out less than perfect? This list includes common problems and their solutions.

- Bitter pickles indicate too much vinegar; check the recipe. Note: This can also be caused by using salt substitutes.
- Cloudy pickles are a warning that your pickles may have spoiled—especially if they were fresh packed. The introduction of an airborne yeast, using metal pans, adding table salt, and using hard water during production can also have this effect. If the pickled item seems greasy or smells funny, throw it out.

- Discolored pickles are usually the fault of the pan or hard water, but strong spices can also bleed over into pickles, giving them a different hue.
- Green- or blue-tinted garlic isn't cause for concern. It just means that the garlic absorbed the metals in your cooking utensils or the garlic you used was young. It's still perfectly safe to eat.
- Hollow cucumbers are safe to eat. The cucumber may have been too big or may have been hollow when canning. If a cucumber floats in water, it's not a good pickling cucumber. The brine may also have been too weak or too strong.
- Pale coloring may mean your produce was exposed to light or was of poor quality.
- Dark coloring may result from minerals in the water, the use of different vinegar (like malt vinegar), overcooking, or the use of iodized salt in processing. If you didn't change any components, darkening may indicate spoilage. When in doubt, throw it out!
- Bubbly brine is a sign that your food has begun to spoil. Throw these pickles out.
- Pink pickles may result if you use overly ripe dill in your pickle blend. The introduction of yeast is another possible reason. If the pickles are soft, the liquid cloudy, or the food feels slimy, it's likely a yeast problem and the pickles should be discarded.
- Slimy pickles can be the result of a variety of causes. The amount of salt or vinegar used in the mix may not have been sufficient, the pickles may not have been totally covered by brine, the canning process may not have been followed correctly, yeast may have been introduced, moldy spices may have been used, jars may have been improperly sealed, or the pickles may have been kept in too hot an area (70°F is the best temperature to encourage proper pickling). These are not safe to eat.
- Bland pickles may result from use of cucumbers that were not meant for pickling. Store-bought cucumbers often have a waxy coating. The brine can't penetrate this; pickles are less flavorful. If you must use this type of cucumber, slice and salt it for about 1 hour, then rinse and pickle. This will open the pores, letting the brine in.

- Shriveled pickles may mean the vinegar is too strong, the salt concentration too high, or the pickles overprocessed. Measure carefully and watch the clock!
- Mixed flavors usually mean the size of the vegetables wasn't even. The larger the cut, the more time a vegetable takes to accept flavor.
- Mushy pickles can result from using the wrong type of cucumber or overprocessing. If you have a choice of what to buy or grow, look for lemon cucumbers, little leafs, saladin, and Edmonson. You can use food-grade alum or grape leaves in the bottom of the jar to improve crispness.
- Mold or dirt on a jar often indicates it wasn't properly sealed; some of the brine has gotten out onto the rim, meaning that bacteria can also get into the jar. Don't eat these.

Whenever you're confronted with a jar you don't feel quite right about, it's usually best to err on the side of caution and throw it out.

Chapter 6

Condiments

Garlic Honey Mustard

MAKES 2 CUPS

INGREDIENTS
¼ cup freshly ground mustard
½ cup honey
¼ whole dark mustard seed
½ cup malt or white vinegar
1 tablespoon yellow mustard powder
1 tablespoon finely ground garlic
salt to taste (optional)
pepper to taste (optional)

Use this zesty honey mustard on pork, chicken, or your next hoagie. Orange blossom may be substituted for honey to add a nice aromatic note.

1. Thoroughly mix all ingredients. Taste test and adjust for personal preferences.

2. To make the mustard thinner, add more vinegar; to make it thicker, add more mustard powder or honey.

3. This mustard may be frozen, but canning offers a longer shelf life and better textural/taste results. Use a hot pack, hot water method, leaving at least ¼" space at the top of each jar and immersing the jars for 15 minutes.

4. Move to a cooling surface, leaving plenty of space between the jars. Check all the lids when cool, tightening as needed. If any of the jars did not seal, refrigerate or freeze instead.

The Lore of Mustard
People in the Far East consider mustard an aphrodisiac that also supports well-being. In India, a wife might spread mustard seeds around her house to keep out malevolent spirits. In Germany, brides carefully place mustard seed in their wedding dress to safeguard their authority in the home, and in Denmark mustard seed is said to improve passion, especially when mixed with mint and ginger.

Onion Bourbon Mustard

If you can find apple-flavored whiskey, the resulting flavor is really amazing with pork. Make sure to choose a piece of horseradish root that's firm and dense.

1. Sauté the onions in the olive oil. As they begin to brown, sprinkle them with sugar to caramelize.

2. Mix the onions, honey, sugar, vinegar, mustard, horseradish, and whiskey in a blender on low until well incorporated.

3. Pour the resulting mix into a saucepan.

4. Heat the mustard over low heat until it comes to a boil. Continue boiling until the mustard reaches the desired consistency.

5. Cool and taste, adding salt and pepper if desired.

6. Store in a freezer-safe container for up to 6 months.

Mustard Grains

There are two common types of mustard seed, brown and white. The good news for home preservers is that mustard grows easily up to zone three. Wait until your weather is steadily above 55°F to sow seeds (1 inch apart, ¼ inch deep). You will need to thin them later. Come late summer, the seed pods turn yellow and they're ready to harvest.

MAKES 2 CUPS

INGREDIENTS

¼ cup onions, diced

1 tablespoon olive oil

½ teaspoon sugar

½ cup pure honey

½ cup dark brown sugar, packed

½ cup apple cider vinegar

4 tablespoons yellow mustard

2 tablespoons whole mustard seed

2 tablespoons freshly ground mustard seed

2 tablespoons freshly ground horseradish

½ cup bourbon whiskey

salt to taste (optional)

pepper to taste (optional)

Heirloom Mustard Pickles

MAKES 4 QUARTS

INGREDIENTS

4 cups onions

4 cups cucumbers

4 cups small green tomatoes

1 medium cauliflower

2 sweet peppers

2 cups salt

1 gallon water

pinch alum (optional)

4 cups sugar

3 tablespoons celery seed

⅔ cup mustard

4¼ cups vinegar

These are the kinds of pickles often seen on our grandparent's tables. While the spices may change a little, the passion these pickles inspire remains consistent.

1. Cut vegetables into 1" pieces. Put in a large bowl; cover with water, salt, and alum.

2. Put a plate over top of vegetables so they stay below brine; leave at room temperature 24 hours.

3. The next day, warm entire mixture to scalding; remove from heat and drain vegetables. Immediately put into sterilized jars (if canning) or freezer-safe containers (if freezing).

4. Put remaining ingredients in a large pot; simmer until thickened. Pour sauce evenly over pickles. Make sure to get all the air bubbles out if canning. Leave ¼" headspace in the jars; process 10 minutes in a hot-water bath. If freezing, remember to leave extra space for freezer expansion.

5. Canned pickles have a shelf life of 1 year. Frozen pickles last 6–8 months.

Alum Issues?

Alum (potassium aluminum sulfate) has been used as a crisper for canned pickles for ages, but its popularity has waned recently. It gives some people indigestion and can irritate sulfate allergies. You may want to leave it out if you have any doubts over how it will affect your tummy or your dinner guests'.

Burmese-Style Mustard Greens

This type of blend is very popular throughout Asia and the Eastern world as an appetizer, side dish, or snack. Try it with Chinese five-spice powder in place of the gingerroot.

1. Thoroughly rinse the mustard greens; blanch for 30 seconds; and dunk in an ice bath. Soak the greens in hot water so they wilt; cut into ¼-inch slices.

2. Mix the remaining ingredients in a large bowl; add the greens and turn to coat evenly.

3. Cover with a plate for weight; secure with plastic wrap. Let sit for 24 hours. Greens can be refrigerated, frozen, or canned. Flavor improves with aging. If canning, pack to within 1" of a quart container, secure the lid, and put in a hot-water bath for 15 minutes. Test lids when cool.

MAKES 2 QUARTS

INGREDIENTS
1½ pounds mustard greens
3 cups carrots, thinly sliced
½ pound shallots, peeled
2 fresh red chilies, seeded and diced
2 teaspoons salt
2 teaspoons brown sugar
1 teaspoon fresh gingerroot, grated
⅓ cup dark ale
⅔ cup malt vinegar

Very Berry Mustard

MAKES ABOUT 1½ CUPS

INGREDIENTS

½ cup dark mustard seeds

2 tablespoons mustard powder

½ cup filtered water

1 cup mixed blackberries and raspberries

⅓ cup balsamic or malted vinegar

4 tablespoons raspberry vinegar

3 teaspoons dark honey

salt to taste

pepper to taste

This mustard has a beautiful color and tastes fantastic on both pork and chicken, especially as part of a glaze. For the best flavor, age this for about a week before using.

1. Using an herb grinder or a mortar and pestle, finely grind all but about ⅛ cup of the mustard seed. Mix the powdered mustard with the mustard powder. Add water to mustard mixture and move to a non-metallic pot.

2. Carefully wash and mush the berries. Add berries, vinegar, and honey to a cooking pot. Warm over a low flame, stirring regularly for 15 minutes.

3. Taste and add more vinegar or honey to personal taste. Salt and pepper to taste. Fold in the remaining whole mustard seeds.

4. Pour into hot, sterilized ½-pint canning jars, leaving ¼"–1" headspace. Process immediately in a hot-water bath for 15 minutes.

5. Move to a cooling surface, leaving plenty of space between the jars. Check all the lids when cool, tightening the rim as needed. If any of the jars did not seal, refrigerate or freeze instead.

Louisiana-Style Mustard

This piquant mustard works as a fabulous braise for pork and chicken, not to mention a sizzling spread for your favorite ham sandwich. If you really like things hot, add some flaked red pepper and/or cloves.

1. Heat a skillet over medium heat and toss in the whole mustard seeds. When the seeds begin to pop, remove the pan from heat and cover with a heavy, clean cloth until the seeds cool.

2. Coarse-grind the seeds using either a rolling pin or mortar.

3. In another pan, mix the wine, garlic, celery, allspice, salt, Worcestershire, and hot sauce. Bring to a simmer, stirring regularly for five minutes.

4. While the wine blend simmers, mix the mustard seed with vinegar, stirring to make an even paste.

5. Bring the wine blend to a full boil, then slowly add the mustard paste until all ingredients are well incorporated.

6. Pour the mustard into sterilized jars, leaving ¼" headspace. Cap.

7. Let sit overnight before freezing. Use within 6 months. Refrigerate after opening.

MAKES 2½ CUPS

INGREDIENTS

1 cup mustard seeds, toasted

1 cup dry white wine or champagne

1 clove garlic, peeled and minced

1 teaspoon celery seeds

1 teaspoon ground allspice

½ teaspoon salt

½ teaspoon Worcestershire sauce

½ teaspoon hot sauce

2 tablespoons white vinegar

2 tablespoons malt vinegar

Green Tomato Relish

MAKES 12–15 QUARTS

INGREDIENTS
20–25 pounds solid hard totally green tomatoes
10–12 pounds onions
1 container Morton's Pickling Salt
4 large green peppers
4 large sweet red peppers
4 large sweet orange peppers
4 large sweet yellow peppers
½ gallon cider vinegar
2–3 gallons white vinegar
10 cups white sugar
½ cup mixed pickling spice
2–4 dried hot peppers
8 bay leaves

This is a great condiment to go with hot dogs and bratwursts.

1. Wash tomatoes in cold water. Drain and dry with paper towels. Core and cut into bite-sized chunks.

2. Layer tomatoes in a very large stockpot. Sprinkle each layer well with pickling salt. Cover with a clean white cotton dishcloth. Let sit in a draft-free area for 2 to 4 hours. The pickling salt draws moisture from the hard tomatoes. If it is a very warm day, 2 hours is sufficient to soften tomatoes a bit.

3. Rinse in cold water at least twice. Drain well. Divide into 2 large stockpots.

4. Slice onions. Wash and dry peppers. Seed and cut into slices. Divide equally between two stockpots.

5. Divide the cider vinegar and white vinegar between the stockpots to cover vegetables. Divide sugar evenly between stockpots. Stir well.

6. Fold a square of cheesecloth twice and place half the mixed pickling spice, half the dried hot peppers, and four of the bay leaves onto it. Gather up the corners and tie with kitchen string. Repeat with remaining pickling spice, hot peppers, and bay leaves. Place one spice ball into each stockpot. Sink it down toward the middle.

7. Stir ingredients in each stockpot well. Cover and bring to a boil over high heat. Reduce heat and simmer 30 to 45 minutes until tomatoes are tender but not mushy.

8. Remove and discard spice balls.

9. Use a slotted spoon to fill each jar with veggie mixture, packing down with plastic knife to remove air pockets.

10. Cover with hot brine, leaving 1" headspace. Wipe rims and place sterilized lid on each jar. Tightly screw on sterilized band. Process in boiling-water bath for 20 minutes.

Caramelized Red Onion Relish

This is absolutely delightful when mixed with extra-virgin olive oil and used as a vinaigrette on a salad of lettuce, tomatoes, fresh basil, scallions, and a handful of blueberries.

1. In a heavy nonstick skillet, combine onions and sugar with olive oil; heat over medium-high heat.

2. Cook uncovered for 25 minutes, or until onions turn golden and start to caramelize, stirring frequently.

3. Stir in wine, vinegar, salt, and pepper; bring to a boil over high heat. Reduce heat to low; cook 15 minutes, or until most of the liquid has evaporated, stirring frequently.

4. Ladle into sterilized jars, leaving ½" headspace. Remove air bubbles. Wipe rims. Cap and seal. Process in a water-bath canner for 10 minutes.

MAKES 6 PINTS

INGREDIENTS

6 large red onions, peeled and sliced very thinly

¾ cup brown sugar, firmly packed

1 tablespoon extra-virgin olive oil

3 cups dry red wine

½ cup aged balsamic vinegar

½ teaspoon fine sea salt

½ teaspoon freshly ground black pepper

End of Summer Chow Chow

As the title implies, this is a tasty way to enjoy your garden for many months after the harvest. If you've got a farmers market, get those end-of-season sales and preserve them!

1. Place cabbage, tomatoes, peppers, and onions into a large stockpot. Sprinkle with pickling salt.

2. Cover and let stand for 4 to 5 hours. Rinse and drain well.

3. In a separate pot, combine remaining ingredients. Heat to a boil.

4. Pour over the rinsed and drained vegetables. Boil gently for about 5 minutes.

5. Ladle into sterilized jars. Wipe rims. Cap and seal. Process in a water-bath canner for 10 minutes.

MAKES 4 QUARTS

INGREDIENTS

1 large head green cabbage, finely chopped

12 large green tomatoes, cored and diced

6 sweet green peppers, chopped

3 medium red onions, chopped

3 large sweet red peppers, chopped

½ cup pickling salt

6 cups granulated sugar

2 tablespoons mustard seed

1 tablespoon celery seed

1½ tablespoons Herbes de Provence

2 teaspoons black pepper

1½ teaspoons turmeric

4 cups cider vinegar

2 cups water

Sassy Summer Chutney

MAKES 4 PINTS

INGREDIENTS

1 pound fresh apricots

1 pound fresh peaches

1 pound fresh nectarines

1 pound fresh pears

2 small seedless oranges

2 tablespoons freshly ground ginger

20 cloves garlic, minced

1 cup golden raisins

1 cup dried cranberries

1 cup apple cider vinegar

1 cup light brown sugar, firmly packed

3 cups sweet onions, finely diced

2 cups orange juice

½ teaspoon ground cinnamon

½ teaspoon ground clove

1 teaspoon salt

½ teaspoon cinnamon

½ teaspoon freshly ground allspice

This is a sweet-savory blend that can be used as a condiment, side dish, or sauce. If you'd like to can it, use the hot-water bath method for 15 minutes.

1. Peel and chop the apricots, peaches, nectarines, and pears; put into a large pot. Carefully remove the peel from the orange and add to the pot.

2. Chop oranges, ginger, and garlic; add to the pot. Add all remaining ingredients. Bring to a boil, stirring constantly.

3. Reduce heat to low; simmer for 45 minutes, continuing to stir regularly. The chutney will begin to thicken.

4. Cool and move into freezer-safe containers, leaving ¼" headspace for expansion. Use within 6–8 months.

Chutney Facts
Chutney is a mix of fruits, vegetables, sugar, and spices cooked down in vinegar. It appears somewhat like jam. Chutney originated in India, where it was originally called *catni*, meaning "to taste." Some of the most popular ingredients used in chutneys include apple, chili peppers, cinnamon, lemon, garlic, ginger, onion, mango, mint, and tomato.

Trish's Tropical Temptation Salsa

This is an incredibly fast and easy salsa that kids and adults alike love. If you want to can this recipe, leave ½" headspace in your jars and process for 10 minutes.

1. Combine all ingredients in a large pot. Slowly bring to a boil, stirring regularly. Let boil 5 minutes.

2. Reduce heat and simmer another 5 minutes. Cool and store in freezer-safe containers.

Helpful Hint
Many preservers like using covered ice cube trays for freezing things like salsa and other sauces in single-serve sizes. In this form, you just pop out what you need and cover the remaining cubes back up for future use.

MAKES ABOUT 8 PINTS

INGREDIENTS
2 cups ripe mango, diced
2 cups ripe pineapple, diced
2 cups ripe passion fruit, diced
2 cups sweet pepper, diced
½ cup finely chopped onion
½ teaspoon crushed red pepper flakes
2 teaspoons garlic, finely chopped
2 teaspoons freshly grated ginger
2 banana peppers, finely diced
1 cup light brown sugar
1¼ cups cider vinegar
½ cup water

Lively Salad Topping

INGREDIENTS

1½ cups sweet pepper, diced

1 cup green onion, diced

1 cup red onion, diced

1 cup celery, chopped

1 cup carrots, chopped

1 cup cherry tomatoes, quartered

1 cup cabbage, diced

½ cup banana pepper, diced (optional)

1 teaspoon Worcestershire sauce

1 teaspoon garlic powder (optional)

1 teaspoon salt

1 teaspoon ground pepper

2 tablespoons sesame seeds

2 tablespoons sunflower seeds

½ cup chow mein noodles

You do not have to be exactly precise with this recipe. Just use up your vegetable ends and pieces and toss them with a little seasoning.

1. Preheat oven to 150°F. If you are using a dehydrator, follow the manufacturer's suggested setting for vegetables.

2. In a bowl, mix all ingredients except the sesame and sunflower seeds and noodles; toss vegetables to evenly coat in the spices.

3. Spread mixture evenly onto nonstick cooking trays. Dry in the oven; stir periodically to make sure nothing sticks or burns.

4. When the mixture is crunchy (about 3–4 hours), cool and mix with sesame seeds, sunflower seeds, and noodles.

5. Store in an airtight container with the rest of your spices. The topping has a shelf life of 6 months.

Shallot Confiture

This is delightful to use as a condiment served either warm or cold with meats, or apply as a marinade.

Day one: Peel the shallots, leaving the root ends intact. Place them in a nonmetallic bowl; sprinkle with canning salt. Add enough water to cover, stirring carefully to dissolve the salt. Put a plate on top of the shallots to submerge them completely. Cover with a clean cotton dish towel; put in a cool place and let sit for 24 hours.

Day two: Drain and rinse the shallots thoroughly in cool water; dry on paper towels. Pour the vinegar and sugar into a stockpot; stir well. Make a spice ball using a doubled square of cheesecloth and all the spices except the caraway seeds. Add the spice ball to the stockpot; pour in the caraway seeds. Heat on medium heat until sugar has completely dissolved. Raise the heat and bring to a boil; boil for 10 minutes. Add the shallots; simmer gently for 15 minutes. Remove stockpot from heat; cover, and let sit for 24 hours.

Day three: Slowly bring the shallots to a boil; turn down heat and simmer for 15 minutes. Remove stockpot from heat; cover, and let sit for 24 hours.

Day four: Slowly bring the shallots to a boil once more. Simmer gently until the shallots are golden brown and translucent. Discard spice ball. Ladle into sterilized jars. Use a plastic knife to remove air pockets. Cap and seal. Process in a water-bath canner for 10 minutes. Store in a cool, dark, dry place for 2–3 months to allow flavors to meld.

The Scuttle on Shallots

Shallots originated in Asia Minor. Europeans were introduced to them after Crusaders brought them back from their travels. They are part of the onion family and are best stored in mesh bags in a well-ventilated area. Nutritionally, shallots are a good source of potassium.

MAKES 7 PINTS

INGREDIENTS

3 pounds shallots, peeled, root ends intact

1½ level cups canning salt

8 cups cider vinegar

4½ cups granulated sugar

4 cardamom pods, crushed

2 teaspoons dried lemon zest

2 cinnamon sticks

4–6 small dried red chili peppers

2½ teaspoons whole cloves

1 tablespoon whole black peppercorns

½ cup caraway seeds

Asian Vinaigrette

MAKES 5–6 PINTS

INGREDIENTS

1 cup soy sauce

1 cup rice vinegar

1 cup sesame oil

1 cup virgin olive oil

4 tablespoons honey

4 teaspoons orange zest

4 teaspoons ginger

2 teaspoons coarsely ground black pepper

1 large bunch green onions, finely diced

4 teaspoons sesame seeds

This vinaigrette is good on noodles, as a dipping sauce for dim sum, or as a salad dressing. It goes together very quickly. Refrigerate and shake well before using.

1. Whisk all ingredients together in a saucepan over low heat. Cook for 10 minutes to allow the blend to reduce.

2. Ladle hot dressing into sterilized jars. Wipe rims. Remove air bubbles. Cap and seal. Process in a water-bath canner for 15 minutes.

History of Salad Dressing

Soy sauce is probably the oldest salad dressing; it has been used for 5,000 years in China. The Babylonians, also salad lovers, used oil and vinegar 2,000 years ago. Romans topped their salads with salt, while Egyptians followed the Babylonian example and added Asian spices.

Peanut Sauce

MAKES 1 CUP

INGREDIENTS

1 medium shallot, minced

1 teaspoon peanut oil

¼ cup peanut butter

2 teaspoons soy sauce

1 teaspoon dark sesame oil

1 teaspoon rice wine vinegar

1 tablespoon brown sugar or honey

1 tablespoon fresh lemon or lime juice

1 clove garlic, crushed

½ teaspoon powdered ginger

½ teaspoon red chili flakes

½ cup water

1 tablespoon fresh lemon or lime juice

Peanut sauce tastes excellent on many items, including chicken, grilled beef, pork, noodles, rice, and even breadsticks. Add more water if you prefer a thinner consistency.

1. Sauté the shallot in peanut oil. In a saucepan, combine shallot with remaining ingredients, except lemon or lime juice.

2. Whisk over medium heat until mixture comes to a very soft boil. Taste; adjust red pepper, then add the lemon or lime a few drops at a time to balance out the flavors.

3. Cool. Pour into 2½-pint freezer containers or add to meat as a marinade in an appropriate airtight container; freeze. Use within 6–8 months.

Brown Sauce Sheets

These roll-up–style sauce sheets can be sliced and placed over meat while it's cooking or used a little at a time in soups and stews for additional flavor.

1. Heat olive oil in a frying pan. Add onions; sauté until soft. If you like a sweeter sauce, sprinkle a few pinches of sugar on them as they sauté.

2. Put onions and all remaining ingredients in a large saucepan; bring to a boil. Stir regularly.

3. Reduce to a simmer. Continue to stir regularly over the next 2–3 hours until it reduces by about 1 cup. Increase simmering time for a thicker sauce with more concentrated flavors.

4. Place an even coating of the sauce on waxed paper or the fruit roll-up sheets of your dehydrator. For the latter, follow the manufacturer's recommended temperature. If drying in the oven, set the temperature for 150°F; cook until no longer sticky. This can take up to 12 hours depending on the environment.

5. Slice to preferred sizes. Wrap in waxed paper; store in a jar or food-storage bag for future use.

Not Just Brown Sauce Anymore
Brown sauce is a traditional condiment throughout Europe, like steak sauce in the United States. It began in the late 1800s as HP sauce, invented by Frederick Gibson Garton in England. Since then, it has taken on various flavors.

MAKES 5 CUPS

INGREDIENTS

1 tablespoon olive oil

2 large sweet onions, roughly chopped

½ cup tamarind paste

2 tablespoons garlic, minced

2 tablespoons ginger, minced

¼ cup tomato paste

2 tablespoons freshly cracked black pepper

½ cup dark corn syrup

1 cup black strap molasses

2 cups white vinegar

1 cup balsamic vinegar

1 cup dark beer

½ cup orange juice

¼ cup soy sauce

2 tablespoons coarsely ground mustard

2 tablespoons Liquid Smoke

2 cups low-fat beef stock

Pickled Ginger Sauce

MAKES 2 CUPS

INGREDIENTS

½ cup rice wine vinegar

¼ cup fresh lime juice

1 tablespoon dried onion flakes

½ tablespoon chives

1 teaspoon freshly ground pepper

1½ teaspoons pickled ginger, minced, plus 1 cup juice

1 teaspoon dark soy sauce

This is a wonderful Asian-style dipping sauce that can be canned or frozen. If you cannot find enough pickled ginger juice, many stores carry regular ginger juice.

1. Mix all the ingredients together in a nonaluminum pan over medium heat.

2. Let the sauce come to a low rolling boil; reduce by about ½ cup.

3. Cool and preserve. Add fresh chopped green onion when serving.

Pickled Dressing

MAKES 2 CUPS

INGREDIENTS

1 cup wine vinegar

½ cup sugar

5 teaspoons kosher salt

¼ cup extra-virgin olive oil

¼ cup chopped fresh basil

2 garlic cloves, pressed

1½ tablespoons Parmesan cheese

2 teaspoons sweet pimento, finely chopped

Try this dressing over noodles with spinach, garnishing with some sesame seeds and alfalfa spouts. If you choose to can this, leave out the Parmesan cheese and add fresh cheese when you're ready to serve the dressing.

1. Whisk together all ingredients except cheese and pimento.

2. Bring to a boil over low heat.

3. Remove from heat. Stir in cheese and pimento.

4. If freezing, let cool before transferring to freezer-safe containers. If canning, pour into sterilized jars and process in a hot-water bath for 15 minutes.

Chapter 7

Marinades and Sauces

Burnt Onion Concentrate

MAKES 8 PINTS

INGREDIENTS

3 pounds onions, peeled and
coarsely chopped

7½ cups cold water

3 cups brown sugar

7½ cups cider vinegar

3 tablespoons dried French
tarragon

1 teaspoon salt

1 teaspoon coarsely ground
black pepper

This recipe was adapted from a Victorian-era blend that can act as either a sauce or a marinade. It's also great for flavoring gravies, soups, and stews.

1. In a large stockpot, combine onions and water. Cover; bring to a boil. Lower heat; simmer until onion is soft. Add sugar; stir well.

2. Continue to simmer until mixture has turned a very dark brown and has reduced by about half. This will take at least 1 hour. Stir occasionally to prevent sticking.

3. In a separate pan, bring vinegar, French tarragon, salt, and pepper to a boil. Lower heat; simmer 10 minutes.

4. Slowly pour vinegar mixture into onion mixture; stir well. Bring to a boil; lower heat, and simmer 10 minutes.

5. Ladle into sterilized pint jars, leaving 1" headspace. Wipe rims. Cap and seal. Process in a water-bath canner 10 minutes.

Buffalo Chicken Marinade

This marinade is good on any poultry and also makes a zesty grilling blend for vegetables. To adapt it for beef, simply substitute red wine and red wine vinegar for the white wine and the cider vinegar.

1. Place all the ingredients in a saucier. Warm the marinade over medium flame until it boils. Maintain a low rolling boil until the mix reduces by about ½ cup.

2. Pour into hot canning jars, leaving ½" headspace. Wipe the rims and apply lids. Process in a hot-water bath 15 minutes.

Natural Tenderizers
The best tenderizing marinades are those that have ingredients with a high acid content. Included in this list are juices like pineapple, mango, and papaya; fruits like figs, kiwi, honeydew, lemon, and orange; liquids like vinegar, yogurt, wine, and buttermilk; and spices like ginger. The acid helps relax protein in meat, making it tender. In the process, the flavors of these items penetrate the food.

MAKES 2 PINTS

INGREDIENTS
4⅛ cups cider vinegar
2 cups virgin olive oil
½ cup dry white wine
1 tablespoon hot sauce
3 teaspoons salt
1 teaspoon sugar
1 teaspoon lemon juice
1 teaspoon black pepper
1 teaspoon paprika
¼ teaspoon cayenne
¼ teaspoon garlic powder
¼ teaspoon onion powder
¼ teaspoon ground oregano
¼ teaspoon ground thyme
¼ teaspoon ground sage
¼ teaspoon ground basil
¼ teaspoon rosemary
1 bay leaf

All-Purpose Dry Marinade

MAKES 1½ CUPS

INGREDIENTS

Fresh Ingredients for Drying

1 medium onion, diced

5 cloves garlic, diced

¼ cup fresh oregano, diced

¼ cup chives, chopped

1 orange

1 lemon

1–2 chili peppers

Remaining Base Ingredients

⅓ cup brown sugar

⅓ cup paprika

⅓ cup kosher salt

⅓ cup coarse peppercorns

2 tablespoons dry mustard

2 tablespoons dry Worcestershire sauce powder

To use the dry marinade, simply sprinkle 1–2 teaspoons on each side of your meat, poultry, fish, or vegetables and let sit. Meat and poultry improves from a full day in the refrigerator with the dry marinade rubbed in. Fish and vegetables can go on the stove or grill almost immediately.

1. Place the onion, garlic, oregano, and chives, evenly spaced, in the dehydrator or on a lightly oiled baking sheet.

2. Zest the orange and lemon peels; put them on a second layer or sheet.

3. Finely dice the orange and lemon; place on a third layer or sheet.

4. Carefully seed the hot pepper(s); dice. Place on a fourth layer or sheet.

5. Dry the herbs, fruit, and pepper in the oven at 150°F until crunchy. The mixture will dry in about 2 hours, but make sure that everything is crunchy (not rubbery). Any rubbery items should remain in the heat until fully dried. If using a dehydrator, follow the manufacturer's recommended time and temperature guidelines, leaving longer if the items aren't fully crunchy.

6. Place all the freshly dried goods in a spice grinder and grind for consistency.

7. Add spices to the remaining base ingredients; mix well. Store in an airtight container located in a cool, dark area. Dry marinade is good for approximately 1 year.

Dry Marinade

Most dry marinades are used as flavor enhancers. As in this recipe, a dry marinade consists of various spices rubbed into fish, meat, or poultry, which is why it's also called a dry rub. Grilling and broiling are the two most popular applications for dry marinade.

Raspberry Reduction Marinade

Fruited meats were very popular on the finest of tables in the Middle Ages and Renaissance.

1. Gently sauté the minced onions in oil until golden brown.

2. Add the remaining ingredients to the onions; simmer.

3. Let the liquid reduce by about 1 cup; cool.

4. Move to freezer-safe containers or pour over the desired meat and freeze everything together. Use within 8 months.

MAKES 5 CUPS

INGREDIENTS
1 red onion, minced
1 teaspoon olive oil
2 cups juiced raspberries
2 cups dry red wine
½ cup beef broth
½ cup golden raisins
½ cup raspberry vinegar
2 tablespoons fresh ginger, minced
¼ cup sugar
1 tablespoon Dijon mustard

Cola Marinade

Use red wine vinegar for beef and white vinegar for chicken or fish. Pork adapts nicely to cider vinegar. Some chefs don't put cola in the frozen blend and add it just before using.

1. Mix all ingredients in a sauce pan. Simmer over low heat until the aromatics begin to fill the air, about 15 minutes.

2. Cool; remove bay leaf. Store in freezer-safe containers. Use within 8 months.

Reusing Marinade
Some frugal cooks try to reuse leftover marinade to make a baste or sauce. This isn't safe because the raw food on which the marinade was first used could leave behind bacteria. Instead, make extra marinade at the beginning and keep it in a separate container for basting at the end.

MAKES 2½ CUPS

INGREDIENTS
1½ cups cola
½ cup lemon or orange juice
½ cup vegetable oil
½ cup vinegar
1 teaspoon Worcestershire sauce
½ teaspoon onion powder
½ teaspoon garlic powder
½ teaspoon pepper
½ teaspoon paprika
salt to taste
1 bay leaf

Ginger Citrus Marinade

MAKES 4 CUPS

INGREDIENTS

1 freshly squeezed lemon

1 freshly squeezed lime

3 cups orange juice

½ cup water

⅛ cup white vinegar

3 teaspoons peeled finely grated ginger

1 teaspoon lemon zest

1 teaspoon lime zest

1 teaspoon orange zest

3 teaspoons grated sweet onion

2 teaspoons fresh ground pepper

Use this on chicken and pork, marinating the meat for at least 2 hours before cooking. This diet-friendly marinade doesn't have any oil and boasts a tangy flavor (add some sugar if it's too tangy for your taste).

1. Put all ingredients in a saucepan.

2. Bring to a low-rolling boil, stirring regularly.

3. Let mixture reduce by ¼ cup.

4. Pour into hot canning jars, leaving ½" headspace. Wipe rims, apply lids, and process in a hot-water bath for 15 minutes.

South of the Border Beef Marinade

MAKES 2 CUPS

INGREDIENTS

½ cup fresh lime juice

½ cup chopped fresh cilantro

½ cup olive oil

⅓ cup soy sauce

½ cup tequila

7 cloves garlic, finely chopped

2 teaspoons grated lime peel

2 teaspoons grated orange peel

2 teaspoons ground cumin

2 teaspoons dried oregano

1 teaspoon black pepper

This meat is especially yummy for grilled steak or any meat going into tortillas, taquitos, or burritos. Don't forget a side of refried beans!

1. Mix all the ingredients together in a saucepan.

2. Warm over low flame until the mix reaches a gentle boil.

3. Cool and move to freezer-safe containers. Use within 8 months.

Apricot Baste

This is a great topper for Asian noodles with snap peas or as baste for chicken or pork.

1. Lightly toast garlic and sesame seeds in oil.

2. Turn the garlic and sesame into a saucepan; add all remaining ingredients except the orange flower water.

3. Simmer slowly and let the blend reduce by ¼ cup.

4. Cool and stir in the orange flower water.

5. Pour into freezer-safe containers. Use within 6 months.

Apricots
Apricots originated in China and spread to Europe through trade routes. They reached California by the eighteenth century; today, most apricots in the United States come from California. Apricots contain vitamin A, fiber, and iron.

MAKES 1½ CUPS

INGREDIENTS
2 teaspoons sesame oil
3 cloves garlic, minced
1 teaspoon sesame seeds
⅓ cup dried diced apricots
½ cup apricot preserves
1 tablespoon soy sauce
1 tablespoon coarse ground mustard
1 cup apricot nectar
1 tablespoon orange blossom honey
1 tablespoon rice vinegar
1 teaspoon grated gingerroot
1 teaspoon orange flower water

Asian Plum Sauce

MAKES 6–7 PINTS

INGREDIENTS

1 cup granulated sugar

1½ cups brown sugar, packed

1 cup apple cider vinegar

¾ cup onion, finely chopped

2 tablespoons yellow mustard seed

2 tablespoons green chili peppers, finely chopped

1 tablespoon salt

1–2 garlic cloves, minced

1–2 gingerroot pieces, peeled and minced

10 cups plums, pitted and finely chopped

If you're not fond of plums try peaches or tangerines.

1. In a large stockpot, combine sugars, vinegar, onion, mustard seed, chili peppers, salt, garlic, and gingerroot.

2. Bring to a boil; add plums.

3. Return mixture to a boil; boil gently, stirring occasionally, about 1 hour and 45 minutes, or until thick and syrupy.

4. Ladle sauce into sterilized jars, leaving ¼" headspace.

5. Remove air bubbles. Wipe rims. Cap and seal.

6. Process in a water-bath canner 10 minutes.

Sauces in History
Romans were using all manner of items for sauces, including as many as 12 herbs and spices, fish stock, honey, and wheat, flour, or bread thickeners. Most often this was not because the cook was feeling exotic, but rather to cover up the taste of food that may have turned a bit.

Green Taco Sauce

This sauce kicks up nearly any Mexican style dish and infuses it with that piquant edge.

1. Remove the husks from the tomatillos; rinse in cool water. Remove stem and quarter.

2. Drop tomatillos in boiling water; cook 10 minutes. Drain.

3. Remove the stems and seeds from the jalapeño peppers. Roughly chop them.

4. In a food processor, add tomatillos, onion, shallots, garlic, and cilantro; pulse until coarse. This may take 2–3 batches.

5. Heat the olive oil in a stockpot. Add the mixture; cook 5 minutes, stirring constantly.

6. Add the broth, wine vinegar, and honey; stir well. Reduce heat; simmer until thickened, about 20–25 minutes.

7. Ladle into sterilized jars. Wipe rims. Cap and seal.

8. Process at 10 pounds pressure in a pressure canner for 20 minutes.

Pesto Power

Pesto owes its beginnings to condiments made by our ancestors, who mixed ground spices with oil so they could be applied to bread or other foods. This type of mixture was predominant in Persia and throughout the Roman empire. In Italy, basil was the key ingredient. Not surprisingly, *pesto* means "to pound."

MAKES 6 PINTS

INGREDIENTS
2 pounds tomatillos
4 jalapeño peppers
1 cup red onion, chopped
1 cup shallots, chopped
4 teaspoons garlic, minced
2 cups fresh cilantro
¼ cup extra-virgin olive oil
4 cups chicken broth
2 cups red wine vinegar
½ cup honey

Ho-Ho Hot Sauce

MAKES 2 TABLESPOONS
POWDERED SAUCE FOR
EACH ¼ CUP DRIED

INGREDIENTS

2 cayenne peppers

2 habañero peppers

2 banana peppers

2 jalapeño peppers

2 Scotch Bonnet peppers

2 Anaheim peppers

1 sweet red pepper

1 sweet orange pepper

¼ cup onion, diced

3 cloves garlic, finely chopped

1 teaspoon freshly ground ginger

½ cup white vinegar

1 tablespoon dark molasses

2 tablespoons honey

2 tablespoons orange juice

2 tablespoons brown sugar

1 plum tomato

¼ cup spiced dark rum

½ teaspoon chipotle powder

½ teaspoon curry powder

½ teaspoon salt

½ teaspoon freshly ground black pepper

This hot sauce is high in both heat and flavor and offers a smooth finish. This recipe may also be canned from the liquid stage.

1. Seed all the peppers; roast them in the oven or over the grill. Remove blackened skins.

2. Sauté onion gently in a tiny bit of oil until translucent.

3. Process peppers in a food processor to even consistency.

4. In a saucepan, place the peppers and onions with all other ingredients.

5. Simmer over low heat; stir regularly, until peppers are tender.

6. Run the mixture through a sieve; return to the stove to simmer another 10 minutes.

7. Cool. Pour ¼ cup of sauce evenly over the surface of a fruit roll-up tray for the dehydrator. Place the mix on the manufacturer's suggested setting for drying herbs.

8. Check after 1 hour; if peppers have reached a rubbery stage, cool, dice, and run through an herb grinder.

9. Return to the dehydrator for 1 hour, until crunchy. Put through herb grinder again.

10. Store in airtight container in a cool, dark area. Shelf life is about 1 year.

11. Repeat steps 7–10 for the rest of the mix or put into a jar and store in the refrigerator for family use.

Honey Barbecue Sauce

This recipe is highly adaptable to your family's tastes. For example, if you prefer a maple flavor barbecue sauce, use maple syrup in place of honey.

1. In a large stockpot, combine tomatoes, onions, garlic, red pepper flakes, and celery seed. Simmer, covered, until vegetables are soft, about 30 minutes.

2. Press tomato mixture through a fine sieve or food mill; discard seeds and skins.

3. Return tomato mixture to stockpot; add remaining ingredients.

4. Cook over low heat, stirring frequently, until mixture thickens, about 60–90 minutes.

5. Cool; ladle sauce into freezer-safe containers, leaving ¼" headspace. Use within 6–8 months.

Mother of All Sauces
In cooking, there are several sauces known as mother sauces (or grand sauces)—tomato or red sauce, Hollandaise or butter sauce, brown sauce or demi-glace, veloute or blonde sauce, and béchamel or white sauce. They get this designation because once you know how to make them you'll know the fundamental process for all other sauces.

MAKES 6–7 PINTS

INGREDIENTS

20 pounds firm ripe tomatoes, cored and chopped

4 large onions, peeled and finely chopped

6–8 garlic cloves, minced

1¼ tablespoons crushed red pepper

2 tablespoons celery seed

2 cups brown sugar

1 cup honey

2 tablespoons dry mustard

2 teaspoons salt

1½ teaspoons ground mace

1½ teaspoons ground ginger

1½ teaspoons ground cinnamon

½ teaspoon grated orange peel

2 cups white vinegar

⅔ cup lemon juice

1 teaspoon coarse-ground black pepper

Pickled Onion Sauce

MAKES 3 CUPS

INGREDIENTS

1 large red onion, thinly sliced

2 chili peppers, seeded and diced

10 cloves fresh garlic

1½ cups white vinegar

½ cup sugar

1 tablespoon mustard seed

1 tablespoon celery seed

½ cup dark beer

¼ cup dark honey

1 teaspoon salt

This is an intense onion sauce that marries nicely with bratwurst, garlic sausage, and kielbasa. Other herbs worth trying in this blend include cumin, ginger, and allspice.

1. Blanch the onions and peppers 2 minutes.

2. Place onions, peppers, and remaining ingredients in a sauce pan; bring to a boil.

3. Reduce heat; simmer until sauce reduces by ¼ cup.

4. Cool; run through a blender or food processor for consistent texture.

5. Store in freezer-safe containers, leaving space for expansion. Use within 8 months.

How Hot?

Heat is measured in what's called a Scoville unit, which essentially indicates how much dilution is necessary before a person no longer feels the burning sensation caused by the capsaicin in hot peppers. The average Tabasco sauce measures up at about 3,700 Scoville units. By comparison, jalapeño peppers rank 2,000–8,000 on the Scoville range, and cayenne ranges 30,000–50,000 units.

Kicked-Up Kiwi Relish

This is great to serve with chicken, turkey, duck, or goose. You can also spread this over a pork roast as a marinade while baking or for ribs or chicken on the grill.

1. Make a spice bag of black peppercorns, crushed red peppers, and pickling spices.

2. Add the bag and all ingredients to a large stockpot. Bring to a boil; reduce heat to medium-low and simmer uncovered for about 1½ hours, or until mixture is thick.

3. Stir occasionally to prevent sticking and scorching. Discard spice bag.

4. Ladle into hot sterilized jars, leaving ¼" headspace. Remove air bubbles. Wipe rims. Cap and seal.

5. Process in a boiling-water canner 10 minutes.

Pickling Spice?

Making your own pickling spice is very easy. Take 2 teaspoons each cinnamon, freshly grated gingerroot, mustard seed, allspice berries, peppercorns, cloves, dill, and coriander and mix them with 4 crumbled bay leaves and 1 teaspoon dried red pepper. Put in a jar. The spice has a shelf life of 2–3 months.

MAKES 5½ PINTS

INGREDIENTS

½ teaspoon black peppercorns

¼ teaspoon red peppers, crushed

¼ teaspoon mixed pickling spices

4 pounds kiwi, peeled and chopped

2 large apples, cored, peeled, and chopped

1 pound tomatoes, peeled and chopped

2 cups granulated sugar or Splenda

3 cups white wine vinegar

1 teaspoon sea salt

3–6 chili peppers, seeded and chopped

2 teaspoons fresh gingerroot, grated

2 teaspoons cilantro or parsley, finely minced

Apple Maple Sauce

MAKES 3 CUPS

INGREDIENTS

4 large firm apples, diced

water to cover

2 whole cloves

1 teaspoon wine vinegar

½ cup real maple syrup

¼ cup apple jelly

2 teaspoons minced garlic

1 cup chicken stock

This reduction is delicious on ham and pork. If you're short on time, substitute 1½ cups of applesauce for the fresh apples.

1. Place apples and cloves in a saucepan; cover with water.

2. Simmer, stirring regularly until apples are soft.

3. Put the apple mixture through a sieve.

4. Return the applesauce to your pan and add all remaining ingredients.

5. Bring to a rolling boil, stirring regularly. Allow liquid to reduce by ½ cup.

6. Pour into sterilized jars, leaving ¼" headspace. Wipe the rims and cap, and process for 15 minutes in a hot-water bath.

English Mint Sauce

MAKES 6 PINTS

INGREDIENTS

4 cups fresh mint, washed and finely chopped

4 cups sugar

⅓ cup lemon or lime juice

2 12-ounce bottles English malt vinegar

2 cups white vinegar

1 teaspoons ground black pepper

This recipe is traditionally served with lamb or pork.

1. Add all ingredients to a large stockpot. Bring to boil and simmer until mint leaves are softened.

2. Ladle into jars leaving 1" headroom. Wipe rims and place sterilized lids on each jar. Screw on sterilized band tightly. Process in boiling-water bath for 15 minutes.

Spiced Tomato Paste

This recipe uses a dehydrator to make tomato paste roll-ups that are best either kept in a dark airtight container or well wrapped in the freezer. Rehydrate the paste as needed.

1. Dice the tomatoes and put them through a food processor, then use a sieve to remove the seeds.

2. Add tomatoes and remaining ingredients to a pan; simmer over low heat until mix thickens.

3. Keep stirring for another 30 minutes or until the consistency thickens and becomes paste-like.

4. Spread the paste on a lightly oiled fruit roll-up sheet for the dehydrator. Paste should be no more than ¼" thick.

5. Dry at about 115–120°F for 12 hours or until the paste is not sticky. Store as desired.

Tomato Talk

Tomatoes are the world's most consumed fruit; we eat more than 60 million tons a year globally. There are more than 4,000 kinds of tomatoes ranging in size from ¾" in diameter to 3-pounders. The largest tomato ever grown weighed more than 7 pounds, and the largest tomato plant was more than 65 feet tall.

MAKES 12 PASTE ROLL-UPS

INGREDIENTS
2 quarts ripe Roma tomatoes
1 teaspoon oregano
½ cup finely diced onion
¼ teaspoon garlic powder
1 teaspoon garlic purée
1 teaspoon fresh basil leaves
⅓ cup dry white wine

Chapter 8

Broths, Soups, and Stews

8

INGREDIENTS

3–4 medium lamb shanks

2 pounds lamb stew (with bones)

8 cups beef stock

2 pounds carrots, peeled and cut into large chunks

2 cups celery, cut into chunks

2 large onions, peeled and diced

2 tablespoons mixed peppercorns

1 tablespoon whole allspice berries

4 tablespoons dried mixed soup greens

8 large bay leaves

cold water to cover ingredients

2 tablespoons oregano

2 teaspoons Greek seasoning

6 lamb or beef bouillon cubes

Lamb Stock

Lamb stock is essential if you enjoy Greek food. It's also great when making bean casseroles or as a baste for chops and full legs of lamb.

1. Divide lamb shanks and stew meat evenly between 2 large stockpots.

2. Brown lamb with a little olive oil.

3. Add 4 cups beef stock per stockpot; simmer 15 minutes.

4. Add ½ the carrots and celery and 1 chopped onion to each pot.

5. Make 2 spice balls with the peppercorns, allspice berries, mixed soup greens, and bay leaves. Put one in each pot.

6. Cover with cold water. Bring to a rapid boil; cover, reduce heat to low, and simmer 3 hours.

7. Skim off any foam; discard. Skim off excess fat; discard. Add oregano, Greek seasoning, and bouillon. Cook on low for another 15 minutes.

8. If canning, strain and ladle into sterilized jars. Wipe rims. Cap and seal.

9. Process in a pressure canner at 10 pounds pressure for 20 minutes for pints or 25 minutes for quarts.

Alphabet Soup
The word *soup* comes from a Latin term *suppare*, meaning *soak*. It's related to the Germanic *sup*, which is also where we get the word *supper*. The word originally meant "bread soaked in liquid" (or a pottage). By the eighteenth century, soups began appearing on tables as a common appetizer or first remove.

Dill Pickle Soup Stock

Use this as the base for Pickled Soup (page 111).

1. Put everything in your stockpot; cook until it reduces by ½ cup.

2. Strain and freeze. If canning, leave 1" headspace and process at 10 pounds of pressure for 25 minutes for pints.

MAKES 3 CUPS

INGREDIENTS
3 cups basic stock
½ cup dill pickle brine
3 large pickles, diced
1 medium onion
2 carrots, chopped

Ham Stock

Try this stock the next time you make scalloped potatoes and ham. Garnish with a bit of melted cheese.

1. Combine all ingredients in a large pot. Cover; simmer 40 minutes.

2. Open the pot; let mixture reduce by 1 cup. Strain broth; discard residue. Cool; skim off fat.

3. If freezing, it's ready now. To can, pour into sterilized glass containers, wipe the rims, and cap. Process at 11 pounds of pressure for 25 minutes for pints or 30 minutes for quarts.

Dried Stock
While you can try to dehydrate soup stock so it can be powdered, it's not recommended. It takes too long to be financially viable compared to ready-made items at the supermarket. This is often true with other food items that have a high liquid content.

MAKES 4 CUPS

INGREDIENTS
2 pounds ham, with ham bone
5 cups water
1 large carrot, sliced into large chunks
1 large onion, quartered
2 stalks celery, coarsely diced with leaves
½ teaspoon dried parsley, crushed
½ teaspoon celery seed
½ teaspoon onion powder
1 bay leaf

Garlic Stock

MAKES 6 CUPS

INGREDIENTS

1½ tablespoons olive oil

½ head garlic, peeled and chopped

½ head elephant garlic, peeled and chopped

6 cups vegetable stock

1 bay leaf

¼ teaspoon dried thyme

1 pinch dried sage

salt to taste

pepper to taste

Have fun experimenting with different types of garlic in this broth. For a milder but rich garlic taste, bake the garlic in olive oil before using it for the stock.

1. Warm the oil in a frying pan and very lightly sauté garlics.

2. Combine all ingredients; boil.

3. Reduce heat; simmer 30 minutes.

4. Strain; taste for saltiness.

5. Preserve as desired. If canning, use 10 pounds of pressure for 30 minutes for pints.

Broth or Brew?

Linguistically, the root word for *broth* is the very same one used for *brewing*. In part, it's because both methods include boiling liquid, which made the blend healthier to eat. Up until the seventeenth century, broth typically referred to liquid in which meat had been boiled. It's related to bouillon, except that bouillon has far more salt.

Traditional Beef Broth

The red wine in this recipe is optional, but it is an excellent touch if you plan to use the broth for gravies or reductions.

1. Broil beef. Put into a large pot with the marrow bones.

2. Sauté onion in olive oil until translucent. Add to stockpot. Add wine, salt, garlic, and celery leaf and cover with water (about 12 cups).

3. Bring the water to a simmer and cook for at least 2½ hours. If necessary, add water during the process to keep bones covered.

4. Cool and strain, skimming off as much fat as possible, then return stock to stove to heat.

5. If canning, use hot-pack method, leaving 1" of headspace in the jars. Pressure can at 11 pounds of pressure for 25 minutes.

MAKES 4 QUARTS

INGREDIENTS

3 pounds shank or pot roast cut into 2-inch pieces

2 pounds marrow bones, smashed

1 medium onion, diced

1 tablespoon olive oil

¼ cup red wine (optional)

¼ teaspoon salt

¼ teaspoon pepper

2 whole cloves garlic

handful celery leaf (about 1 cup)

water

Classic Chicken Stock

Nothing is as versatile as chicken stock. The best thing here is that you don't need expensive meat—get whatever's on sale!

1. Rub the chicken with olive oil, salt, and pepper. Brown chicken. Reserve juices and set aside.

2. Add remaining ingredients to a stockpot. Simmer for 30 minutes, then add the chicken with juice.

3. Bring to a low rolling boil, skimming the fat off regularly.

4. Cool in the refrigerator. Remove oil once it separates from the stock.

5. Freeze as is or reheat the stock for canning. Ladle into jars, leaving 1" headspace and process at 11 pounds of pressure for 25 minutes for quarts.

MAKES 1 QUART

INGREDIENTS

2 pounds chicken, cut up in pieces

1 tablespoon olive oil

salt to taste

pepper to taste

1 onion, diced

2 teaspoons salt

1 quart water

2 bay leaves

½ teaspoon poultry seasoning (optional)

Vegetable Stock

MAKES 8 QUARTS

INGREDIENTS

14 quarts cold water

2 pounds peeled carrots, cut into 1-inch pieces

2 pounds peeled parsnips, cut into 1-inch pieces

1 bunch leeks, rinsed well and chopped finely

12 stalks celery, cut into 1-inch pieces

3 large onions, peeled and quartered

4 large sweet red peppers, seeded and cut into 1-inch pieces

4 large tomatoes, seeded and diced

4 medium turnips, peeled and diced

6 cloves garlic, peeled and minced

6 bay leaves

2 teaspoons dried thyme

1 cup fresh parsley, chopped

1 tablespoon black peppercorns

2 teaspoons fine sea salt

When you know you're going to be making vegetable stock, prepare ahead of time. Keep your clean vegetable ends and pieces in a food-storage bag in the freezer and add them to the stock water for increased flavor.

1. Combine all ingredients in a large stockpot. Bring to a boil.

2. Cover and reduce heat to low. Simmer for 2 hours.

3. Uncover and simmer for 2 additional hours to concentrate flavors.

4. Strain stock through several layers of cheesecloth in a colander. Discard veggies and seasonings.

5. If canning, ladle stock into sterilized jars, leaving 1" headspace. Wipe rims. Cap and seal. Process in a pressure canner at 10 pounds pressure for 30 minutes for pints or 35 minutes for quarts.

Ukrainian Cabbage Soup

MAKES 7–8 QUARTS

You can thicken the soup before freezing or after defrosting by making a butter-flour roux consisting of 4 tablespoons butter or margarine and 4 tablespoons all-purpose flour.

1. Put neck bones in a large stockpot.

2. Add bay leaves and pepper; cover with water. Start on high heat to boil; reduce heat and cook 1 hour.

3. Add shredded cabbage, sauerkraut (including juice), and chopped onions. Continue to cook about 45 minutes; meat will start falling off bones.

4. Add caraway seeds. Remove and discard bay leaves. Remove bones with slotted spoon.

5. After cooling bones, remove meat and discard bones. Add meat back to soup.

6. Freeze. If canning, ladle soup into sterilized wide-mouth quart jars, leaving 1" headspace. Wipe rims. Cap and seal.

7. Process in a pressure canner at 10 pounds pressure for 1 hour and 5 minutes.

INGREDIENTS

5–6 pounds pork neck bones

2 whole bay leaves

2 teaspoons ground black pepper

water to cover neck bones

1 large head cabbage, cored and shredded

2 28-ounce cans sauerkraut

2 large onions, finely chopped

4 tablespoons whole caraway seeds

Cabbage Chronicles

The biggest cabbage ever grown was in England in 1865. It weighed 123 pounds. The world's greatest fans of cabbage live in Russia, whose citizens consume seven times as much of this vegetable as their counterparts in the United States.

Ukrainian Borscht

MAKES 8 QUARTS

INGREDIENTS

4–5 pounds smoked pork shoulder or smoked butt

4–6 carrots, peeled and chopped

2 medium onions, chopped

4 parsnips, peeled and chopped

4 celery stalks, chopped

3 bay leaves

water to cover

½ medium head of cabbage, finely shredded

3–4 pounds beets, peeled and cut into small pieces

1 whole head of garlic, peeled and chopped

½ teaspoon sour salt or 2 tablespoons red wine vinegar

1 teaspoon salt

½ teaspoon caraway seeds

½ teaspoon black pepper

1 cup sour cream

If you want to can this, do not add the sour cream. You can add that when you are ready to eat—about ¼ cup per quart of soup. Serve with dark rye bread.

1. In a large stockpot, place smoked shoulder or smoked butt, carrots, onions, parsnips, celery, and bay leaves; cover with water. Bring to a boil; turn heat down and cook 1½ hours, until meat is fork-tender.

2. Remove meat; discard bay leaves.

3. Add remaining ingredients to broth, except sour cream, and cook another hour, until all vegetables are fork-tender.

4. Remove from heat; let cool, about 45 minutes to 1 hour.

5. Meanwhile, if using butt, remove meat from bones; set aside. If using smoked pork shoulder, debone it.

6. Cut meat into bite-sized pieces with the least amount of fat on them. Add meat back to stockpot.

7. If freezing, in a small bowl, add 1 cup sour cream to 2 cups of the soup liquid; whisk until well blended. Pour blended liquid back into soup. Cool and freeze.

8. If canning, turn heat back on and simmer until soup is hot. Ladle meat and veggies into sterilized jars. Fill with hot liquid, leaving 1" headspace.

9. Process at 10 pounds pressure for 75 minutes for pints or 90 minutes for quarts.

Borscht Bulletin

Borscht is made primarily of beets. It originated in Eastern Europe and Russia as a soup for common people because it was inexpensive to make. The first recipes for what was then called *borchch* appear in the medieval era.

Broccoli-Cauliflower Leek Soup

Serve this dish with a sprinkling of your favorite cheese on top.

1. Sauté the leeks and mushrooms in olive oil.

2. Put all the remaining ingredients in a stockpot; cover with broth. Bring to a full boil.

3. Meanwhile, purée half of the leeks. Add puréed leeks, sliced leeks, and mushrooms to boiling soup.

4. Simmer another 15 minutes, stirring constantly. Cool and freeze. If canning, move into sterilized jars. Wipe rims. Process in a pressure canner at 10 pounds pressure for 1 hour and 15 minutes for pints or 1 hour and 30 minutes for quarts.

Curious Cauliflower

Historians believe that cauliflower originated in Asia Minor, but it really didn't make much of an impact on recipes until it reached Italy and England in the sixteenth century. Before that, three types were grown in Spain in the twelfth century; today, there are about a dozen varieties.

MAKES 6–8 QUARTS

INGREDIENTS

3 large leeks, cleaned and sliced

½ pound of mushrooms, cleaned and sliced

1 tablespoon olive oil

6 medium-size potatoes, peeled and cubed

1 head broccoli, cleaned and chopped

1 head cauliflower, cleaned and chopped

1 cup diced onion

6 carrots, peeled and diced

2 cloves garlic, minced

1 tablespoon basil

salt to taste

pepper to taste

16 cups chicken broth

Sweet Potato Ham Soup

MAKES ABOUT 2 QUARTS

INGREDIENTS

4 large sweet potatoes, cubed

2 pounds ham steak, diced

4 cups ham broth

1 cup water

salt to taste

pepper to taste

This recipe tastes great if you add a pinch of brown sugar and ginger to bring out the sweet potatoes. Alternatively, add a little cornstarch and milk when warming for a scalloped-potato-and-ham-type base.

1. Place all your ingredients in a stockpot. Bring to a full boil; reduce to a simmer, until water has reduced off and the potatoes are fork-tender. If you are canning, do not make the potatoes that tender; they need more firmness for the pressure cooker. They should be slightly firmer than those used in potato salad, but time will vary based on size.

2. Cool; move into freezer-safe containers. Alternatively, can, leaving 1" headspace, in a pressure cooker at 11 pounds of pressure for 90 minutes for quarts.

Beef Barley Bliss

MAKES 11–12 QUARTS

INGREDIENTS

2 cups pearl barley

3-pound boneless rump roast, diced

3 tablespoons oil

1¾ gallons water

4 medium onions, chopped

15 large carrots, diced

8 stalks celery, chopped

9 cloves garlic, chopped

3 bay leaves

1 tablespoon tarragon

2 tablespoons oregano

2 tablespoons salt

1 tablespoon black pepper

If you are canning this recipe, omit the pearl barley and add it when you rewarm the soup for serving.

1. Prepare the barley according to the instructions on the box.

2. Brown the beef in a stockpot using minimal oil. Scrape the bottom to loosen the little pieces.

3. Add remaining ingredients into the stockpot, bring to a boil, then simmer for 1 hour over low heat. Test for flavor and adjust spices accordingly.

4. Cool and put into containers for freezing or can using a hot-pack method. Process at 10 pounds pressure for 60 minutes for pints or 75 minutes for quarts.

Veal Stew

Try this over a thick slice of buttered French bread with parsley.

1. Dice meat; dust lightly with flour. Sauté veal and onions in olive oil.

2. Put all ingredients in a stew pot; simmer over low heat 3 hours. If you need more liquid, add more wine.

3. Cool and freeze; otherwise, can using the hot-pack method, leaving 1" headspace, for 75 minutes for pints or 90 minutes for quarts at 10 pounds of pressure.

Canning Stews

The stews in this cookbook are not as thick as traditional stews. This allows them to be canned safely. You can freeze thicker stews, but you may find the gravy is a little lumpy upon warming. Stews are found in almost every culture; they were invented as a way to use up leftovers.

MAKES 2 QUARTS

INGREDIENTS

3 pounds veal, cut in 1-inch cubes

¼ cup flour

3 onions, peeled and thickly sliced

¼ cup olive oil

2 cups port wine

1 teaspoon salt

1 teaspoon pepper

Beef Burgundy

MAKES 8 QUARTS

INGREDIENTS

5 pounds roast beef

1 beef bone with marrow

1 tablespoon olive oil

5 medium onions

15 small whole shallots

2 cloves garlic crushed

6 slices of thick bacon cooked, drained, and crumbled

3 cups diced carrots

2 teaspoons salt

1 teaspoon cracked black pepper

3 cups beef stock

3 mushrooms, cleaned and halved

3 cups Burgundy wine

Prior to serving this dish, run 2 cups of onion-shallot-mushroom stock through a blender. Slowly pour this back into the base to thicken the stew and create a fuller flavor throughout.

1. Trim beef and cut into 1" cubes.

2. Brown meat and marrow bone in a stew pot using minimal olive oil for 10 minutes.

3. Add onions and continue browning for 10 more minutes.

4. Add remaining ingredients and simmer for 3 hours; remove the marrow bone.

5. Cool, skim off excess fat, and put into containers if freezing. If canning, return to the heat after removing fat and place hot into jars with 1" headspace. Process at 10 pounds of pressure for 75 minutes for pints and 90 minutes for quarts.

Beef Veggie Soup

You can add any other root vegetables to this dish. Just peel them, slice them, and throw them in. Make your own *fines herbes* by combining equal parts fresh chervil, chives, parsley, and tarragon.

1. Trim fat from beef and cut into chunks. Put beef bones, beef, water, carrots, onion, and celery into large stockpot. Include additional root vegetables if you choose to use them.

2. Make a spice ball with peppercorns, bay leaves, dill seed, and *fines herbes*. Add to the stock and bring to a boil.

3. Cover and simmer on medium heat for 75 minutes.

4. Remove from heat and discard bones, spice ball, and bay leaves.

5. Divide beef and vegetables into sterilized jars.

6. Allow broth to cool and skim off any fat. Return broth to heat until boiling. Pour into jars, leaving 1" headspace. Wipe rims. Cap and seal. Process in a pressure canner at 10 pounds pressure for 75 minutes for pints or 90 minutes for quarts.

7. If freezing, add meat and vegetables back into the stock and then divide among containers.

MAKES 7–8 QUARTS

INGREDIENTS

2–3 pounds lean beef chuck or pot roast

2–4 pounds beef bones

8 quarts cold water

4 stalks celery, chopped

6 large carrots, peeled and sliced

2 quarts chopped tomatoes with juice

1 large onion, peeled and chopped

1 teaspoon whole black peppercorns

4 bay leaves

1 teaspoon dill seed

1 teaspoon *fines herbes*

4 tablespoons dehydrated beef stock or 4 beef bouillon cubes

Black Turtle Bean Soup

MAKES 6 QUARTS

INGREDIENTS

2 pounds dried black beans

water to cover

2 ham hocks or ½ pound salt pork

1 cup chopped onion

1 cup chopped celery

1 cup chopped carrots

1 large green pepper, seeded and chopped

4 cups chopped and peeled tomatoes with juice

2 tablespoons minced garlic

2–3 beef, vegetable, or chicken bouillon cubes, crushed

2–3 whole bay leaves

½ teaspoon dried basil

½ teaspoon dried oregano

½ teaspoon dried thyme

½ teaspoon chili powder or dried hot pepper flakes or 1 teaspoon Tabasco sauce

½ teaspoon dried cilantro flakes

salt to taste

pepper to taste

Add 2 pints or 1 quart of previously cooked and/or home-canned black turtle beans to the puréed mixture for extra flavor.

1. Cover beans with cold water and soak 12 to 18 hours in a cool place. Drain.

2. In a large stockpot, cover beans with 2 inches of water. Add remaining ingredients and bring to a boil. Cover and simmer 1½ hours until beans are tender.

3. Remove and discard bay leaves. Remove meat and cut into small pieces.

4. Press remaining ingredients through a sieve or food mill or purée in a food processor or blender. Combine meat with puréed bean/veggie mixture.

5. If necessary, add boiling water to reach desired consistency. Season to taste.

6. If freezing, cool and put in freezer-safe containers leaving space for expansion. If canning, ladle hot into sterilized jars, leaving 1" headspace. Wipe rims. Cap and seal. Process pints in a pressure canner at 10 pounds pressure for 75 minutes and quarts for 90 minutes.

Ballpark Hot Dog Soup

If you're not fond of baked beans, substitute your favorite chili or creamed corn instead. All three options yield a soup that tastes like a day at the ballpark!

1. Gently sauté the hot dogs, onion, and carrots until onions are translucent, about 7–10 minutes. Stir regularly to prevent sticking. Put sautéed meat and vegetables in a soup pot with remaining ingredients.

2. Bring to a full rolling boil; reduce heat and simmer for 20 minutes, stirring regularly.

3. Cool to freeze; otherwise, pour the hot soup into prepared jars, processing 90 minutes at 10 pounds of pressure for quarts.

MAKES 4 QUARTS

INGREDIENTS

1 package hot dogs, in ¼-inch slices

1 medium onion, diced

2 carrots, diced

½ teaspoon butter

4 cups baked beans

1 teaspoon ketchup

1 teaspoon stone-ground mustard

5 cups chicken, vegetable, or beef stock

Taco Soup

Serve this with tortilla chips, shredded cheese, and a teaspoon of sour cream.

1. Brown beef and remove excess fat. Place beef and all remaining ingredients in a stockpot. Simmer 45 to 60 minutes over low heat.

2. Divide into individually labeled and dated freezer-safe containers. If canning, ladle soup into sterilized wide-mouth quart jars, leaving 1" headspace. Wipe rims. Cap and seal. Process in a pressure canner at 10 pounds pressure for 65 minutes.

MAKES ABOUT 3 QUARTS

INGREDIENTS

1½ pounds lean ground turkey

1 14-ounce can diced tomatoes

1 4-ounce can diced chili peppers

2 15-ounce cans kidney beans, drained

1 medium onion, diced

1 teaspoon garlic, diced

4 cups water or chicken stock

1 package taco seasoning mix

Poor Man's Minestrone

MAKES 3–4 QUARTS

INGREDIENTS

1 pound ground beef

1 large onion, chopped

1 clove garlic, minced

1 16–ounce can low-fat beef broth

9 cups water

1 6-ounce can tomato paste

1 16-ounce can kidney beans, drained

1 cup sliced celery

1 cup sliced carrots

½ teaspoon salt

⅛ teaspoon pepper

¼ teaspoon oregano

1 cup chopped cabbage

1 cup frozen peas

1 large zucchini, sliced

Use your leftover vegetable ends and pieces in this recipe; tie them in cheesecloth and let them soak in the soup.

1. Brown ground beef, onion, and garlic; drain off fat.

2. Add broth, water, tomato paste, kidney beans, celery, carrots, and seasonings. Bring to a boil.

3. Cover and reduce heat; simmer 10 minutes.

4. Cool to freeze, or can hot in a pressure canner 1 hour and 15 minutes for pints or 1 hour and 30 minutes for quarts at 10 pounds pressure.

Minestrone Musings?
The word *minestrone* means "big soup" in Italian. It likely got its name because of its vast number of ingredients. In the beginning, it didn't actually have a set recipe; rather, it was created out of whatever was available and in season.

Dried Vegetable Soup Mix

This recipe can be made in bulk and put into food-storage bags with instructions for gift giving. While it takes time to dry the vegetables, the resulting product saves a lot of shelf space.

1. Place each vegetable on a separate layer of your dehydrator. Set dehydrator to appropriate temperature as specified by the manufacturer (otherwise use your lowest oven setting). If you are drying vegetables in the oven, dry each type of vegetable separately because some will dry faster than others. Bake at 150°F. On average, vegetables take 6–12 hours to dry completely to a crunchy texture. Beets, carrots, and onions take 3–6 hours; corn and garlic take 6–8 hours; and potatoes, mushrooms, and peas take 8–11 hours.

2. Mix all vegetables together with soup stock. Store in a cool, dry area for use in flavoring soup or stews or as instant soup mix.

Pickled Soup

This recipe is traditionally thickened with an egg and a flour roux, but this step should be left until just before you serve the dish. Top with 1 tablespoon of sour cream.

1. In large pot, combine broth, bouillon cubes, carrots, potatoes, and celery.

2. Cook until potatoes are tender, about 10 minutes.

3. Add grated dill pickles. Continue cooking about 15 minutes more.

4. Taste, adding salt and pepper if desired. Soup can be cooled and frozen or transferred into canning jars, leaving 1" headspace, and pressure cooked at 10 pounds for 75 minutes.

MAKES 4 CUPS

INGREDIENTS

2 stalks celery, chopped
2 carrots, chopped
1 cup diced broccoli
1 cup diced cauliflower
1 cup diced cabbage
1 cup thinly sliced potatoes
1 cup diced onion
1 cup diced mixed sweet peppers
1 cup cherry tomatoes, quartered
½ cup diced leeks
1 cup fresh peas
1 cup powdered vegetable soup stock

MAKES 12 CUPS

INGREDIENTS

8 cups Dill Pickle Soup Stock (page 97)
2 chicken bouillon cubes
2 medium carrots, coarsely grated
2 cups potatoes, cubed
1 cup celery, thinly sliced
5 large dill pickles, grated
salt to taste
pepper to taste

Sweet Pickle Stew

MAKES 2 QUARTS

INGREDIENTS

2 pounds ground beef or turkey

1 pound mixed diced potatoes, onions, and carrots

1 16–ounce can tomato sauce

1 cup water

½ cup sweet pickles

½ cup pickle juice or wine

salt to taste

pepper to taste

This is another neat twist on hamburgers. This stew is complete with your favorite homemade sweet pickles to top off the flavor. Serve with a generous slice of fresh bread and a pickle/olive tray.

1. Pan fry the ground meat until cooked; drain fat.

2. Turn cooked meat into a slow cooker with all remaining ingredients; cook 6 hours on low.

3. Cool to freeze; otherwise, can mixture hot, leaving 1" headspace. Pressure can at 10 pounds of pressure for 75 minutes for pints and 90 minutes for quarts.

What Makes a Pickle Kosher?

In order for a pickle to be considered kosher, it must be made under the scrutinizing eye of a rabbi, and it cannot come in contact with any utensil or food that is not kosher. Additionally, the traditional kosher pickle has a liberal amount of garlic in the brine.

Chapter 9

Vegetables

9

Green Tomato Raspberry Jam

MAKES 8–9 PINTS

INGREDIENTS

8 cups shredded green tomatoes

½ cup lemon juice

2 teaspoons orange extract

3 tablespoons homemade dried, grated orange peel

8 cups white sugar

2 6-ounce packages raspberry-flavored gelatin mix

You can use whatever type gelatin you like in this. No one will ever know there are tomatoes in it!

1. Combine tomatoes, lemon juice, orange extract, dried orange peel, and sugar in a large saucepan; bring to a boil over medium heat. Stir and cook about 10 minutes.

2. Add gelatin; reduce heat to low and simmer 20 minutes. Spoon into hot, sterilized jars. Cap and seal.

3. Process in water-bath canner for 10 minutes or pour into freezer containers and freeze.

Corn Relish

MAKES 5–6 PINTS

INGREDIENTS

10 cups uncooked sweet baby corn kernels

1 cup sweet red pepper, diced

1 cup sweet green pepper, diced

1 cup celery, diced

½ cup red onion, sliced

½ cup Vidalia onion, diced

1½ cups sugar

2½ cups white vinegar

2 cups water

1 teaspoon salt

2 teaspoons celery seed

2 teaspoons mustard seed

This is a bright beautiful dish, both visually and flavor-wise. Try it served with crab cakes.

1. Place all ingredients in a large pan over a medium flame. Bring to a fast boil; lower heat and simmer 15 minutes.

2. Hot pack into pint jars with ½" headspace. Cap and seal; process in boiling water 15 minutes. Check lids after cool for proper sealing.

Corny

It was some 10,000 years ago that people began eating wild corn. Some 5,000 years ago, people began to plant it and harvest it in specific areas. Today, there are numerous types of corn that have been designed to yield a good crop throughout temperate zones. This corn is used for everything from food to making clothing and ethanol.

Sauerkraut

This recipe is based on a traditional method of making kraut in a brine crock. You'll need a large, 3-gallon crock.

1. Wash the cabbage head; remove any leaves that have dark spots.

2. Cut cabbage into quarters; remove core and shred into ¼-inch pieces.

3. Mix cabbage with salt; pack firmly into brine crock.

4. Fill crock, leaving 5" of headspace. If the brine has not covered the cabbage, boil some water, cool it, and then add it to the crock until the cabbage is completely covered.

5. Use a small bowl, plate, or other weight at the top to push the cabbage down; cover crock with an airtight lid.

6. Leave cabbage 5 weeks to ferment (75°F is the best temperature).

7. Move sauerkraut to a nonaluminum pan; simmer until heated through.

8. Pack hot into jars, leaving ½" headspace. Process 20 minutes in hot-water bath for quarts.

MAKES 4 QUARTS

INGREDIENTS
12 pounds cabbage
¼ pound salt

Spiced Artichoke Hearts

MAKES 4½ PINTS

INGREDIENTS

2½ cups frozen artichoke
hearts, defrosted

¼ cup white wine vinegar

¼ cup red wine vinegar

½ cup water

4 whole cloves garlic

¼ teaspoon thyme

¼ teaspoon parsley

¼ teaspoon rosemary

½ teaspoon basil

½ teaspoon oregano

⅛ teaspoon dried red pepper
flakes

Serve these as appetizers or as a topping to either green salad or pasta salad to shake things up a bit. The flavor improves if served with a little olive oil.

1. Blanch the artichoke hearts; chill and drain.

2. Place hearts in equal quantities in four ½-pint jars.

3. Mix together remaining ingredients; heat in a saucepan to boiling.

4. Pour over hearts, leaving ½" headspace; cap and seal.

5. Process 15 minutes in hot-water canner. Let cool; then check lids.

Artichoke Flower

The artichoke is a kissing cousin to the sunflower, and it probably originated somewhere in the Mediterranean. The part we eat is really a flower bud that could blossom into a 7-inch array if not harvested for food. Currently, there are more than forty commercial varieties cultivated worldwide.

Jumpin' Vegetable Juice

This is a healthy beverage that can be canned and drunk just like you would commercial vegetable drinks. It can also be frozen.

1. Put all ingredients in a nonreactive pot; simmer 45 minutes. Stir periodically.

2. Put entire blend through a sieve or juicer to remove any fibers, skins, and seeds. Repeat to get a fine consistency.

3. Return to pan; boil. Pour liquid into hot quart jars, leaving ½" headspace.

4. Process in hot-water canner 30 minutes. Let cool, then test lids.

Tomato, Tomahto

The tomato is really a fruit, a member of the nightshade family. Yet the tomato, in its almost infinite number of sizes, shapes, and colors, complements savory ingredients. It's also one of summertime's biggest hits, and although flavorful tomatoes are occasionally available throughout the year, their peak essence comes in mid- to late summer.

MAKES ABOUT 6 QUARTS

INGREDIENTS

15 pounds fresh, ripe tomatoes, cut up

1 small yellow, orange, or red pepper, chopped

1 small green pepper, chopped

1 cup diced celery

2 diced carrots

2 bay leaves

2 teaspoons dried basil

1 tablespoon salt

1 tablespoon freshly grated horseradish root

½ teaspoon pepper

1 teaspoon sugar

2 teaspoons Worcestershire sauce

Candied Sweet Potatoes

MAKES 4 QUARTS

INGREDIENTS

12 pounds sweet potatoes, scrubbed

water to cover

5 medium oranges

1½ cups packed brown sugar

1 cup honey

2 tablespoons pure vanilla extract

1½ tablespoons pumpkin pie spice

These taste delicious heated and served with turkey or chicken. The vanilla extract and pumpkin pie spice add just the right kick.

1. Over medium heat, boil potatoes in water to cover until skins come off easily, about 20 minutes.

2. While potatoes cook, prepare orange sauce. Wash oranges. Grate ¼ cup peel and set aside. Juice oranges and add water to make 2½ cups. In a medium saucepan, combine orange juice mixture, brown sugar, and honey. Bring to a boil over medium-high heat, stirring constantly until sugar dissolves. Stir in vanilla extract, grated orange peel, and pumpkin pie spice. Cover and keep hot.

3. Immerse cooked potatoes in cold water. Rub and pull skins off. Cut potatoes into chunks.

4. Pack potatoes into 1 hot jar at a time, leaving 1" headspace. Ladle ⅓ cup hot syrup into pints and ¾ cup hot syrup into quarts. Remove air bubbles, wipe rims, cap, and seal.

5. Process in a pressure canner at 10 pounds pressure for 65 minutes for pints or 90 minutes for quarts.

Caponata

This is a delightful accompaniment to any meat, fish, or poultry dish. The hint of rosemary in this really ups the flavor.

1. Sauté eggplant, celery, and onion in oil until tender.

2. Combine remaining ingredients in a stockpot. Bring to boil and simmer for 10 minutes.

3. Pack into jars. Remove air bubbles, wipe rims, cap, and seal. Process in pressure canner at 10 pounds pressure for 30 minutes for pints or 40 minutes for quarts.

Caponata's Origins

Caponata is a summery Sicilian dish that gets its hearty flavor and texture from its superstar ingredient—eggplants. It is similar to other Mediterranean vegetable dishes, like ratatouille. This recipe includes some of the traditional staples of Sicilian cuisine, such as olive oil, olives, and capers.

MAKES 4 QUARTS

INGREDIENTS

10 pounds eggplant, peeled and cubed

3½ cups chopped celery

2 cups chopped onion

4 tablespoons extra-virgin olive oil

7 pounds tomatoes, skinned, chopped, and drained

1½ cups red wine vinegar

1 3-ounce can tomato paste

3 tablespoons sugar

2 cups ripe olives, sliced

¾ cup pine nuts or slivered almonds

1 tablespoon minced rosemary

½ cup parsley, finely chopped

3 ounces capers, rinsed and drained

1 teaspoon black pepper

Herbed Corn on the Cob

MAKES 12 EARS

INGREDIENTS

½ cup unsalted butter

1 teaspoon salt and pepper

1 teaspoon parsley

½ teaspoon garlic powder

½ teaspoon onion powder

¼ teaspoon chipotle powder (optional)

12 ears corn, cleaned and blanched

Make these at the fall harvest and warm them up on a cold winter day for a lasting taste of summer picnics.

1. Soften butter; mix in all herbs evenly.

2. Spread the butter evenly over each cob of corn.

3. Wrap cobs tightly with plastic wrap, twisting top and bottom of wrap.

4. Wrap in a layer of aluminum foil. Place in a large resealable food-storage bag in freezer up to 9 months.

5. When ready to use, take out of food-storage bag and grill or broil in oven safely; the plastic will not melt inside the foil. Defrost first, then warm 15–20 minutes.

Discovering Corn
Corn was a major staple in Native Americans' diet when Columbus arrived and introduced Europeans to corn. The word *maize* is thought to originate with the Taino people of the Caribbean Islands. It meant "life source."

Baked Stuffed Potatoes

These go together quickly and make a great snack or side dish that's warm and filling. Serve with sour cream, broccoli, or your other favorite potato toppings.

1. Scoop out insides of potatoes, leaving enough to make a good shell for freezing and baking.

2. Mash potatoes with butter, green onions, bacon bits, and cheese.

3. Refill potato skins, then wrap individually using freezer-safe wrap. Double wrap to avoid freezer burn; label accordingly.

4. To cook, thaw potatoes and warm at 400°F for 30 minutes, until the cheese is fully melted.

Potato Gods?

Archaeologists have discovered potatoes at Peruvian sites dating back to 500 B.C.E. In Incan civilization, potatoes were worshipped and considered a gift from the gods. As such, they were and often buried with the dead to help with the journey to the afterlife.

MAKES 6

INGREDIENTS

6 large Idaho potatoes, prebaked

¼ cup butter

½ cup green onions, diced

¼ cup crumbled bacon bits

1 cup shredded sharp Cheddar cheese

Stuffed Shiitake Mushrooms

MAKES 6

INGREDIENTS

6 4"–5" diameter Shiitake mushrooms, cleaned

¼ cup chopped onions and celery

1 tablespoon freshly minced garlic

3 tablespoons butter

1 teaspoon lemon

1 cup finely diced crab meat, cooked

½ cup herbed bread crumbs

¼ cup dry white wine

olive oil to taste

salt to taste

pepper to taste

When you're ready to warm these, defrost them, preheat the oven to 400°F, and put the mushrooms on a cooking sheet with a slice of mozzarella cheese on top. They'll be ready in about 15 minutes!

1. Blanch mushrooms for 2 minutes; immediately cool on ice.

2. Put onions, celery, garlic, butter, and lemon in a frying pan; sauté until tender. Pour into a mixing bowl; add crab, bread crumbs, and white wine. Mix completely.

3. Oil and lightly season both sides of mushroom caps.

4. Stuff the caps evenly with the crab mixture. Wrap carefully with freezer-safe wrap. Label and put away. Best used within 4 months.

Honey Almond Carrots

MAKES 3 QUARTS

INGREDIENTS

8 pounds carrots

6 cups water

3 cups orange juice

¾ cup honey

2 tablespoons pure vanilla extract

½ cup orange peel

⅓ cup sliced almonds

1 tablespoon crystallized ginger

This is a delightful side dish for any meal. The orange juice and peel marry well with the sweetness of the carrots.

1. Peel and slice carrots. Cook carrots until they are tender but not mushy. Drain and set aside.

2. Prepare syrup by combining water, orange juice, and honey in a saucepan. Bring to a boil and simmer for 10 minutes until syrup starts to thicken slightly. Remove from heat and stir in vanilla. Pack pre-cooked carrots into hot jars.

3. Divide orange peel, sliced almonds, and crystallized ginger evenly among jars. Pour hot syrup over carrots, leaving 1" headspace. Remove air bubbles, wipe rims, cap, and seal.

4. Process in pressure canner at 10 pounds pressure for 30 minutes for quarts.

Stuffed Sweet Blackened Peppers

Peppers are a good source of vitamins A and C and also have antioxidants that build the immune system.

1. Preheat broiler. Place peppers in oven. When skins are bubbly and black, turn over. Remove and cool.

2. Remove blackened exterior of skins. Halve each pepper; season lightly with olive oil, salt, and pepper. Set aside.

3. In a frying pan, heat 1 tablespoon olive oil and butter; add onions, celery, and crushed garlic. When tender, add tomato sauce, Worcestershire, and herbs; simmer 15 minutes.

4. Add ground beef; remove from heat and cool.

5. Mix in cheese; generously stuff each pepper half with blend.

6. Wrap individually in freezer-safe container and label. Best used within 4 months.

MAKES 12 APPETIZERS

INGREDIENTS

6 large sweet peppers

1 tablespoon olive oil, plus more for seasoning

pepper to taste

1 tablespoon butter

½ cup chopped onion

½ cup chopped celery

1 clove garlic, crushed

1 cup tomato sauce

1 teaspoon oregano

½ teaspoon dried leaf basil

2 teaspoons salt, or to taste

½ teaspoon ground black pepper

1 teaspoon Worcestershire sauce

1½ pounds lean ground beef, cooked and drained

¾ cup shredded cheese

Vegetable Lover's Lasagna

MAKES 12 SERVINGS

INGREDIENTS

1 20-ounce bag mixed
blanched vegetables

1 medium red onion, sliced

3 cloves garlic, minced

⅛ cup fresh diced basil

1 tablespoon olive oil

1 16-ounce can tomato or
spaghetti sauce

2 teaspoons Italian
seasoning

1 12-ounce container ricotta
cheese

2 eggs, beaten

5 cups mixed shredded
Italian cheeses

1 12-ounce package lasagna
noodles, cooked

3 cups Alfredo sauce
(optional)

This is a great recipe for the cheese lovers in your family. You can certainly add meat if you wish, but it's very rich without. Note that you can simply freeze large slabs of this lasagna rather than single servings if you prefer.

1. Cook the mixed blanched vegetables and set aside.

2. Saute the onion, garlic, and basil in olive oil.

3. Mix the spices with the vegetables, tossing to coat evenly.

4. Blend ricotta, eggs, and Italian cheeses.

5. Line the bottom of a 9" × 13" pan with aluminum foil. Cover with a layer of tomato or spaghetti sauce.

6. Put down one layer of noodles, followed by vegetables, ricotta blend, and Alfredo sauce. Repeat the layering until you fill the pan.

7. Cover and place in the freezer until it's solid enough to cut into 12 pieces.

8. Slice and double-wrap each piece in plastic wrap and aluminum foil and put into a food-storage bag for single servings.

9. To warm, remove from the wrappings and place in an ovenproof pan. Cover with aluminum foil and bake at 350°F for about 30 minutes for a single piece. Uncover and bake another 10 minutes to finish.

Vegetable Medley

This dish is braised in the oven before being moved to single-serve aluminum foil containers—perfect for camping trips or any day you need a side dish.

1. Preheat your oven to 400°F. Oil a large roasting tray and set aside.

2. Toss vegetables with half the vinaigrette, coating them evenly.

3. Transfer vegetables to tray and cook for 20 minutes, stirring regularly. They will not be completely tender.

4. Set out 10 pieces of aluminum foil about 12–14" long. Put equal portions of the vegetable blend on each piece of foil.

5. Add 1 teaspoon fresh vinaigrette to each package. For extra flavor, include a sprig of fresh rosemary or other herb. Wrap the herbs into an envelope-style bundle and wrap with a second layer of aluminum foil. Label and freeze.

6. To cook, defrost and return to a 400°F oven or a hot grill for another 20 minutes.

MAKES ABOUT
10 SERVINGS

INGREDIENTS

1 pound baby carrots, peeled

1 pound young parsnips, halved

1 pound fingerling potatoes, halved

1 red onion, sliced

10 stalks celery cut in 1" pieces

1 12-ounce container cherry tomatoes

10 teaspoons vinaigrette

2 teaspoons garlic, chopped

salt to taste

pepper to taste

Dried Hot Pepper Flakes

MAKES 1 CUP

INGREDIENTS

5 cups fresh hot peppers, any variety

This is a good way to use up those leftovers from the garden, or a reason for a trip to the farmers market. It doesn't matter how many varieties you mix together.

1. Rinse any lingering dirt off peppers.

2. Remove pepper stems and ends; clean off seeds.

3. Chop peppers no more than ¼" thick.

4. Line a cookie sheet with heavy-duty aluminum foil; lightly spray with cooking spray. Evenly spread chopped peppers onto cookie sheet.

5. Place in 200°F oven. Leave oven door slightly ajar. Bake 3–4 hours, turning with a long-handled spatula every 30 minutes. Peppers should be bone dry.

6. Leave on kitchen counter for a few days to make sure flakes crumble when picked up. Store in a Mason jar with a tight-fitting cover. Label clearly.

Hot Pepper Safety

Hot peppers can be dangerous if you do not handle them properly. Always wear disposable rubber gloves when you handle them, and never touch your eyes or mouth. Hot peppers leave behind an oily residue that can cause a burning sensation if it comes into contact with your skin, eyes, or mouth.

Vegetable Chips

This makes a healthy snack that has a long shelf life and can also double as the base for a vegetable soup or stew.

1. Blanch vegetables for 1 minute; drain.

2. Toss slices with olive oil, salt, garlic powder, and any other spices you like.

3. Sort in layers by vegetable type and transfer to a dehydrator, using the temperature setting recommended by the manufacturer. Dry about 6 hours, until crispy.

4. Store in airtight container.

MAKES ABOUT 10 CUPS

INGREDIENTS

2 large potatoes, thinly sliced

1 sweet potato, peeled and thinly sliced

3 large radishes, peeled and thinly sliced

2 thick carrots, peeled and thinly sliced

2 thick parsnips, peeled and thinly sliced

2 tablespoons olive oil

½ teaspoon salt

1 teaspoon garlic powder

Traditional Dilly Beans

These are often a seasonal favorite. For a change of tastes, try using these pickles as the base for a green bean casserole.

1. Cut beans to fit the jars. Blanch beans for 3 minutes, then move to an ice bath. Drain. Pack beans into sterilized jars. Place two sprigs of dill and one clove of garlic in each jar.

2. In a saucepan, mix the vinegar, salt, and water; bring to a boil. Pour over the beans, leaving ½" headspace.

3. Fit the lids and process for 10 minutes in a hot-water bath.

MAKES 4 PINTS

INGREDIENTS

2 pounds fresh green beans, trimmed

4 cloves garlic

8 dill weed sprigs

4 teaspoons pickling salt

2 cups white vinegar

½ cup red wine vinegar

2½ cups water

Green and Bean

Green beans are part of a group that science calls common beans, and probably originated in the Peruvian region. Beans were introduced to the rest of the world by Portuguese and Spanish traders in the sixteenth century.

Sweet Minted Eggplant

MAKES ABOUT 3 CUPS

INGREDIENTS

1 pound small eggplants, cut into ½-inch thick rounds

1 tablespoon pickling salt

2 tablespoons lemon juice

2 tablespoons distilled white vinegar

2 tablespoons honey

½ cup extra-virgin olive oil

2 tablespoons minced garlic

⅓ cup chopped fresh mint

grated zest of 1 lemon

¼ teaspoon dried red pepper flakes

salt to taste

pepper to taste

These pickles do not need to be chilled for serving. In fact, they're tastiest at room temperature.

1. Sprinkle eggplant slices with salt; let stand 30 minutes.

2. Preheat oven broiler.

3. Mix lemon juice, vinegar, honey, olive oil, and herbs together; toss eggplant pieces to coat evenly.

4. Remove eggplant; grill lightly 3 minutes on each side.

5. Toss back into honey-vinegar blend; pack into a small jar. Pickles can be refrigerated for several months.

Selecting the Perfect Eggplant

Eggplant is a member of the nightshade family, so it is related to tomatoes and potatoes. When you shop for eggplants, look for fruits with smooth, firm skin. The skin should give when you press it gently, but it should not be mushy or discolored.

Green Tomato Piccalilli

This can be served as a side dish or as a brightly colored condiment, especially for hamburgers and hot dogs.

1. Combine vegetables and salt; cover with water and soak overnight. Drain and rinse vegetables.

2. In a large pot, combine remaining ingredients; bring to a boil. Add drained vegetables; return mixture to a boil. Reduce heat; simmer until vegetables are tender, about 30 minutes.

3. Pack hot mixture into sterilized pint jars. Cover; process in boiling bath for 15 minutes.

Piccalilli

Traditional piccalilli is a mixture of chopped vegetables with piquant spices such as mustard. Common components include cabbage, tomato, cauliflower, carrot, and onion, but nearly anything can go into the pickling mixture. The first recipe of this nature showed up in the eighteenth century, and some historians believe that Napoleon's chef is responsible for the blend.

MAKES 6–8 PINTS

INGREDIENTS

16 cups green tomatoes, finely chopped

½ head green cabbage, finely chopped

½ cup pickling salt

water to cover vegetables

4 cups cider vinegar

1½ cups dark brown sugar

½ tablespoon yellow mustard seed

½ tablespoon ground cinnamon

1 tablespoon black pepper

⅛ teaspoon crushed red pepper flakes

½ tablespoon ground allspice

1 tablespoon ground ginger

1 tablespoon dill seed

Gracious Garlic Dills

Nothing goes together quite so well as dill and garlic.

MAKES 8 QUARTS

INGREDIENTS

8 pounds pickling cucumbers
4 cups white vinegar
12 cups water
⅔ cup pickling salt
16 whole cloves garlic
4 teaspoons minced garlic
16 sprigs fresh dill weed
4 teaspoons dry dill weed

1. Wash cucumbers and soak in ice water for 2 hours. If you're planning to slice these, wait until just before canning.

2. Bring the vinegar, water, and salt to a boil.

3. Place 2 cloves of garlic, 2 sprigs of dill, ¼ teaspoon minced garlic, and ¼ teaspoon dry dill into each of the 8 quart jars. Pack each jar with approximately 1 pound of cucumbers.

4. Fill jars with brine, leaving 1" headspace and making sure the cucumbers are fully covered.

5. Cap and process jars for 15 minutes in a hot-water bath. Age for 2 months before eating.

Dad's Freezer Pickles

This recipe is highly adaptable; you can tinker with other spices and add other vegetables to the blend.

MAKES 2 QUARTS

INGREDIENTS

12 cups thinly sliced cucumber
4 cups thinly sliced sweet onion
3 cups sugar
3 cups vinegar
1 teaspoon canning salt
1 teaspoon mustard seed
1 teaspoon celery seed

1. Place cucumbers and onions in a large nonreactive bowl.

2. Mix remaining ingredients in a saucepan; bring to a boil. Stir to dissolve sugar.

3. Pour over cucumbers. Put a plate on top of cucumbers so they stay below brine; let sit at room temperature 24 hours.

4. Move into freezer-safe containers. This blend can be successfully canned using a hot-water bath method for 15 minutes.

Chapter 10

Fruit

10

Persimmon Butter

MAKES 5–6 PINTS

INGREDIENTS

8 cups persimmon purée
1 cup orange juice
1½ cups honey
grated zest of 1 orange

This recipe comes together nearly instantaneously, making a unique treat for the family and guests alike.

1. Combine all ingredients in a large stockpot; cook over medium-high heat until thick, about 10–15 minutes.

2. Ladle into sterilized jars, leaving ¼" headspace. Wipe rims; cap and seal. Process in water-bath canner 10 minutes.

Berry Bliss

MAKES 4 PINTS

INGREDIENTS

4 cups Monin sugar syrup
8 cups mixed fresh berries

To improve the flavor, mix the sugar syrup with berry-flavored juice instead of water. Make sure you use real juice and not juice drinks.

1. Wash berries in cold water; remove any bruised spots.

2. Heat sugar syrup to boiling; fill each jar with ½ cup of liquid. Add berries, leaving ½" headspace and making sure berries are covered in liquid. Remove any air bubbles.

3. Put on lids; process 15 minutes in hot-water bath.

Syrups for Fruit
Many fruit recipes call for a sugar syrup. You make a light syrup by mixing 2 cups of sugar with 1 quart of water (yields 5 cups). A medium syrup is 3 cups of sugar to 1 quart water (5½ cups) and a heavy syrup is 4¾ cups sugar to 1 quart water (6 cups).

Lemon Zesty Pears

The pears and lemon combine to make a topper, side dish, or dessert. The syrup can also be used as part of bastes and marinades if tempered with some vinegar or more lemon juice.

1. Wash pears and drain. Peel, core, and halve or quarter. Treat with Fruit Fresh mixed in water to prevent darkening.

2. To make syrup, in a large stockpot, combine sugar, lemon zest, and water; stir well. Heat until boiling; reduce heat to medium. Cook pears until they are tender, 5–6 minutes. Ladle hot pears into sterilized jars, leaving ½" headspace.

3. Ladle hot syrup over pears, leaving ½" headspace. Wipe rims; cap and seal. Process in water-bath canner 20 minutes for pints or 25 minutes for quarts.

MAKES 3 QUARTS

INGREDIENTS

8 pounds pears

¼ teaspoon Fruit Fresh (ascorbic acid)

2 cups sugar

⅛ teaspoon grated lemon zest for every 3 pounds pears

4 cups water

Raspberry Salsa

This fruity salsa works for snacking and as a topping for meat.

1. Put half the raspberries in a large stockpot and mash lightly. Add the remaining raspberries and the remaining ingredients. Bring to a boil, stirring constantly to prevent scorching. Boil gently for 5 minutes.

2. Ladle into sterilized jars, leaving ¼" headspace. Wipe rims. Cap and seal. Process in water-bath canner for 15 minutes.

MAKES 7 HALF PINTS

INGREDIENTS

6 cups fresh raspberries

1¼ cups red onion, chopped

4 jalapeño peppers, seeded and finely chopped

1 large sweet red pepper, seeded and chopped

¾ cup cilantro, loosely packed and finely chopped

juice and grated zest of 2 limes

½ cup white vinegar

4 tablespoons balsamic vinegar

3 tablespoons honey

3 cloves garlic, finely minced

1½ teaspoons ground cumin

½ teaspoon cayenne pepper

1 teaspoon ground coriander

½ teaspoon black pepper

INGREDIENTS

4 20-ounce cans crushed
pineapple with juice

1¼ cups yellow onion,
chopped

4 jalapeño peppers, seeded
and finely chopped

1 28-ounce can diced
tomatoes with juice

¾ cup cilantro, loosely
packed and finely chopped

juice and grated zest of
2 limes

½ cup white vinegar

4 tablespoons white
balsamic vinegar

3 tablespoons honey

3 cloves garlic, finely minced

1½ teaspoons ground cumin

½ teaspoon cayenne pepper

1 teaspoon ground coriander

½ teaspoon coarse-ground
black pepper

Pineapple Salsa

Pour this salsa over softened cream cheese as an appetizer or scoop it up with your favorite tortilla chips. Pour some over chicken and roast it for a delightful taste sensation.

1. Combine all ingredients in a large stockpot. Bring to a boil, reduce heat to medium-low, and let simmer for 5 minutes. Stir constantly to avoid sticking.

2. Ladle into sterilized jars, leaving ¼" headspace. Wipe rims. Cap and seal. Process in water-bath canner for 15 minutes.

Pineapples in Hawaii

Pineapples and palm trees are both synonymous with Hawaii, but only one of them is native to the islands. Pineapples originally came from South America, but the first commercial crops came from Hawaii, which is why they are often associated with it. Hawaii still produces pineapples; it supplies about 10 percent of the total world market.

Apple Butter

Fruit butters are a wonderful way to dress up bread, and they can also be used in other ways. In this case, try slathering the butter on a ham or pork chop.

1. Wash apples. Cut off stem and blossom end. Do not peel or core. Cut into small pieces.

2. Add apples and apple cider to a large stockpot. Cover and simmer until apples are soft. Reserve cooking liquid. Press apples through a sieve or a food mill.

3. Return pulp to the stockpot and add the remaining ingredients. Add half the reserved cooking liquid. Cook slowly on medium-low heat 45 to 60 minutes.

4. As pulp thickens, stir frequently to prevent sticking. If mixture gets too thick, add reserved cooking liquid until you get the desired consistency.

5. Ladle into sterilized jars, leaving ¼" headspace. Wipe rims. Cap and seal. Process in a water-bath canner for 10 minutes.

MAKES 10 PINTS

INGREDIENTS
8 pounds apples
4 cups apple cider
4 cups brown sugar
4 cups granulated sugar
4 tablespoons ground cinnamon
1 tablespoon ground cloves
1 tablespoon ground nutmeg
1 teaspoon ground cardamom
½ cup lemon juice

Blueberry Vinegar

MAKES 2 QUARTS

INGREDIENTS

3 cups fresh blueberries

3 cups rice vinegar

2 cinnamon sticks, about 2" each

4 whole allspice berries

2 tablespoons honey

This makes a very unique and beautiful vinegar that has a sweet-sour quality.

1. In a stainless-steel or enamel saucepan, combine 1½ cups blueberries with rice vinegar, cinnamon sticks, and allspice berries. Bring to a boil; reduce heat.

2. Simmer uncovered for 3 minutes. Stir in honey. Remove from heat.

3. Pour mixture through a fine-mesh strainer and let it drain into a bowl. Discard blueberries.

4. Divide remaining 1½ cup blueberries evenly between two jars. Add 1 cinnamon stick and 2 whole allspice berries to each jar.

5. Ladle half of the vinegar into each jar. Remove air bubbles. Wipe rims.

6. Cap and seal in a hot-water bath for 10 minutes. Let sit in a cool place for 2–3 weeks before opening.

7. Strain through a colander lined with cheesecloth twice and discard berries and spices before using.

Kiwi-Pineapple Preserve

This makes a big batch, but it won't last long once people get a taste!

1. Cut kiwis in half and scoop out pulp with a teaspoon. Put in a large stockpot. Drain pineapple chunks. Reserve juice. Add to stockpot. Add sugar, pepper, and lemon or lime juice. Stir well.

2. Cover and bring to a boil on high heat. Reduce heat and simmer about 30 to 45 minutes until kiwi and pineapple are tender but not mushy.

3. Mix ClearJel with 1 cup reserved pineapple juice. Add to stockpot and stir well. Simmer another 8 minutes or until mixture thickens.

4. Place in freezer-safe containers with ½" headspace.

5. To can, ladle into sterilized jars, leaving ½" headspace. Wipe rims. Cap and seal. Process in boiling-water bath for 20 minutes.

MAKES 15–20 QUARTS

INGREDIENTS

60 ripe kiwis

4 8-ounce cans pineapple chunks

1 8-ounce can crushed pineapple

10 cups granulated sugar

4 tablespoons coarse-ground black pepper

1 cup lemon or lime juice

1 cup ClearJel

Mouthwatering Mangos

MAKES 4 PINTS

INGREDIENTS

6 cups ripe mangos

½ tablespoon powdered cloves

½ tablespoon freshly grated allspice

½ tablespoon ginger

1½ cups white wine or Champagne vinegar

1½ cups water

6 cups Hawaiian sugar

4 peppercorns (optional)

These mangos are so tasty you might have trouble getting them into the canning jars before you eat them.

1. Peel, pit, and slice the mangos.

2. Combine all the ingredients except the peppercorns in a pot. Bring to a boil; reduce heat.

3. Simmer for about 10 minutes or until the mangos look semitransparent.

4. Put one peppercorn into each jar, then add mangos with hot syrup, leaving ½" headspace

5. Seal. Process in boiling-water bath for 20 minutes. Check lids when cooled.

Mango Madness

If you eat mangos often, it might be worth it to invest in a mango splitter to help you get rid of the pesky pits. This specialized kitchen tool works just like an apple corer and removes the pit in one easy motion, saving you the trouble of hacking the fruit apart with a knife.

Summer Strawberry Ice Cream

Ice cream is a wonderful treat, especially during the warm months. If you want to personalize this recipe, try adding some flaked coconut to the egg yolk mixture or mixing strawberries and raspberries.

1. Place the berries into a blender or food processor; purée until smooth.

2. Heat 1¼ cups cream in a saucepan over medium heat until it begins to bubble at the edge of the pan.

3. In a separate bowl, whisk together sugar, egg yolks, remaining ¼ cup cream, vanilla, and corn syrup.

4. Slowly pour the cream into the egg yolk mixture, whisking constantly.

5. Return the mixture to the saucepan. Simmer until mixture is thick enough to coat the back of a wooden spoon, about 5 minutes. Do not boil!

6. Mix berries and custard together; refrigerate until chilled.

7. Use an ice cream maker to get a really smooth dessert. If you don't have an ice cream maker, you can transfer the custard into a mixing bowl and put it in the freezer. After 30 minutes, beat thoroughly and return to freezer. Repeat until you achieve the desired texture.

MAKES 4 CUPS

INGREDIENTS

1¼ quarts fresh strawberries, hulled

1½ cups heavy cream, divided

¾ cup white sugar

½ teaspoon vanilla extract

3 egg yolks

3 tablespoons light corn syrup

Minty Nectarine Pear Preserves

MAKES 5–6 PINTS

INGREDIENTS

2 pounds ripe nectarines, peeled and pitted

2 pounds pears, peeled and cored

¾ cup cold water

¼ cup lemon juice

1 teaspoon whole cloves

1 teaspoon whole allspice berries

2 whole cinnamon sticks

5 cups sugar or Splenda

½ cup fresh mint leaves, chopped or 2 tablespoons dried mint

Use this for summer pasta salads, poured over pork while it roasts, and or as a side dish with various poultry dishes.

1. Peel and pit nectarines; cut into chunks.

2. Peel pears; core. Put in a large stockpot with water and lemon juice.

3. Make a spice ball with cloves, allspice berries, and cinnamon sticks. Add to stockpot; cook over medium heat 10 minutes.

4. Crush nectarines with a potato masher. Add sugar or Splenda and mint leaves; stir well.

5. Bring mixture to a boil; simmer 15 minutes, until mixture is thick. Remove and discard spice ball.

6. Put into freezer-safe containers with ½" headspace.

7. Alternatively, can this by ladling hot preserves into sterilized jars, leaving ½" headspace. Wipe rims; cap and seal. Process in water-bath canner 15 minutes.

Nectarines

Nectarines are related to peaches, but their skin is clear, while peaches have fuzz. Peaches and nectarines have histories that mix and mingle. Nectarines have been documented in China more than 2,000 years ago, just like peaches! The word itself simply means "sweet nectar." Nectarines have a sweet, tangy flavor.

Cranberry-Raspberry Sauce

This is a unique adaptation of a Thanksgiving favorite that's yummy all year.

1. Combine sugar, raspberry vinegar, and water in a large nonreactive pan over medium heat; bring to a boil, stirring constantly until sugar dissolves.

2. Add cranberries, raspberries, cinnamon stick, vanilla bean, and orange peel.

3. Reduce heat to low; cover partially and simmer 10 minutes, or until cranberries burst.

4. Remove from heat; take out the cinnamon stick and cool completely.

5. Place in freezer-safe containers, leaving ½" headspace.

Cows and Cranberries

The botanical name for cranberry, *vaccinium*, comes from a Latin word that means "cow." This apparently happened because cows love the stuff! In England, the word *cranberry* was originally *craneberry* because the flowers resemble this bird. Additionally, like cows, cranes apparently love cranberries! A folk name for cranberry is *bounceberry*; when they're fresh they tend to bounce when dropped.

MAKES 5–6 CUPS

INGREDIENTS
1¼ cups sugar
½ cup raspberry vinegar
¼ cup water
1 12-ounce package fresh cranberries
1 cup fresh raspberries
1 cinnamon stick
¼-inch vanilla bean
1 tablespoon thinly sliced orange peel

Wine-Poached Figs

MAKES 6 CUPS

INGREDIENTS

1 750-milliliter bottle Pinot Noir or Burgundy

1 cup dark honey

½ cup red wine vinegar or fig vinegar

2 cinnamon sticks

2 ¼-inch slices gingerroot

1 tablespoon whole cloves

2½ pounds fresh ripe figs, quartered

Be sure to get firm, ripe figs for this recipe. If they're too ripe, they turn to mush when cooking. When you serve these, warm them up and top with some sweet cream.

1. Bring the wine, honey, vinegar, cinnamon sticks, ginger, and cloves to a simmer in a nonreactive saucepan.

2. Simmer until mixture is reduced to a light syrup, approximately 30–40 minutes. Remove from heat; strain.

3. Return reduction to saucepan; add figs and salt.

4. Cook over low heat until figs are just tender, approximately 5–10 minutes. Remove from heat; cool before transferring to freezer-safe containers.

5. Make sure figs have enough sauce to cover.

Give a Fig

Figs complement the tangy flavors of balsamic vinegar and wine, which is what makes this dish so delightful. Balsamic vinegar flavored with figs is delicious on everything from salads to pound cake. It's often very expensive to buy because it takes so many figs to make a relatively small amount of vinegar.

Fundamental Fruit Leather

This basic process will work for nearly any fruit that you'd like to make into roll-up leather. They have a great shelf life and make wonderful healthy snacks.

1. Wash and peel fruit; make sure to remove any overripe parts.

2. Purée fruit in food processor or blender.

3. Taste; sweeten to preference.

4. Heat entire mix to a low rolling boil; cool.

5. Coat fruit-leather tray for your dehydrator with spray-on oil.

6. Cover the oiled surface with purée no more than ⅛-inch thick. Dry at 135°F about 12 hours.

7. Wrap in plastic for storing.

8. This process can work in a conventional oven on the lowest setting, but the dehydrator circulates the air so the leathers dry evenly.

YIELD VARIES

INGREDIENTS

apples, pears, berries, peaches, or a mixture of your favorite fruit

honey or sugar to taste

Watermelon Pickles

MAKES 5 PINTS

INGREDIENTS

4 pounds watermelon rind

½ cup pickling salt

8 cups water

4 cups sugar

2 cups white vinegar

5 ½-inch cinnamon sticks

10 whole cloves

5 ¼-inch slices gingerroot, peeled

1 lemon, sliced into 5 pieces

This is a Southern favorite that has a fresh, thirst-quenching quality.

1. Trim the pink parts off the watermelon rind; cube rind.

2. Soak the rind in pickling salt and water overnight; drain and rinse thoroughly.

3. Place rind in a large pot and cover with water; simmer until tender, being careful not to overcook.

4. In a large stockpot, mix remaining ingredients; simmer 10 minutes.

5. Add watermelon rind, cooking over low heat until nearly transparent.

6. Transfer rind and liquid to ½-pint jars. Leave ½" headspace; process in hot-water bath 10 minutes.

Desert Watermelon

An African explorer by the name of David Livingston found that the Kalahari Desert held an abundance of watermelon. This is the area where this fruit may have originated. Other evidence suggests that watermelon cultivation began around the second millennium B.C.E. in the Nile Valley.

Pickled Peaches and Pears

Prepare your sterilized quart jars beforehand by putting 1 whole stick of cinnamon, 2 whole cloves, and 1 slice of gingerroot in each.

1. Combine sugar, vinegar, water, and spices; bring to a boil.

2. After 10 minutes add fruit; cook until partially tender.

3. Pack fruit into jars, pouring syrup over top and leaving ½" headspace.

4. Add tops; process 10 minutes in hot-water bath.

Just Peachy

Peaches had their beginning in China, where they were favored by the royal family. They appear in Chinese writings dating to the tenth century B.C.E. Peaches traveled with Persian merchants, who introduced them to Europe. Peaches were one of the fruits brought to America by the Spanish in the seventeenth century.

MAKES 4 QUARTS

INGREDIENTS

5 cups sugar

2½ cups vinegar

2½ cups water

4 cinnamon sticks

8 whole cloves

4 ¼-inch slices fresh ginger

8 cups peaches, peeled and pitted

8 cups pears, peeled and pitted

Green Tomato Mincemeat

MAKES 10 PINTS

INGREDIENTS

2 tablespoons pickling salt

2 quarts green tomatoes, cored and chopped

water to cover

4 tablespoons dried orange peel

⅔ cup peeled, seeded, and chopped orange

2½ quarts peeled, cored, and chopped apples

1 pound golden yellow raisins

1½ cups chopped suet

3½ cups packed dark brown sugar

½ cup cider vinegar

juice of 1 lemon

2 teaspoons cinnamon

1 teaspoon pure vanilla extract

1 teaspoon nutmeg

1 teaspoon ginger

1 teaspoon cloves

While this is not a traditional pickling recipe, it does use pickling salt and vinegar as preservatives.

1. Sprinkle salt over green tomatoes and let sit for 1 hour.

2. Rinse well in cold water and drain. Cover tomatoes with boiling water and let sit for 5 minutes. Drain.

3. Combine tomatoes and remaining ingredients in a large stockpot. Bring to a boil. Ladle into sterilized jars, leaving 1" headspace. Wipe rims. Cap and seal. Process in a pressure canner at 10 pounds pressure for 25 minutes.

Fruit or Vegetable?

Have you ever wondered why the tomato is classified as a fruit? When we cook, we generally use fruits when we want a sweet dish. But tomatoes are more savory and are often used with vegetables. Technically, tomatoes are in the fruit family because they contain the seeds of the plants; vegetables do not.

Candied Fruit Rinds

Candied fruit rinds were enjoyed during the Middle Ages as a way to sweeten the breath.

1. Peel citrus fruit; remove as much pith as possible. Place peels in enough water to cover. Bring to a full boil; reduce heat and simmer 30 minutes. Change water and repeat; this reduces bitterness.

2. Cool; slice citrus into strips about ¼-inch thick.

3. Mix water, salt, honey, and sugar; bring to a simmer. Put peels in syrup; continue simmering about 25 minutes.

4. Turn off heat; let rinds sit in syrup. Remove rind pieces from syrup; dry on a rack over waxed paper. Sprinkle with fine sugar; store in an airtight container.

MAKES 20 SLICES

INGREDIENTS
1 large navel orange
1 medium grapefruit
2 lemons or 2 large limes
¼ cup water
dash salt
¾ cup sugar
¼ cup honey
fine sugar (optional)

Candied Pineapple Chunks

YIELD VARIES

INGREDIENTS

1 medium ripe pineapple

1 cup water

2 cups granulated sugar

1 teaspoon powdered ginger (optional)

⅓ cup light corn syrup

This makes a luscious snack all by itself, or you can use it for making fruitcake!

1. Peel pineapple and slice into bite-sized chunks.

2. Bring sugar, water, ginger, and corn syrup to a boil. Add pineapple and simmer until pineapple turns translucent.

3. Drain on a rack, then store in an airtight container.

Pineapple Passion

Americans began importing pineapples in the seventeenth century, and by the Victorian era a pineapple carved into serving trays, a doorway, or other decorative items had come to represent hospitality and welcome to all guests.

Chapter 11

Meat, Poultry, and Fish

Chili with Meat

MAKES 6 QUARTS

INGREDIENTS

10 pounds ground beef

3 cloves garlic, minced

4 cups chopped onions

1 tablespoon olive oil

4 quarts canned chopped tomatoes, with juice

½ cup chili powder

1 teaspoon cumin seed

2 jalapeño peppers, seeded and minced

2 teaspoons oregano

4 teaspoons honey

2 teaspoons onion powder

1 teaspoon coarse-ground black pepper

When you're ready to serve this as a meal, add cooked pinto or kidney beans and heat through.

1. In a large stockpot, sauté ground beef, garlic, and chopped onions in olive oil until meat is browned. Drain excess fat; return to stockpot.

2. Add remaining ingredients; simmer 20 minutes.

3. Ladle into sterilized jars, leaving 1" headspace. Wipe rims; cap and seal.

4. Process in pressure-canner pints 1 hour and 15 minutes and quarts 1 hour and 30 minutes.

Ground Meat Basics
To safely can ground meat, you can season it and sauté loosely or shape it and sauté before layering it into jars. In both instances, the meat should be drained afterward, placed hot into jars, covered with a matching broth leaving 1" headspace, and processed at 11 pounds pressure for 75 minutes for pints and 90 minutes for quarts.

Barbecued Turkey Drumsticks

If you find you don't have sufficient sauce for canning, add an equal amount of ketchup and water.

1. Combine all ingredients except turkey legs and scallions. Whisk together until well combined. Stir in chopped scallions.

2. Skin drumsticks. Place in baking pan sprayed with cooking spray.

3. Pour marinade over turkey. Cover with heavy-duty aluminum foil; refrigerate overnight.

4. Bake in 350°F oven 1–1½ hours, or until drumsticks are tender and done.

5. Remove drumsticks from sauce; allow to cool. Reserve sauce.

6. Debone turkey; cut into bite-sized pieces. Put back in sauce; ladle into sterilized jars, leaving 1" headspace. Wipe rims; cap and seal.

7. Process in pressure canner 1 hour and 15 minutes for pints or 1 hour and 30 minutes for quarts at 10 pounds pressure.

MAKES 7–8 QUARTS

INGREDIENTS

2 cups of your favorite commercial BBQ sauce

2 cups ketchup

2 tablespoons white vinegar

2 tablespoons granulated sugar

salt to taste

pepper to taste

1 tablespoon finely minced garlic

2 beef bouillon cubes, crumbled

6–8 large turkey drumsticks, skinned

1 bunch scallions, finely chopped

Shellfish Stock

INGREDIENTS

2 tablespoons butter

2 large onions, chopped

1 bunch leeks, rinsed well and chopped

4 or 5 chopped garlic cloves

3–4 stalks chopped celery

1 pound carrots, peeled and roughly chopped

4–5 pounds lobster or crab shells

¼ cup lemon juice

½ cup chopped parsley

1 teaspoon whole black peppercorns

3–4 bay leaves

½ teaspoon dried basil leaves

½ teaspoon dried oregano leaves

½ teaspoon dried tarragon leaves

½ teaspoon dried thyme leaves

1 cup dry white wine (optional)

1 gallon cold water

This shellfish stock is a prime ingredient for crab or lobster bisque.

1. Melt butter in bottom of stockpot; sauté onion, leeks, garlic, and celery about 5 minutes, or until soft.

2. Add remaining ingredients; simmer about 1 hour. Periodically skim off foam that will appear at top of pot.

3. Strain; ladle into sterilized jars. Wipe rims; cap and seal.

4. Process in pressure canner at 10 pounds pressure for 30 minutes for pints or 35 minutes for quarts.

Oysters in "R" Months?

There's a myth that claims shellfish are only safe in "R" months, but it's only an urban legend. While some European shellfish breed young in months whose names contain the letter "R," that only makes the fish a little less tasty. Additionally, there are regulations in place for the gathering and distribution of shellfish by the health department that make commercial shellfish safe to eat.

Ready-to-Go Ribs

The process is a little lengthy, but it's well worth the time and effort. When you take these out of the freezer, they only need a quick broil or toss on the grill.

1. Remove membrane from underside of ribs. Trim off any loose fat; rub both sides with seasoning.

2. Wrap in plastic wrap, followed by aluminum foil; cook 4 hours at 200°F. Cool.

3. While ribs cook, prepare sauce; simmer over a low flame about 1 hour. The sauce will reduce a bit during this time.

4. Heat up grill and cook ribs until internal temperature reaches 145°F. Brush with sauce on each turn.

5. Cut into single-serving sizes, wrapping with freezer-safe plastic wrap and covering again with aluminum foil. Label and date. The ribs are good for 6 months.

MAKES 3 POUNDS

INGREDIENTS

Rub Ingredients

3 pounds pork spareribs
½ cup brown sugar
¼ cup paprika
1 tablespoon black pepper
1 tablespoon salt
1 tablespoon chili powder
1 tablespoon garlic powder
1 tablespoon onion powder
1 tablespoon lemon zest
1 tablespoon orange zest
1 tablespoon basil
1 teaspoons mesquite powder
1 teaspoon cayenne

Sauce Ingredients

1 cup ketchup
¼ cup whiskey
¼ cup molasses
¼ cup vinegar
2 tablespoons olive oil
1 tablespoon chili powder
1 tablespoon ginger powder
1 tablespoon Worcestershire sauce
1 tablespoon hearty mustard
2 cloves garlic, minced
½ teaspoon red pepper flakes

SERVES 8

INGREDIENTS

1½ pounds lean ground beef

½ cup bread crumbs

1 onion, minced

¼ cup minced green pepper

2 tablespoons molasses

1 tablespoon steak sauce

1 egg, slightly beaten

2 celery stalks, finely chopped

1 tablespoon Worcestershire sauce

2 cloves garlic, chopped

1½ teaspoons salt

pepper to taste

¼ cup spaghetti sauce

Mama's Meatloaf

If you like, add a portion of mashed potatoes on top of the spaghetti sauce for a heartier meal. This may be frozen whole, but portioning it allows family members to defrost and eat one piece at a time as desired.

1. Thoroughly combine all ingredients except spaghetti sauce.

2. Press into an 8" × 8" baking pan. Top with sauce.

3. Bake at 350°F for 1 hour, or until slightly brown around the edges.

4. Slice into 8 pieces; freeze whole, or freeze individual pieces double-wrapped in freezer-safe wrapping. Label and date.

Mixing It Up with Meatloaf

While it seems like a rather modern food, meatloaf has a very ancient past. When a meat was tough or resources were tight, meat would be ground and mixed with whatever was available before it was baked, fried, or put into pies. Around the nineteenth century, meatloaf as we know it slowly came into American homes. Once popularized, every cook put their personal spin on this very ancient dish!

Pork Dumplings

These are a fantastic snack for company, but be forewarned that you may want to make a double batch—they disappear very quickly. Serve with soy sauce, Chinese mustard, or sweet and sour sauce for dipping.

1. Fry and drain pork.

2. Mix drained pork with all other ingredients except wonton wraps. The blend should be slightly damp but not wet.

3. Place a heaping tablespoon of the mix onto the center of each wonton wrap.

4. Moisten edges of the wrap; fold into a triangle.

5. Place pot stickers in a well-oiled pan in batches of five. When bottoms of pot stickers turn golden brown, pour in ⅛ cup of rice wine or water. Cover; steam until translucent.

6. Cool; chill in the refrigerator 1 hour.

7. Freeze in batches of five.

8. Reheat in oven or frying pan.

MAKES ABOUT 25 POT STICKERS

INGREDIENTS

1 pound ground pork

1 bundle green onions, chopped

½ cup bean sprouts, cut in half

½ cup finely shredded cabbage

½ cup finely shredded carrot

3–4 tablespoons soy sauce

½ teaspoon ginger powder

2–3 drops hot sauce

1 package wonton wraps

oil, rice wine, and water, as needed

Barbecued Pork

MAKES ABOUT 7 QUARTS

INGREDIENTS

2 cups barbecue sauce

2 cups ketchup

2 tablespoons white vinegar

2 tablespoons granulated sugar

salt to taste

pepper to taste

1 tablespoon finely minced garlic

2 beef bouillon cubes, crumbled

1 bunch scallions, finely chopped

6–8 pounds boneless pork roast

Harkening back to old-fashioned pulled pork, this great recipe can be used for sandwiches or barbecue-flavored stew. You can substitute an equal amount of chicken for the pork if you desire.

1. Combine all ingredients except pork and scallions. Whisk together until well combined; stir in chopped scallions.

2. Cut pork into bite-sized pieces. Place in a baking pan sprayed with cooking spray; pour marinade over top.

3. Cover with heavy-duty aluminum foil; refrigerate overnight.

4. The next day, bake at 350°F for 30–40 minutes, until pork is cooked. Cool.

5. Transfer into freezer-safe containers. Add more barbecue sauce if you need it to cover the meat in the containers.

Mango Steaks

Alternatively, simply marinate the flank steak in the sauce and freeze it before cooking. This allows the steak to marinate while you defrost it. In this case, using a vacuum sealer works great.

1. Mix together all ingredients except for steak. Warm in a saucepan.

2. Pour half the sauce into the bottom of a marinating dish, place the steak on top, and pour the remainder over the top. Cover and marinate in the refrigerator for 24 hours.

3. Prepare the grill, spraying it with oil. Grill the steaks until they reach 120°F internally (rare), brushing with sauce.

4. Cool and wrap in plastic, then place each steak in a freezer-safe bag. Label and date. If you like your steak rare, just do a quick warm on a griddle. Otherwise you can defrost and cook each steak to your liking.

MAKES 4–6 SERVINGS

INGREDIENTS
¼ cup olive oil
2 cups mango juice
1 peach, pulped
1 tablespoon garlic salt
2 tablespoons Worcestershire sauce
2 teaspoons kosher salt
1 tablespoon ground black pepper
¼ cup red wine
¼ cup soy sauce
¼ cup honey
3–4 pounds flank steak

Cider Ham

If you like spices, feel free to add ginger, cloves, or cinnamon to this dish. To serve, simply defrost and warm at 350°F for about 20 minutes.

1. Preheat the oven to 350°F.

2. Mix cider, sugar, mustard, and orange rind.

3. Cut the ham into 6 steaks, trimming excess fat. Let steaks soak in the cider mixture overnight in the refrigerator, turning occasionally.

4. Individually wrap each steak with a slice of pineapple and a tablespoon of butter and brush the top with marinade. Place steaks in a freezer-safe container. Label and date. Use within 6–8 months.

MAKES 6 SERVINGS

INGREDIENTS
4 cups cider
½ cup light brown sugar
1 teaspoon dry mustard or stone-ground mustard
1 teaspoon grated orange rind
4-pound cooked whole ham
6 pineapple rings
6 tablespoons butter

Healthy Taco Sauce with Meat

MAKES 6 QUARTS

INGREDIENTS

10 pounds ground beef

2–4 cloves garlic, minced

4 cups chopped onions

1 tablespoon extra-virgin olive oil

3–4 jalapeño peppers, seeded and minced

4 quarts canned chopped tomatoes with juice

½ cup Salt-Free Taco Seasoning Mix (page 179)

3–4 drops hot sauce

2 teaspoons dried oregano

2 teaspoons onion powder

1 teaspoon coarse-ground black pepper

Taco sauce isn't just for tacos. It can also be the foundation for a Mexican chili or a dip for chips.

1. In a large stockpot, sauté ground beef, garlic, and onions in olive oil until meat is browned. Drain excess fat in a colander. Return to stockpot.

2. Wearing rubber gloves, remove stem and blossom ends of jalapeño peppers. Chop finely.

3. Add remaining ingredients and simmer for 20 minutes. Ladle into sterilized freezer-safe containers, leaving 1" headspace. Use within 6 months.

Pepper Popularity

Jalapeño peppers are the most commonly used peppers in the United States. They are small and can be either green or red, depending on when they were harvested. As a precaution, wear rubber gloves when slicing peppers. This prevents the oils in the peppers from burning your hands.

Pasta Sauce

As with taco sauce, a basic pasta sauce comes in very handy for many dishes.

1. Wash tomatoes in cold water. Drain and dry with paper towels. Core and cut into small pieces.

2. Put in food processor or blender and purée in small batches. Put puréed tomatoes into two large stockpots.

3. Wash and finely chop all herbs. Divide equally between two stockpots.

4. In a frying pan, sauté ground beef, green peppers, black pepper, and onions in extra-virgin olive oil until meat is browned and veggies are soft. Drain well in a colander to remove excess fat. Split mixture evenly between two tomato pots.

5. Bring to a boil over high heat. Reduce heat to low and simmer for about 45 to 60 minutes, stirring often.

6. Ladle into properly dated and labeled freezer-safe containers.

Marrying Pasta with Tomatoes
Tomato sauce is a relatively new advancement in pasta's rich history. Tomatoes used to be considered inedible because they are a member of the nightshade family. The first recipe that contained pasta with tomatoes appeared in 1839, and Italians slowly became enamored with the fruit.

MAKES 8 QUARTS

INGREDIENTS
40 pounds tomatoes
2½ cups chopped fresh basil
½ cup chopped fresh thyme
½ cup finely chopped fresh rosemary
1 cup chopped fresh oregano
2 pounds lean ground beef
3 tablespoons freshly ground black pepper
2 green peppers, diced
2 cups chopped onion
3 tablespoons extra-virgin olive oil
1 cup lemon juice
1½ cups sugar or Splenda
salt to taste (optional)

Sloppy Jeannes

MAKES 8 QUART
CONTAINERS

INGREDIENTS

5 pounds ground beef

2 large onions, finely chopped

2 large sweet green peppers, seeded and finely chopped

3–4 tablespoons extra-virgin olive oil

1⅓ cups ketchup

1 cup water

4 tablespoons lemon juice

2 tablespoons brown sugar or brown sugar replacement

2 beef bouillon cubes, crumbled

2 teaspoons fine sea salt

2 teaspoons ground black pepper

1 teaspoon dry yellow mustard

2 teaspoons granulated sugar or Splenda

2 teaspoons white vinegar

1 teaspoon chili powder or Tabasco sauce

Kids and adults alike will love this sloppy, tasty mix. It can be used on rolls a la sloppy Joes or as filling for a unique lasagna!

1. Brown ground beef, green pepper, and onions in olive oil until meat is browned and onions and peppers are tender. Drain well in a colander to remove excess fat.

2. Add remaining ingredients. Simmer on low heat for 20 minutes.

3. Cool and ladle into freezer-safe containers. Use within 6–8 months.

Sloppy Joes
Sloppy Joes are an easy dinner recipe, and children and adults alike think they're fun to eat. This unique take on the classic makes dinnertime even easier. All you have to do is warm up the mix and slap it into a roll!

Homemade Salami

You may substitute onion salt or garlic salt for the powder in this recipe if you like your salami on the salty side. For the recipe to succeed, you must use curing salt or quick cure.

1. Combine all ingredients in a large bowl; knead 5 minutes. Cover tightly with plastic wrap; refrigerate 24 hours.

2. Knead mixture 5 minutes. Cover tightly with plastic wrap; refrigerate another 24 hours.

3. Knead 5 minutes; form into 6–8 small rolls. Place on a broiler pan; bake 8 hours at 150°F, turning every hour. Turn oven off; let salami cool on broiler rack still in the oven until it reaches room temperature.

4. Wrap tightly in plastic wrap. Refrigerate and slice. Serve on crackers or bread.

What Kind of Salami?
Despite the fact that you can buy lunch meat labeled *salami* in the supermarket, *salami* is actually a generic word for any meat product that's encased as part of its processing. *Pepperoni* falls into the same category. *Salami* comes from the Latin *salumen*, or "salted meat."

MAKES 6–8 SMALL ROLLS

INGREDIENTS
5 pounds ground beef
5 teaspoons salt
5 hot peppercorns, crushed
2 teaspoons garlic powder
1½ teaspoons mustard seed
2½ teaspoons Hickory Smoked salt
2 teaspoons onion powder
5 teaspoons Morton's Curing Salt
2 teaspoons ground caraway seed

Pineapple Pork Jerky

MAKES 2 POUNDS JERKY

INGREDIENTS

3 pounds pork

¼ cup soy sauce

½ cup pineapple juice

3 tablespoons brown sugar

1 tablespoon Dijon mustard (optional)

1 tablespoon hot sauce

salt to taste

pepper to taste

1 clove garlic, minced

1 onion, minced

1 tablespoon Worcestershire sauce

2 tablespoons Liquid Smoke

This is a neat twist on jerky. If you're not fond of pineapple, try mango juice, passionfruit, or even cider.

1. Cut meat into thin strips

2. Mix seasoning together; add meat in an airtight container. Marinate at least 24 hours in the refrigerator.

3. Drain. Preheat oven to 150°F or use dehydrator. As with other jerky, put meat on a rack over another pan to catch drippings. Turn meat regularly over the next 6–8 hours.

4. Cool and store in an airtight container or food-storage bag.

Jerked Meat

The original word for jerky was a Spanish term, *charque*. Native Americans had enjoyed jerky long before Europeans discovered America. The meat was simply sun dried to preserve the catch left over from a good hunting expedition or for use when traveling.

Refrigerator-Pickled Herring

This is a common side dish and snack in Scandinavia during Christmas and midsummer celebrations.

1. Soak fillets in water in refrigerator 6 hours; change water and soak 6 hours more. Rinse and slice into bite-sized pieces.

2. In a saucepan, combine remaining ingredients except onion; boil, stirring regularly.

3. Slice onion; layer into jars with fish.

4. Add pickling mixture and cap. Let age about 1 week before serving. Use within 3 weeks.

A Red Herring?

Herring live in temperate shallow waters in the North Atlantic. The phrase "a red herring" came about because of the potent smell of red herrings. Fox hunters could divert their competition by dragging herring across the good trail, confusing the opponents' hounds.

MAKES 2 POUNDS

INGREDIENTS
2 pounds salt herring fillets
¾ cup water
½ cup white vinegar
⅓ cup red vinegar
1 bay leaf
¼ teaspoon black peppercorns
¼ teaspoon whole allspice
¼ teaspoon dill seeds
½ cinnamon stick
⅓ cup granulated sugar
1 red onion

INGREDIENTS

Marinade

1 cup red wine

1 cup red wine vinegar

2 cups water

1 onion, sliced

1 tablespoon crushed peppercorns

1 tablespoon crushed juniper berries

2 bay leaves

1 teaspoon mustard seed

1 teaspoon pickling salt

1 teaspoon freshly grated ginger

Braising Sauce

1½ tablespoons butter

1½ tablespoons virgin olive oil

2 cups red onion, diced

1½ cups diced celery

2 cups diced carrots

flour

water

Sauerbraten

This pickled beef is traditionally served with potatoes, dumplings, or cabbage. It can be frozen or canned using pressure-canning methods for beef.

1. Place ingredients for marinade in a large saucepan; boil 10 minutes. Cool.

2. Find a large container that will hold the beef and marinade. If necessary, add more wine to cover the beef.

3. Marinate in refrigerator 3 days, turning meat regularly.

4. Drain meat; strain marinade and put aside.

5. In a covered oven dish, heat butter; brown meat on all sides. Roast with the reserved marinade at 350°F for 1¼ hours.

6. Toss vegetables lightly in flour; add to pot. You may add water to this if needed at any time to prevent the juices from reducing too much.

Teriyaki Jerky

This recipe is fantastic for any type of meat that you enjoy with a rich teriyaki flavor. Depending on the cut, the shrinkage is minimal and the cost savings are significant.

1. Slice the meat as thinly as possible (a mandolin or meat slicer helps with this). About ³⁄₁₆" is recommended.

2. Mix all the remaining ingredients together and put into a marinating dish with the meat.

3. Cover and refrigerate for at least 24 hours and as long as 48 hours, stirring regularly. Drain meat completely.

4. For a dehydrator, put an even number of slices on each layer, being careful not to let slices touch. Follow manufacturer's recommended temperatures and times.

5. For an oven, put the meat on a rack over a cookie tray and set your oven to 150°F. Turn regularly over the next 6 hours.

6. Cool and store in an airtight container or food-storage bag.

MAKES 3½ POUNDS JERKY

INGREDIENTS
5 pounds meat
2½ cups soy sauce
2½ cups teriyaki sauce
3 tablespoons dark brown sugar
3 tablespoons garlic powder
3 tablespoons onion powder
2 tablespoons powdered ginger
1 5-ounce bottle Liquid Smoke
½ cup honey
5 teaspoons curing salt

Pickled Pigs Feet

MAKES 2 QUARTS

INGREDIENTS

6 pigs feet, halved

salt to taste

2 quarts vinegar

1 small red pepper

2 tablespoons grated horseradish

1 teaspoon whole black pepper

1 bay leaf

2 whole cloves garlic

This is a traditional recipe that people either love or hate. It adapts well to minor tinkering, so add spices according to your personal taste.

1. Scrape and scald pigs feet. Sprinkle lightly with kosher salt. Let stand for 6 hours. Rinse well in clean water.

2. In a large pot, cook the feet in water until tender.

3. Make the vinegar stock with remaining ingredients except garlic. Bring to a boil. Pack feet into canning jars.

4. Fill jars with boiling spiced vinegar, leaving ½" headspace. Clean rim, cap, and tighten the band. Process jars in pressure canner for 30 minutes at 10 pounds of pressure.

Pickled Chicken

MAKES 4 POUNDS

INGREDIENTS

4 pounds chicken, cut into pieces

water to cover

2 cups white vinegar

2 cups balsamic vinegar

1 medium onion, sliced

1 tablespoon canning salt

1 bay leaf

6 whole cloves

12 whole peppercorns

1 head fresh dill

This is a quick pickling method intended for immediate use. Alternatively, cook the chicken as directed, then can it with the brine using a pressure cooker.

1. Place chicken in a large stockpot and cover with water. Add vinegar and heat to boiling point. Skim excess fat off the top of the water.

2. Add remaining herbs and cook until tender.

Chapter 12

Herbs, Spices, and Nuts

Candied Ginger

MAKES 4 PINTS

INGREDIENTS

2 pounds fresh gingerroot

1–2 cups cold water to cover

2 cups cold water

1 tablespoon grated lemon zest

4 cups granulated sugar

2 cups superfine sugar

Candied ginger is wonderful in baking, and it also makes a handy breath mint! Note that this basic process also works effectively for fruit, particularly pineapple.

1. Peel gingerroot; cut into very thin strips across the grain. In a saucepan, cover with cold water. Heat to boiling; simmer 5 minutes. Drain.

2. Repeat procedure a second time. Dry on paper towels.

3. In a stockpot, combine 2 cups cold water, lemon zest, and 4 cups granulated sugar. Heat to boiling; simmer 10 minutes, or until a syrup forms.

4. Add ginger; cook slowly until all syrup is absorbed, about 40–50 minutes. Do not boil.

5. Remove ginger; place on a wire rack to dry.

6. Roll ginger in superfine sugar sprinkled on waxed paper; let ginger stand in the sugar until it crystallizes. Spoon into cold, sterilized jars. Cap and seal.

Nutty Honey Peanut Butter

Try a little vanilla in this recipe for a nice twist. You can also change the base nut to anything you want.

1. Put nuts through a blender or chopper.

2. Add vegetable oil to 1 cup of the nuts; mix thoroughly. Add more oil if mixture is not smooth enough.

3. Add honey; mix thoroughly.

4. Add remaining nuts; mix until evenly distributed.

5. Pack into clean, hot canning jars, leaving 1" headspace.

6. Cap and process in hot-water bath 1 hour.

7. When you serve, mix the peanut butter. The peanut butter is best used within 6 months.

Awe Nuts

In the fifteenth century, Africans were grinding peanuts and using them as a thickener. We also know that soldiers in the Civil War ate a peanut porridge. Nonetheless, it wasn't until the late nineteenth century that George Bayle began producing peanut butter as a healthy addition to the diet.

MAKES ABOUT 3 CUPS

INGREDIENTS
2 cups roasted peanuts
2 tablespoons vegetable oil
1 cup honey
salt to taste

Just Nutty!

MAKES 6 CUPS

INGREDIENTS

1 cup pecans, shelled
1 cup peanuts, shelled
1 cup walnuts, shelled
1 cup almonds, shelled
1 cup filberts, shelled
1 cup Brazil nuts, shelled

This recipe is for nut lovers who just want to relish a pure nutty taste. However, you can season the nuts with butter, Worcestershire sauce, garlic salt, seasoned salt, or another favorite flavoring before canning.

1. Spread nuts evenly over baking pan.

2. Bake at 250°F until nuts are dry. Be careful not to brown or burn them.

3. Put into prepared pint jars with ½" headspace. Cap.

4. Place into hot-water canner, leaving 1 inch of the jars above water.

5. Process 30 minutes. Cool and label.

Pecan Pie Conserve

MAKES 8 PINTS

INGREDIENTS

4 cups coarsely chopped pecans
4 cups granulated sugar
2 cups dark brown sugar
8 cups apple juice or apple cider
½ cup apple cider vinegar
½ cup unsalted butter (½ cup)
1 tablespoon ground coriander
1 tablespoon ground cinnamon
1 tablespoon ground ginger
⅛ teaspoon salt
1 tablespoon black walnut extract
2 packages powdered pectin

Use this conserve on toast or try it as the filling for tarts.

1. Combine granulated sugar, brown sugar, apple juice, and cider vinegar in a large stockpot. Stir well over medium heat and slowly bring to a boil, stirring until sugar dissolves.

2. Add remaining ingredients and bring back to a boil. Cook until thick, stirring frequently to prevent sticking.

3. Ladle hot into sterilized jars, leaving ¼" headspace. Wipe rims. Cap and seal.

4. Process 15 minutes in water-bath canner.

Plum and Walnut Preserve

This is a lovely conserve to enjoy especially in the winter months; the rum-plum blend makes it warm and welcoming.

1. Add plums, limes, raisins, and sugar to a large stockpot. Cook gently for about 45 minutes or until the mixture is thick. Stir constantly.

2. Remove from heat and stir in chopped walnuts and rum. Let stand about 5 minutes.

3. Ladle into sterilized jars. Cap and seal jars. Process for 10 minutes in a water-bath canner.

MAKES 9½ PINTS

INGREDIENTS

4 pounds fresh plums, seeded and quartered

4 fresh limes, very thinly sliced

1½ cups golden raisins

7 cups granulated sugar

2 cups chopped walnuts

8 tablespoons dark rum

Garlic Onion Pesto

This is the foundation for a great white pizza. Just brush it over the crust and add your favorite toppings.

1. Place all ingredients into a nonreactive pan over a low flame; simmer 15 minutes.

2. Cool; transfer to ice cube trays. Freeze.

3. Pop out frozen pesto cubes and put in a food-storage bag in the freezer.

Perfect Pesto

Pesto probably owes its origins to garlic sauces made during the medieval era. Romans were also known to mix spices with oil as a sauce. Strictly speaking, we find mention of something akin to a pesto in Virgil, but it was made without basil. While basil is now the most popular element in most pestos, it was a very late comer to the recipe.

MAKES ABOUT 3 CUPS

INGREDIENTS

2 cups fresh basil, packed

¼ cup pine nuts

¼ cup dried minced onion

⅛ cup minced garlic

¼ cup olive oil

1 tablespoon lemon juice

Sweet Walnuts

MAKES 1 POUND

INGREDIENTS
1 pound walnuts
½ cup butter
½ cup brown sugar
1½ teaspoons cinnamon
¼ teaspoon allspice
¼ teaspoon ginger
¼ teaspoon vanilla

The nice part about this dish is that once you get it started, it pretty much takes care of itself, making a nice snack that can be frozen for up to 6 months.

1. Place all ingredients in a slow cooker; stir.

2. Cook on high setting 15 minutes.

3. Reduce to lowest setting; continue cooking uncovered 2 hours.

4. Nuts are done when glaze isn't sticky and nuts have a crisp texture.

5. Put in containers. Label and freeze.

Walnuts in History
Walnuts have played a role in folk remedies since the time of Rome, when black walnuts were eaten to treat intestinal troubles. They also appeared in Russian and Chinese folk medicine for building strength and overall vitality.

Parsley, Sage, Rosemary, and Thyme

This is a great Italian herb blend if you grow your own herbs or have access to a farmers market.

1. Rinse herbs. Blanch for 2–3 seconds. Remove from water when the color of the leaves is noticeably brighter green. Cool and let drip dry.

2. Remove the stalks and mince the sage, thyme, and parsley.

3. Freeze in small plastic containers or add herbs to olive oil and freeze in ice cube trays.

MAKES 3½ CUPS

INGREDIENTS
½ cup fresh rosemary
1 cup fresh sage leaves
1 cup fresh thyme
1 cup fresh parsley

Snack Happy

If you have frequent drop-in guests, this is a great blend to have in your freezer. It defrosts quickly and tastes great.

1. Melt butter and stir in soup mixes.

2. Add nuts and coat completely.

3. Move nuts to the oven to dry the coating (300°F). Check and turn regularly to keep the nuts from burning.

4. Cool and store in food-storage bags in the freezer for about 4 months.

MAKES 1 POUND

INGREDIENTS
4 teaspoons butter
1 package onion soup mix
1 package garlic herb dry soup mix
1 pound mixed unsalted nuts

Pickled Garlic and Onions

MAKES 2½ PINTS

INGREDIENTS

12 large garlic cloves

12 pearl onions

2 cups white vinegar

½ cup red wine vinegar

1 cup dry white wine

1 tablespoon pickling salt

1 tablespoon sugar

1 tablespoon oregano or basil (optional)

This recipe makes a nice snack or may be used in garnishing various beverages.

1. Blanch garlic and onions 30 seconds. Immediately transfer to ice bath; drain and peel.

2. Bring vinegars, wine, salt, sugar, and spices to a boil for 1 minute.

3. Separate garlic and onions evenly between prepared canning jars.

4. Pour hot brine over onions and garlic, leaving ½" headspace. Cap.

5. Process in hot-water bath 10 minutes. Cool; label and store.

Pickled Capers

MAKES 1 QUART

3 cups capers

4 cups white vinegar

2 teaspoons pickling salt

1 medium red or Spanish onion, thinly sliced

½ lemon, thinly sliced

1 teaspoon pickling spice

2 cloves garlic, minced

5 peppercorns

½ teaspoon celery seed

½ teaspoon mustard seed (optional)

If you buy salted capers, rinse them before you pickle them or they'll be way too salty. In pickled form, capers are a nice addition to many Mediterranean dishes.

1. Combine all ingredients in a pan; bring to a boil for 5 minutes.

2. Pour into a quart container; cap and process 15 minutes in a hot-water bath.

3. Cool; label and store.

Caper Capers

Capers come from a shrub native to the Mediterranean. It's actually a fruit and is seen predominantly in Italian cuisine, where it is often combined with cream cheese, smoked salmon, and certain salsa blends. In ancient times, the Greeks used this herb to treat rheumatism.

Pickled Walnuts

Pickled walnuts make a unique addition to barbecued meats, especially venison and other game animals. You can also mix them with cheese or toss them into Thai and Indian recipes.

1. Pierce each nut with a fork in several places. Place walnuts in a bowl, covering with water and salt. Place a weight on top so the nuts stay below the brine. Let set 7 days.

2. Drain and make a fresh brine. Let stand another 7 days.

3. Dry the walnuts on a tray using a light cloth over the top to keep dust and dirt out. When the nuts turn black, they're ready for the pickle solution.

4. Combine vinegar, sugar, and spices and bring to a boil.

5. Add nuts, reduce heat, and simmer for 15 minutes.

6. Pack into canning jars, covered with syrup, leaving ½" headspace.

7. Process in a hot-water bath 10 minutes for pints, 15 minutes for quarts.

MAKES 5 POUNDS

INGREDIENTS

5 pounds fresh black walnuts

water to cover

2 cups pickling salt

1 quart malt vinegar

1 pound brown sugar

1 teaspoon allspice

1 teaspoon cloves

1 teaspoon cinnamon

1 teaspoon ginger

Homemade Vanilla Extract

MAKES 1 PINT

INGREDIENTS

4 split vanilla beans, cut into
1-inch pieces

1 pint cognac or vodka

The beans in this recipe can be dried and placed in your sugar jar to make vanilla sugar.

1. Place vanilla beans and cognac or vodka in a sterilized pint jar. Cap and seal.

2. Let stand in a cool dark place 1 month. Shake bottle gently from time to time.

3. Pour liquid through a cheesecloth-lined sieve into a sterilized pint jar. Seal tightly; store in a cool dark place.

Vanilla Beans

Vanilla beans grow primarily in Madagascar, Indonesia, Mexico, and Tahiti. Madagascar vanilla is considered the best quality. In terms of taste, Indonesian vanilla has a sharp undertone, Mexican vanilla is a bit spicy, and Tahitian bears a floral note. Vanilla isn't just used for cooking; it's also an important ingredient in various perfumes.

Herb-Garlic Blend

Mix this with butter for garlic bread beyond compare.

1. Put all ingredients into a blender or food processor; whirl until fine.

2. Store in a jar with an airtight cover.

MAKES 1 CUP

INGREDIENTS
4 tablespoons minced basil
4 tablespoons tarragon
4 tablespoons chervil
5 tablespoons minced thyme
1 teaspoon garlic powder

Chervil
Chervil comes from Eastern Europe, where Romans embraced it and introduced it to the rest of the world via Roman trade routes. According to superstition, this herb brings happiness, improves focus, and increases longevity. For cooking, chervil accents eggs, cheeses, and potatoes.

Sloppy Joe Seasoning Mix

If you are canning your sloppy Joe mix, eliminate the cornstarch so the sauce isn't too thick to process properly. Use 3 tablespoons of the mix to 1 pound of ground meat.

Combine all ingredients until well blended. Store in a jar with a tight-fitting cover.

MAKES ABOUT 1¼ CUPS

INGREDIENTS
1 cup dried minced onion flakes
3 tablespoons green pepper flakes
4 teaspoons sea salt
3 tablespoons cornstarch
4 teaspoons garlic powder
2 teaspoons dry mustard
2 teaspoons celery seed
2 teaspoons chili powder

Joe Who?
No one knows for sure where the first sloppy Joe recipe originated. Most people believe, however, that there's actually no real Joe behind the dish. Instead, it got that name because it was a dish for everyday folk that was simple and inexpensive.

Apple Pie Spice

MAKES 4 TABLESPOONS

INGREDIENTS

1 tablespoon ground cinnamon

1½ teaspoons ground nutmeg

1 teaspoon ground allspice

¼ teaspoon ground cloves

If you ever want to scent your home, toss a bit of this in boiling water; it will act like a potpourri.

1. Place all ingredients in a jar; cover tightly and shake well to mix.

2. Store in airtight container in cool, dark location.

Pie in Your Eye

Pie as we know it today didn't really come into common use until a few hundred years ago, when sugar became readily available. The first recipe for a modern apple pie with quince, butter, saffron, eggs, and ginger appeared in the sixteenth century, and the first American recipes for apple pie came out in 1796.

Pumpkin Pie Spice

MAKES ¾ CUP

INGREDIENTS

½ cup cinnamon

¼ cup ground ginger

2 tablespoons nutmeg

2 tablespoons ground cloves

Mark Twain disliked European cooking, remarking that he was looking forward to getting home and enjoying such treats as pumpkin pie in his 1880 book *A Tramp Abroad*.

1. Combine all ingredients; seal in a spice jar.

2. Use 3¼ teaspoons per 1½ cups canned pumpkin.

Salt-Free Taco Seasoning Mix

This recipe makes about 6 batches of tacos (3½ teaspoons mix to 1½ pounds meat). If you use this in canning, eliminate the cornstarch.

1. Measure all ingredients into a 1-pint Mason jar. Put on lid and screw band and shake until well combined.

2. Store in a jar with a tight-fitting lid in a cool, dark area. This can also be frozen.

MAKES 1¼ CUPS

INGREDIENTS

6 tablespoons chili powder

4 tablespoons onion powder

2 tablespoons ground cumin

2 tablespoons garlic powder

2 tablespoons oregano (preferably Mexican)

2 tablespoons cornstarch

2 tablespoons paprika

1 teaspoon celery seed

Chili Seasoning Mix

Use ½ cup of this mix with every 1 pound ground beef.

1. Measure all ingredients into a 1-pint Mason jar. Put on lid and screw band and shake until well combined.

2. Store in a jar with a tight-fitting lid in a cool, dark area.

MAKES 2¾ CUPS

INGREDIENTS

1 cup sweet green pepper flakes

2 tablespoons Mexican oregano

¾ cup chili powder

¼ cup ground cumin

½ cup onion flakes

¼ cup parsley flakes

2 teaspoons garlic flakes

½ teaspoon red pepper flakes

Spaghetti Herb Mix

MAKES 3 CUPS

INGREDIENTS

2 cups dry minced onion

3 tablespoons Italian oregano

2 tablespoons dried green pepper flakes

4 teaspoons dried basil

1 tablespoon dried minced garlic

4 teaspoons sea salt (optional)

4 tablespoons dry parsley

2 teaspoons rosemary

2 teaspoons thyme

2 teaspoons marjoram

Use ½ cup dry mix for every 1 pound ground meat in your spaghetti sauce.

Mix all spices together in a blender or food processor. Store in an airtight container.

Spaghetti: The Food of Love

Nearly all the herbs in spaghetti sauce were once regarded as "love" herbs and they often showed up in love potions. Basil was once given as a token of love, marjoram was part of wedding rituals (to inspire joy and strengthen emotions), and rosemary was burned to inspire love and friendship.

Old Bay Seasoning

MAKES ½ CUP

INGREDIENTS

1 tablespoon ground bay leaves

2½ teaspoons celery seeds

½ teaspoon dry mustard

1 ½ teaspoons black pepper

¾ teaspoon ground nutmeg

½ teaspoon ground cloves

½ teaspoon ground ginger

½ teaspoon paprika

½ teaspoon red pepper

¼ teaspoon ground mace

¼ teaspoon ground cardamom

Try adding a little dried lemon rind to this mix. It adds the perfect flavor when you use it to season fish.

1. Measure all ingredients into a 1-pint Mason jar. Put on lid and screw band and shake until well combined.

2. Store in a jar with a tight-fitting lid in a cool, dark area.

Herbes de Provence

This spice blend comes from southern France, where people used it to flavor their food much as we use salt and pepper. Try using some on your next chicken cookout for an amazing flavor and aroma.

Mix all spices together in a blender or food processor. Store in an airtight container.

MAKES 1¼ CUPS

INGREDIENTS

2 tablespoons dried basil

4 teaspoons dried oregano

2 teaspoons dried marjoram

2 teaspoons dried tarragon

2 teaspoons dried thyme

2 teaspoons dried savory

1½ teaspoons bay leaves, crushed

1 teaspoon fennel seed

1 teaspoon dried mint

1 teaspoon ground sage

1 teaspoon dried rosemary

1 teaspoon dried lavender

Greek Seasoning Blend

Great on beef or chicken, this mix can also become the base of a fantastic marinade; just add chicken or beef stock and vinegar.

1. Rub Greek oregano, spearmint, and parsley flakes between the palms of your hands over a mixing bowl.

2. Add remaining ingredients and whisk until well combined.

3. Store in a container with a tight-fitting cover.

It's Greek to Me
Mint is one of the predominant herbs in Greek cooking. It's used in everything from tomato sauce, stuffed vegetables, and cheese pies to teas and beverages. If you don't have mint, fresh parsley with a splash of basil can do the trick.

MAKES 1¼ CUPS

INGREDIENTS

6 tablespoons dried Greek oregano

1½ tablespoons dried spearmint

2 teaspoons dried parsley flakes

2 tablespoons garlic powder

2 tablespoons onion powder

1½ teaspoons fine sea salt

2 teaspoons cornstarch

2 teaspoons coarse-ground black pepper

¼ teaspoon ground nutmeg

¼ teaspoon ground cinnamon

2 teaspoons beef bouillon granules

Mexican Seasoning

MAKES 5 TABLESPOONS

INGREDIENTS
2 tablespoons paprika
2 teaspoons finely crushed dried oregano
1 teaspoon ground cumin
1 teaspoon ground turmeric
1 teaspoon garlic powder
¼ teaspoon cayenne pepper

As the name implies, this is a foundational spice blend for Spanish and Mexican dishes. It will also give soups and stews a hint of hot.

Mix all spices together in a blender or food processor. Store in an airtight container.

Italian Seasoning

MAKES 1 CUP

INGREDIENTS
⅓ cup dried crushed oregano
⅓ cup dried basil
2 tablespoons rosemary
¼ cup thyme
1 tablespoon garlic powder
¼ dried onion flakes

Kitchen gardens are common in Italy, where people prefer fresh herbs for cooking. If you have your own garden, you can make this blend from fresh herbs, add olive oil, and freeze the mix.

Mix all spices together in a blender or food processor. Store in an airtight container.

Basil
Basil was a very important herb in the ancient world. The Greeks in particular felt that only a ruler using a golden sickle should harvest it. In Romania, if a girl accepts basil from a young man, she's accepted his proposal. In India, Hindus are buried with a basil leaf, which grants entry into Paradise.

Herb and Spice Blends

These specific herb and spice blends complement their respective meats perfectly.

1. Put all ingredients into a blender or food processor; whirl until fine.

2. Store in a jar with an airtight cover.

Mix and Match
These herb and spice blends are designed to bring out the flavors of specific meats or vegetables. However, you can try adding a little of your own favorite herbs or spices to the mixes to suit your tastes. You can also try using the beef blend with chicken or the fish blend with vegetables.

MAKES ⅓ CUP OF EACH BLEND

INGREDIENTS

For Beef

1 tablespoon coarsely ground black pepper

1 tablespoon red pepper flakes

2½ tablespoons garlic powder

1 tablespoon dried minced onions

For Fish

2 tablespoons dried dill weed

2 tablespoons crumbled bay leaves

2 tablespoons freeze-dried chives

For Vegetables

2 tablespoons dried thyme

2 tablespoons dried oregano

2 tablespoons dried basil

For Chicken

2 tablespoons curry powder

2 tablespoons paprika

2 tablespoons dried lemon rind

For Lamb

1½ tablespoons dried marjoram

1 tablespoon crumbled dried rosemary

1 tablespoon white pepper

2 tablespoons garlic powder

Chapter 13

Jams, Jellies, Conserves, and Marmalade

Maple-Apple Jam

MAKES 8½ PINTS

INGREDIENTS

6 pounds mixed apples, chopped

6 cups sugar

1 cup maple syrup

½ teaspoon cinnamon

½ teaspoon allspice

½ teaspoon nutmeg

½ teaspoon ginger

¼ teaspoon cloves

Just for fun, leave ½" of space at the top of the jars, sprinkling hard-crack caramel and chopped nuts on top of the jam. The tasty result is similar to a candy apple at the fair.

1. Combine all ingredients in a large nonreactive pot. Bring to a boil over medium low heat.

2. Continue boiling, stirring frequently, until the jam holds its shape when put on a cold platter.

3. Pour hot into hot jars, leaving ¼" headspace. Cap and process in a hot-water bath 10 minutes.

Apple Pie Jelly

MAKES 6–7 PINTS

INGREDIENTS

4 cups apple juice

4 tablespoons maple syrup

3 teaspoons apple pie spice

1 box powdered pectin

5 cups granulated sugar

Try serving this hot with a drizzle of sweet cream on top.

1. Place apple juice, maple syrup, and apple pie spice in a large stockpot.

2. Add the pectin and bring to a hard boil over high heat until it dissolves into the juice.

3. Slowly stir in the sugar and bring back to a rolling boil over high heat. Boil for 1 full minute.

4. Remove from heat and skim off foam with a metal spoon. Ladle into sterilized jars, leaving ¼" headspace.

5. Remove air bubbles. Wipe rims. Cap and seal.

6. Process in a water-bath canner for 15 minutes.

Garlic Jelly

This different kind of jelly can be used as a condiment. It's wonderful added to a marinade or brushed directly on meat while cooking.

1. Blend garlic and ½ cup vinegar in a food processor or blender until smooth.

2. Combine garlic mixture, remaining vinegar, and sugar in a stockpot. Bring mixture to a boil over high heat, stirring constantly.

3. Quickly stir in pectin; return to a boil and boil hard 1 minute, stirring constantly.

4. Remove from heat; ladle into sterilized jars, leaving ¼" headspace. Wipe jar rims; cap and seal.

5. Process in a water-bath canner 10 minutes.

Garlic

The word *garlic* originates with the Old English term *garleac* (literally, "spear leek"). This plant can be traced back more than 6,000 years in central Asia, where it was an important part of cuisine. It was also worshipped by Egyptians, who used garlic as a type of currency.

MAKES 5½ PINTS

INGREDIENTS
¼ pound peeled garlic cloves
2 cups white vinegar
5 cups granulated sugar
1 3-ounce pouch liquid pectin

Dandelion Jelly

MAKES 2–3 PINTS

INGREDIENTS

4 cups yellow parts of dandelion blossoms

3 cups boiling water

4½ cups sugar

2 tablespoons freshly squeezed lemon juice

1 3-ounce package powdered pectin

20 drops yellow food coloring

What we consider a pesky weed has been used for centuries in cooking. Be very careful to get all the green parts off of the flowers or the result will be very bitter.

1. Place the flowers and water in a large pan; simmer over low heat 10 minutes. The flowers must be covered with water; if there are too many, break this step into batches. Warning: If the water begins to boil, the flavor of this jelly really suffers.

2. Strain the water, extracting as much of the juice from the flower as possible. Make sure your final measure is 3 cups of juice; add water if needed.

3. Bring to a boil; add sugar, food coloring, and lemon juice. Add pectin and boil 1 more minute.

4. Pour hot into jars. Cap and seal; use hot-water bath 10 minutes.

Lemon-Lime Marmalade

This makes a great marmalade that can double as a fish and poultry marinade if you blend it with a little vinegar to offset the sweetness.

1. Wash lemons and limes in warm water. Cut in half, squeezing out juice; reserve juice.

2. Remove zest from skins in thin strips, avoiding bitter white pith. Put zest, juice, and water in a pan.

3. Bring to a boil; simmer until skins are tender, about 15 minutes.

4. Add sugar, stirring constantly; boil again until mixture reaches 220°F.

5. Pour into hot clean jars. Cover and process in hot-water bath 10 minutes.

What's in a Name?
Jams, jellies, and preserves are all made from fruit, sugar, and fruit pectin. So what makes them different? With jam, fruit pulp remains in the mix for a thicker but less solid final product. Fruit juice is used in jelly, and fruit chunks and syrup blend together to provide the unique texture of preserves.

MAKES 6 PINTS

INGREDIENTS
5 lemons
6 limes
8 cups water
8 cups white sugar
½ cup candied ginger

Cantaloupe Conserve

MAKES 7½ PINTS

INGREDIENTS

6 pounds cantaloupe, peeled, seeded, and cut into ½-inch cubes

8 cups granulated sugar

2 teaspoons lemon zest

½ cup lemon juice

2 cups golden yellow raisins

1½ cups toasted almonds, chopped

¼ teaspoon almond extract

Cantaloupe can be tricky to cook with, so follow this recipe carefully.

1. Toss cantaloupe with sugar. Cover with plastic wrap; leave standing at room temperature 8–10 hours.

2. Add cantaloupe to stockpot with remaining ingredients except nuts and extract. Bring to a boil; cook until mixture starts to thicken, 15–20 minutes. Stir constantly.

3. Remove from heat; stir in almonds and almond extract. Quickly skim off foam with a metal spoon.

4. Ladle into sterilized jars, leaving ½" headspace. Wipe rims; cap and seal. Process in water canner 10 minutes.

Blackberry Preserves

MAKES ABOUT 6 PINTS

INGREDIENTS

3 quarts blackberries

7½ cups granulated sugar

2 3-ounce pouches liquid pectin

This recipe is flexible; use raspberries or a blend of raspberries and blackberries if you prefer.

1. Rinse fully ripe blackberries in cold water and drain.

2. Place blackberries into a stockpot.

3. Crush with a potato masher to extract juice. Stir in the sugar and mix well.

4. Bring to a full rolling boil over high heat, stirring constantly.

5. Add pectin and return to a full rolling boil. Boil hard for 1 minute. Remove from heat.

6. Skim off foam. Ladle preserves into sterilized jars. Wipe rims. Cap and seal. Process in water-bath canner for 5 minutes.

Fig-Walnut Conserve

Try this conserve warm on bread to release its great aroma.

1. Cover figs with boiling water; let stand 10 minutes. Drain, stem, and chop.

2. In a large sauce pot, combine figs, sugar, spices, and apple juice. Bring slowly to a boil; stir until sugar dissolves. Cook rapidly until thick. Stir frequently to prevent sticking.

3. Add lemon juice; cook 1 minute longer. Remove from heat; stir in chopped walnuts.

4. Ladle hot into sterilized jars, leaving ¼" headspace. Cap and seal.

5. Process 15 minutes in water-bath canner.

Fig Facts
Figs arrived in America in the sixteenth century on Spanish boats. They are native to Asia Minor, where they appear in ancient writings dating back to 2500 B.C.E. Fig trees live up to 100 years, and the fruit is rich in iron and potassium.

MAKES 6 PINTS

INGREDIENTS
5 pounds chopped figs
6 cups white sugar
⅛ teaspoon cinnamon
⅛ teaspoon allspice
⅛ teaspoon cardamom
⅛ teaspoon ginger
¾ cup apple juice
¼ cup lemon juice
1 cup chopped walnuts

MAKES 3 PINTS

INGREDIENTS

1 quart Bing cherries, chopped and pitted

1 3-ounce package powdered pectin

¼ cup lemon juice

¼ cup cherry liqueur

4½ cups sugar

Very Cherry

Some people like this jam with cinnamon, allspice, or cloves. If you want to add spices, about ½ teaspoon each does the trick.

1. Put all ingredients except sugar in a large pan.

2. Bring to a boil, stirring regularly. Add sugar; continue stirring until completely dissolved.

3. Continue boiling 2 minutes after sugar dissolves; ladle into hot jars, leaving ¼" headspace.

4. Cap and process 10 minutes in hot-water bath.

Cheering for Cherries

Cherry trees originated in Eastern Europe and Western Asia. They're actually part of the rose family. They were cultivated as early as 300 B.C.E., making them one of the oldest cultivated fruits. While there are thousands of types of cherries in the world, the Bing cherry, developed in the late nineteenth century, is the best seller.

Prickly Pear Cactus Marmalade

While oranges are the most popular fruit for marmalade, the prickly pear packs a very pleasant and flavorful surprise.

1. Combine oranges, lemons, and water in a large saucepot; simmer 5 minutes. Remove from heat and cover. Let stand 12–18 hours in a cool place.

2. Stir in prickly pears; add sugar and lemon zest. Bring to a boil over medium low heat, stirring until sugar dissolves. Cook rapidly to jelling point (220°F).

3. As mixture thickens, stir frequently to prevent sticking. Remove from heat. Skim foam if necessary.

4. Ladle hot marmalade into sterilized jars, leaving ¼" headspace. Cap and seal.

5. Process 15 minutes in boiling-water canner.

A Prickly Situation

Prickly pears come from a type of cactus native to North America. All the cacti in this family have flat pads as branches, and these are often cooked as a vegetable, while the pears themselves are gathered and sold with the name *tunas*. Modern experiments tell us that prickly pear may help keep blood sugars stabilized.

MAKES 6½ PINTS

INGREDIENTS

3 cups oranges, chopped and seeded

1 cup thinly sliced lemon

4 cups water

4 cups prickly pears, chopped, peeled, and seeded

6 cups granulated sugar

2 tablespoons grated lemon zest

Apricot-Raspberry Jam

MAKES 7½ PINTS

INGREDIENTS

2 pounds fresh apricots, peeled and pitted

1 pint red raspberries

6 cups granulated sugar

¼ cup lemon juice

1 teaspoon grated lemon peel

1 tablespoon unsalted butter

1 3-ounce pouch liquid pectin

This makes a great tart filling, especially if you add your favorite chopped nuts to it.

1. In a large stockpot combine apricots and raspberries. Crush with a potato masher.

2. Stir in sugar, lemon juice, lemon peel, and butter. Bring to a boil over high heat, stirring constantly.

3. Cook for 15 minutes until mixture starts to thicken, stirring constantly. Add pectin.

4. Bring to a rolling boil and boil for 1 minute, stirring constantly.

5. Ladle into sterilized jars, leaving ¼" headspace. Remove air bubbles with a plastic stirrer. Wipe rims. Cap and seal.

6. Process in a water-bath canner for 15 minutes.

Brandied Plum Jam

The addition of the blackberry brandy really brings out the flavor of the plums, but you can use other flavors of brandy.

1. Combine plums, water, lemon juice, and pectin in a large stockpot. Bring to a rolling boil over high heat, stirring constantly.

2. Add sugar and return to a rolling boil. Boil hard for 1 minute, stirring constantly.

3. Remove from heat and stir in blackberry brandy.

4. Ladle into sterilized jars, leaving ¼" headspace. Wipe rims. Cap and seal.

5. Process 10 minutes in a water-bath canner.

Brandy Beginnings

Wine was among the most popular items for trade throughout Europe. In the sixteenth century a clever Dutch trader found a way to ship more wine—he removed the water! This concentrated wine came to port in Holland where it was called *bradwin* (burnt wine), which later became our *brandy*.

MAKES 4 PINTS

INGREDIENTS

4 pounds plums, pitted and chopped

¾ cup water

2 tablespoons lemon juice

1 package powdered pectin

7 cups sugar

1 cup blackberry brandy

Butterscotch Peach Preserves

MAKES 5–6 HALF PINTS

INGREDIENTS
6 cups peaches, peeled, cored, and chopped
⅓ cup lemon juice
5 cups dark brown sugar

This preserve is wonderful for tarts or over ice cream!

1. Combine peaches and lemon juice in a stockpot.

2. Crush fruit with a potato masher. Bring to a boil over medium heat. Cover and simmer for 10 minutes, stirring occasionally.

3. Stir in brown sugar. Increase heat to medium high and cook 20–25 minutes until slightly thickened. Stir often.

4. Remove from heat and stir jam for 3–5 minutes. Skim off foam if necessary.

5. Ladle preserves into hot, sterilized jars, leaving ¼" headspace. Wipe rims clean. Cap and seal. Process jars in a water-bath canner for 10 minutes.

Pomegranate Jelly

MAKES 3½ PINTS

INGREDIENTS
3½ cups pomegranate juice
2 tablespoons lemon juice
6 cups sugar
1 3-ounce pouch liquid pectin

This jelly taste good but is rich in antioxidants and vitamins A, C, and E.

1. In nonreactive pan, mix pomegranate and lemon juices, and sugar.

2. Over medium heat, bring to full rolling boil. Stir regularly.

3. Stir in pectin and continue to boil for 1 minute.

4. Ladle hot jelly into hot jars, leaving ¼" headspace.

5. Cap and process in boiling-water bath for 10 minutes.

Pineapple-Strawberry Delight

One cup of strawberries provides 140 percent of the daily recommended amount of vitamin C. This fruit also fights bad cholesterol.

1. In a large stockpot, combine strawberries and pineapple with juice. Bring to a boil on medium heat, stirring frequently.

2. Stir in the sugar or Splenda, lemon juice, and lemon rind. Bring to a boil over high heat, stirring constantly.

3. Cook for 15 minutes until mixture starts to thicken, stirring constantly. Add the pectin. Bring to a rolling boil and boil for 1 minute, stirring constantly.

4. Ladle into sterilized jars, leaving ¼" headspace. Remove air bubbles with a plastic stirrer. Wipe rims. Cap and seal.

5. Process in a water-bath canner for 10 minutes.

MAKES 8½ PINTS

INGREDIENTS

1 pound strawberries, hulled and sliced

2⅓ cups crushed pineapple with juice

5 cups granulated sugar or Splenda

3 tablespoons lemon juice

1 teaspoon grated lemon rind

1 3-ounce package liquid pectin

Jeanne's Elder-blueberry Jam

MAKES ABOUT 7 PINTS

INGREDIENTS

1 quart crushed elderberries

1 quart crushed blueberries

6 cups granulated sugar

¼ cup white vinegar

2 teaspoons dried orange peel

2 teaspoons pure vanilla extract

Some studies indicate that elderberries may help the body recuperate from the flu.

1. Combine all ingredients in a large stockpot. Slowly bring to boil, stirring until the sugar dissolves. Continue to boil until thick, stirring frequently to prevent sticking.

2. Ladle into sterilized jars, leaving ¼" headspace. Wipe jar rims. Cap and seal.

3. Process in a water canner for 10 minutes.

Purple Plum Preserves

MAKES 5 PINTS

INGREDIENTS

5 pounds purple plums, pitted and chopped

7 cups granulated sugar

1 cup honey

½ cup lemon juice

1½ cups water

1 teaspoon ground mace

Honey and mace make these plum preserves really yummy. They are a pretty shade of purple.

1. Combine all ingredients in a large stockpot. Bring slowly to a boil, stirring until sugar dissolves.

2. Cook rapidly for 15 minutes until mixture thickens, stirring occasionally to prevent sticking.

3. Ladle into sterilized jars, leaving ¼" headspace. Wipe rims. Cap and seal.

4. Process 15 minutes in a water-bath canner.

Raspberry Surprise Preserves

No one can guess that there are beets in this scrumptious preserve. The color is a bright red and the flavor is delightful. It can be made healthier by using Splenda and sugar-free Jell-O.

1. Cook beets in water until tender. Remove from stockpot with slotted spoon. Reserve juice. When beets are cool, peel, cut into chunks, and purée in a food processor.

2. Measure 7½ cups of reserved beet juice. Add water if necessary.

3. Combine puréed beets, beet juice, lemon juice, grated lemon peel, and pectin. Stir until combined and heat to a boil over medium-high heat.

4. Add sugar or Splenda and powdered Jell-O. Boil for 8 to 10 minutes, stirring frequently to prevent scorching. Skim off foam, if necessary.

5. Ladle into sterilized jars, leaving ¼" headspace. Remove air bubbles. Wipe rims. Cap and seal.

6. Process in a water-bath canner for 10 minutes.

MAKES ABOUT 7 PINTS

INGREDIENTS
10 pounds large beets
cold water to cover
7½ cups reserved beet juice
½ cup lemon juice
2 teaspoons grated dried lemon peel
2 packages powdered pectin
5 cups granulated sugar or Splenda
2 3-ounce packages raspberry Jell-O

Wild Strawberry Preserves

MAKES 8 HALF-PINTS

INGREDIENTS
4 cups ripe strawberries, mashed
4 cups sugar
1 tablespoon lemon juice (optional)

This classic recipe transports you from your kitchen to the countryside every time you open the lid.

1. Mix sugar and berries in a bowl and let sit at room temperature for about 1 hour so they begin getting juicy.

2. Transfer to a pan. Add lemon juice and bring to a full rolling boil for 7 minutes, stirring constantly.

3. Pour into 8 pre-sterilized half-pint jars with ¼" headspace. Process in a boiling-water bath for 10 minutes. May be kept for one year in dark, cool area. May also be frozen.

Persimmon Jam

MAKES 7 CUPS

INGREDIENTS
5 cups persimmon purée
3 cups sugar
¼ cup lemon juice
½ teaspoon fresh lemon zest
pinch nutmeg
pinch ground cloves

It's vital that you use ripe persimmons in this jam or it will be very tart. Test the fruit and give it time if it isn't ripe yet.

1. Place persimmons, sugar, lemon juice, and lemon zest together in a nonreactive pan. Boil 30 minutes, stirring regularly.

2. Cool and pour into freezer containers. Leave out overnight before freezing.

In Pursuit of Persimmons
The botanical name for persimmons is *diospyros*, which translates as "food of the gods." There are two versions—the hachiya variety and the fuyu variety. The hachiya are best when mushy and bright orange in color. The fuyu should be firm and eaten with the skin on.

Mango Madness

This is a lovely, fresh jam perfect for a hot summer day.

1. Mix mangos with juice and sugar. Let sit for 15 minutes.

2. Mix water and pectin in a saucepan. Boil for 1 minute.

3. Add in the fruit mixture and continue boiling for 3 minutes, until sugar dissolves.

4. Cool slightly and place in freezer containers, leaving ½" headspace. Do not freeze for 24 hours. Use within 1 year.

MAKES ABOUT 6 CUPS

INGREDIENTS

3 cups mashed ripe mango

¼ cup fresh lemon juice

5 cups sugar

½ cup water

¼ cup mango or passion-fruit juice

1 1.75-ounce package powdered fruit pectin

Fruit Punch Jelly

This recipe is very fast and easy and you can use any soft drink mix you wish!

1. Dissolve drink mix in water. Bring to a boil, stirring constantly.

2. Mix the pectin with sugar. Add drink mixture slowly and boil for 1 more minute.

3. Cool slightly, then transfer into freezer containers, leaving ½" headspace. Let sit overnight before freezing.

MAKES ABOUT 4 CUPS

INGREDIENTS

1 envelope unsweetened mixed fruit soft drink mix

3 cups water

3 cups sugar

1 1.75-ounce package powdered fruit pectin

Perfect Peaches and Pears

MAKES 10 CUPS

INGREDIENTS

3 ripe pears, not mushy

3 small ripe peaches

1 teaspoon orange juice

1 teaspoon orange peel

1 teaspoon lemon peel

1 tablespoon freshly grated gingerroot

2 cups sugar

2 cups water

1 pouch dry pectin

Some recipes for freezer jelly use cornstarch as a thickener. Cornstarch, however, lends the jelly a completely different texture, so this recipe relies on pectin.

1. Peel the pears and peaches and dice them.

2. Combine pears, peaches, juice, orange and lemon peels, and ginger in a saucepan. Cook over medium-low heat until the fruit is fully tender.

3. Add sugar and water and bring to a boil for 15 minutes. Add pectin and boil for 1 minute more.

4. Remove from heat and cool slightly before transferring to freezer containers. Leave ½" headspace. Use within 3 months.

Banana Jam

MAKES 6 CUPS

INGREDIENTS

6 ripe bananas

½ cup brown sugar

2 tablespoons grated fresh ginger

⅔ cup citrus juice

This is a great way to use up bananas that are just about to be overripe. If you want other spices in the mix, add some allspice or cinnamon.

1. Slice bananas into a pot.

2. Add remaining ingredients; cook over low heat, stirring regularly, 2 hours. To avoid stirring, cook in a slow cooker on low heat for 5 hours.

3. Cool and put into jars, storing in the refrigerator for immediate use.

Pineapple-Rhubarb Jam

Look for crisp, young rhubarb that's firm and brightly colored.

1. Boil rhubarb, sugar, and water 15 minutes. Reduce heat. Add pineapple; simmer another 10 minutes.

2. Add gelatin; mix well. Refrigerate.

Radical Rhubarb
Rhubarb comes from Tibet, China, and Mongolia, where it was often used in folk medicine. It wasn't until about the eighteenth century that this vegetable made its way into food, but it is often treated like a fruit. In fact, rhubarb bears the nickname pie plant for just that reason.

MAKES ABOUT 6 CUPS

INGREDIENTS

5 cups rhubarb, cleaned and diced

5 cups sugar

1 cup water

1 cup crushed pineapple, drained

1 3-ounce package powdered pectin

Plumberry Jam

You can substitute 1 cup blueberries for strawberries.

1. Mix the fruit together with the sugar and let stand for 15 minutes.

2. Place the fruit in a pan with corn syrup and water. Bring to a boil.

3. Add pectin and continue boiling for 1 minute. Cool and put into containers. This can be refrigerated or frozen; leave ½" headspace if freezing.

Plum Dandy
There are about twelve different species of cultivated plums in the world. Plums originated in Europe and came to America with the Pilgrims. When shopping, look for plums with a bright, rich color that are at the peak of ripeness for making jam.

MAKES 4 PINTS

INGREDIENTS

2 cups red raspberries

1 cup strawberries

1 cup peeled, diced ripe plum

5 cups sugar

½ cup light corn syrup

¾ cup water

1 3-ounce package powdered fruit pectin

Chapter 14

Sides and Sundries

Sweet and Sassy Beans

MAKES 8 CUPS

INGREDIENTS
2 cups white beans
2 cups red beans
2 cups black beans
1 cup finely diced onion
1½ teaspoons salt
1½ cups packed dark brown sugar
1 cup molasses
¼ pure maple syrup
2 tablespoons garlic
1 tablespoon Worcestershire sauce
1 tablespoon ginger powder
1 tablespoon spicy brown mustard
1 tablespoon red pepper flakes
hot sauce to taste
⅓ pound thick bacon, cut in 1-inch pieces

You can make this recipe hotter by using fresh chili peppers. Experiment with various types of beans; each creates a different texture in this recipe.

1 Rinse beans. Place in a large pot with 3 quarts water; soak 12 hours.

2. Drain beans. Place back in pan with 3 fresh quarts water and salt. Boil over medium heat; reduce heat and simmer 1 hour.

3. Drain, reserving 2 cups of water for use later.

4. Combine all remaining ingredients; cook slowly, until ingredients are well combined, about 7–10 minutes. Pour over beans along with reserved water.

5. Place in a baking dish; cook at 250°F for 6 hours, stirring periodically. Taste; adjust spices to your liking.

6. Ladle into hot jars with 1" headspace. Remove all air bubbles.

7. Put on tops; process in pressure cooker at 10 pounds of pressure 1 hour and 20 minutes for pints and 1 hour and 35 minutes for quarts.

Homemade Pectin

Gather your apples in early summer for best results.

MAKES 1½ CUPS

INGREDIENTS
2 pounds small green, immature apples or crabapples
4 cups water

1. Wash apples, trim bad parts, and slice very thinly. Place in a large stockpot; add 2 cups of water for each pound of apples. Cover pan; boil 15 minutes.

2. Strain juice through cheesecloth. Do not squeeze the pulp. Reserve the juice.

3. Put pulp back into pan; add same amount of water. Cook 15 minutes over medium heat.

4. Strain juices through cheesecloth, without squeezing the pulp. When pulp cools, you can press some more juice from it.

5. Heat stock to boiling point. Ladle into sterilized jars, leaving ½" headspace. Remove air bubbles. Cap and seal.

6. Process in water-bath canner 10 minutes.

Is It Sugar?
Sugar substitutes are usually artificially made. The exceptions are sorbitol and xylitol, both of which are natural sugar substitutes found typically in fruits and vegetables. There is some question about the potential health risks in synthetic sugar substitutes, so if you're considering dramatically changing your diet, it's good to check with your physician first.

Spicy Star Fruit

MAKES 6 PINTS

INGREDIENTS

6 pounds star fruit, washed and sliced

4 cups granulated sugar

4 cups cold water

¼ cup lemon juice

6 3-inch whole cinnamon sticks

12 whole allspice berries

12 whole cloves

6 whole star anise

yellow or green food coloring (optional)

This is a fun fruit to serve to children because of the star shape. It also makes a pretty topping for a homemade cheesecake.

1. Wash and slice star fruit.

2. In a large stockpot, combine sugar, water, lemon juice, cinnamon sticks, allspice berries, cloves, and star anise. Bring to a boil; simmer 5 minutes.

3. Remove from heat; add sliced star fruit. Let stand 10 minutes.

4. Return to a boil. If desired, stir in a few drops of food coloring. With a slotted spoon, ladle cooked fruit into sterilized pint jars.

5. Divide spices equally between jars. Ladle hot syrup into the jars, leaving ¼" headspace. Wipe rims; cap and seal.

6. Process in water-bath canner 15 minutes.

A Star Is Born
Star fruit comes to us from Sri Lanka. It's been cultivated in Southeast Asia for hundreds of years. Sometimes called a star apple, this fruit loves a warm environment. There are actually two types of star fruit, one of which is sour, but both contain good amounts of vitamin C.

Asparagus Appetizer

When you serve this, try it on a bed of baby greens, drizzled with some fresh oil and vinegar and topped with crumbled feta. It's tasty warm or cold.

1. Rinse, dice, and mix asparagus. Pack into jars with 1" headspace.

2. Mix remaining ingredients together in a pan; gently warm. Spoon into jars evenly; cover everything with boiling water, making sure to leave 1" headspace.

3. Process in pressure canner 40 minutes at 10 pounds of pressure for quarts.

MAKES 1 QUART

INGREDIENTS

1½ cups diced white asparagus

1½ cups diced green asparagus

1 tablespoon extra-virgin olive oil

2 teaspoons lemon juice

zest of ¼ lemon, thinly sliced

¼ teaspoon canning salt

1 bundle scallions, chopped

¼ pound lean ham, cut into tiny bits

boiling water to cover

Gourmet Almond Honey

You can play with this concept. For example, use rose and lavender water instead of almond extract for a highly aromatic honey.

1. Place all ingredients in a saucepan; warm.

2. Stir regularly until well incorporated, about 7 minutes.

3. Pour into hot jars; cap and seal using hot-water bath for 15 minutes.

MAKES 1 CUP

INGREDIENTS

1 cup orange blossom honey

½ cup almond paste

1 teaspoons almond extract

Honey Facts

It takes 2 million flowers for a bee to create 1 pound of honey. During the process of going from flower to flower, the bee will fly more than 50,000 miles at an average speed of 15 miles per hour. The average person eats 1.3 pounds of honey per year.

Carnival-Style Apple Pie Filling

MAKES 7 PINTS
(3 9-INCH PIES)

INGREDIENTS

4 cups white sugar

¼ cup brown sugar

1 cup cornstarch

¼ teaspoon ground nutmeg

2 teaspoons salt

10 cups water

3 tablespoons lemon juice

1 cup cinnamon hot candy pieces

6 pounds apples, cored and sliced

When you want to use this filling, simply pour it into a pastry crust and bake at 400°F for 50 minutes.

1. Mix sugars, cornstarch, nutmeg, salt, and water in a pan; blend thoroughly.

2. Boil mix until it begins to thicken. Turn off the heat.

3. Add lemon juice; fold in cinnamon candy pieces.

4. Pack apples into hot canning jars, leaving ½" headspace.

5. Cover with syrup; remove air bubbles. Cap and process in hot-water bath 20 minutes for quarts.

Brandied Cherries

MAKES ABOUT 6 PINTS

INGREDIENTS

1 cup sugar

1 cup water

¼ cup lemon juice

6 pounds dark sweet cherries, washed and pitted

1¼ cups brandy

This is a yummy treat that can also become part of various baking efforts.

1. Combine sugar, water, and lemon juice in a large stockpot. Bring to a boil; reduce heat to a simmer.

2. Add cherries and simmer until hot throughout. Remove from heat; stir in brandy.

3. Pack hot cherries into hot jars, leaving ½" headspace.

4. Ladle hot syrup over cherries, leaving ¼" headspace. Remove air bubbles. Wipe rims. Cap and seal.

BBQ Beans

If you like spicier beans, increase the hot pepper sauce to taste.

1. In a large stockpot, cover beans with cold water and let stand in a cool place 12 to 18 hours.

2. Drain and cover with boiling water; boil for 3 minutes. Remove from heat and let stand 10 minutes. Drain.

3. Combine onions, salt, spices, tomato juice, molasses, and hot pepper sauce; heat to a boil.

4. Pack 1 cup beans into sterilized jars. Top with a piece of pork and fill jar about ¾ full with beans.

5. Carefully ladle sauce over beans, leaving 1" headspace. Remove air bubbles. Wipe rims. Cap and seal.

6. Process pints 65 minutes or quarts 75 minutes at 10 pounds pressure in a pressure canner.

MAKES 5 PINTS

INGREDIENTS
2 cups dried pinto beans
2 cups dried navy beans
water to cover
1½ cups chopped onions
2 teaspoons fine sea salt
¼ teaspoon ground cloves
¼ teaspoon ground allspice
4 cups tomato juice
¼ cup dark molasses
½ teaspoon hot pepper sauce
¼ pound salt pork, cut into six pieces

Cherry Pie Filling

MAKES 7 QUARTS

INGREDIENTS

5¾ cups cold water

6 cups granulated sugar

2 cups plus 3 tablespoons ClearJel A

½ cup bottled lemon juice

6 quarts fresh pitted cherries

20 drops red food coloring

1¼ cups Kirsch

This blend also makes a very serviceable dessert topping.

1. Combine water, sugar, and ClearJel in a large stockpot. Stir and cook over medium-high heat until mixture thickens and begins to bubble.

2. Add lemon juice and boil sauce 1 minute more, stirring constantly. Fold in pitted cherries and food coloring and stir well.

3. Continue to heat mixture for 3–5 minutes until mixture is hot throughout. Remove from heat and stir in Kirsch.

4. Ladle into sterilized jars, leaving 1" headspace. Cap and seal.

5. Process in a water-bath canner for 25 minutes.

Cheers for Cherries

Cherries are somewhat related to peaches in that they're considered a stone fruit. We know that some of our most ancient ancestors enjoyed this fruit from the pits found in Stone Age caves. Romans also loved cherries, often taking them with them from town to town.

Drunken Peaches

This recipe needs to be prepared over a three-day period, but it's well worth the time and effort.

1. Dissolve 6 cups sugar, lemon juice, and salt in 4 cups boiling water. Add one layer of peaches at a time and boil gently for 6 minutes.

2. Ladle heated peaches into a large deep bowl.

3. Boil remaining syrup for 5 minutes and pour over peaches. Cover bowl tightly with plastic wrap and let stand 24 hours.

4. The second day, drain syrup into a stockpot and add remaining sugar and water.

5. Boil for 5 minutes and pour syrup over peaches. Cover the bowl tightly with plastic wrap and let stand for 24 hours.

6. The third day, drain syrup into a stockpot and boil until it reaches the consistency of honey.

7. Pack the peaches into six sterilized pint jars and add 3 to 4 tablespoons of peach brandy to each jar.

8. Pour the hot syrup over the peaches, leaving ¼" headspace. Remove air bubbles with a non-metallic utensil. Cap and seal.

9. Process in a water-bath canner for 10 minutes. Leave jars alone for one month so that flavors will meld.

MAKES 6 PINTS

INGREDIENTS

12 cups granulated sugar, divided

½ cup lemon juice

8 cups boiling water, divided

8 pounds whole peeled peaches

2 teaspoons salt

1½ cups peach brandy

Berry Honey Butter

MAKES 3 CUPS

INGREDIENTS
1 pound butter
¼ cup honey
¼ cup crushed raspberries
½ teaspoon vanilla extract

Enjoy this mix with other traditional pie spices, like ½ teaspoon of cinnamon, ginger, or allspice.

1. Soften the butter and put it in a mixing bowl.

2. Add the rest of the ingredients and beat at a low speed until well incorporated, about 5 minutes.

3. Transfer into coverable bowl and refrigerate.

Apricot Balls

MAKES ABOUT 40–42 SNACKS

INGREDIENTS
1½ cups dried apricots, chopped
1 14-ounce package flaked coconut
⅔ cup finely chopped walnuts
1 14-ounce can sweetened condensed milk

These are a perfect little mouthful of goodness!

1. Combine all ingredients in large bowl and mix well with a spoon.

2. Roll tablespoons of mixture into balls. Place in small paper candy or cookie liners and refrigerate.

Garlic Bread Spread

The refrigerated lifespan of this blend is 8 weeks. To use this spread, lightly butter a whole loaf of bread and add this spread on top. Heat under the broiler until cheese melts, about 1 minute.

1. In a large mixing bowl, add 3 cups mozzarella cheese and half of each of the remaining ingredients. Using a large spatula, fold until blended.

2. Repeat with remaining ingredients.

3. Put into sterilized pint Mason jars. Put on sterilized lids and bands. Keep refrigerated.

MAKES 5–6 PINTS

INGREDIENTS

6 cups shredded mozzarella cheese at room temperature

1½ cups grated Parmesan cheese

1½ cups grated Romano cheese

1 tablespoon coarsely ground black pepper

1 cup minced garlic

1 cup extra-virgin olive oil

2 teaspoons freshly squeezed lemon juice

Three-Olive Pâté

This has a shelf life of about 8 weeks in the refrigerator. Try it on crackers or celery or as a sandwich topper.

1. In a large mixing bowl, fold all ingredients together until blended.

2. Put into sterilized pint Mason jars. Put on sterilized lids and bands. Keep refrigerated.

MAKES 4 PINTS

INGREDIENTS

2 cups finely chopped Kalamata olives

2 cups finely chopped Spanish olives with pimentos

2 cups finely chopped black olives

1 tablespoon coarsely ground black pepper

1 cup extra-virgin olive oil

Healthy Yogurt Cheese

MAKES 16 OUNCES

INGREDIENTS

1 32-ounce carton low-fat yogurt

½ teaspoon fine sea salt

2 tablespoons finely minced herbs of your choice

Dill, sage, rosemary, Greek seasoning, and hot peppers are good herbs to use in this recipe. Fresh herbs really set this cheese off, but use dry herbs if they are the only ones you have. Just remember that dried herbs are concentrated and you will need less of them.

1. In a bowl, mix yogurt, salt, and herbs until well combined.

2. Place a colander over a bowl; line colander with two layers of paper towels. Pour mixture into colander.

3. Cover with a paper towel; let sit on kitchen counter 2 days. All the whey will drain out, leaving a yummy soft-spread cheese.

4. Refrigerate and use as desired.

Yearning for Yogurt

Historians believe that the first yogurts happened by mistake. It was produced by wild bacteria in goatskin bags on the backs of nomads. By the Middle Ages, the use of yogurt by monks in Turkey had been documented. It was finally introduced into larger Europe as a cure for stomach ailments, during the reign of the French King Francis I.

Whiskey Barbecue Meatballs

This is a great recipe to keep on hand for when you're asked to bring a finger-food dish to a party. Just defrost and put in a crockpot on low to serve.

1. Mix all meatball ingredients together. Make tablespoon-sized meatballs; bake at 350°F until done, about 45 minutes.

2. While meatballs cook, mix together sauce ingredients; simmer over low heat.

3. Cool both meatballs and sauce.

4. Put some sauce on the bottom of your freezer-safe containers and add the meatballs, surrounding them with more sauce. Leave about ½" headspace. Label and freeze.

MAKES 36 MEATBALLS

INGREDIENTS

Meatball Mix

1 pound lean ground turkey or chicken

1 large egg

1 tablespoon garlic, minced

1 tablespoon Worcestershire sauce

½ tablespoon stone-ground mustard

½ onion, finely minced

½ cup finely minced sweet peppers

⅓ cup bread crumbs

1 teaspoon sugar

salt to taste

pepper to taste

Sauce Ingredients

4 cups smoky barbecue sauce

¼ cup minced green onions

2 cloves fresh garlic, minced

¼ cup whiskey

⅛ cup honey mustard

1 tablespoon Worcestershire sauce

¼ cup white or cider vinegar

¼ cup honey or brown sugar

MAKES 6 SERVINGS

INGREDIENTS

2 cups hot cooked
brown rice

2 cups hot cooked lentils

2 14½-ounce cans stewed
tomatoes

1 10-ounce package chopped
frozen spinach, thawed and
well drained

1 cup chopped green onions

½ cup sliced black olives

⅓ cup herbed bread crumbs

1 teaspoon dried basil

1 teaspoon dried oregano

¼ teaspoon salt

¼ teaspoon pepper

Lentils with Rice

If you'd like, substitute 2 containers of grape tomatoes sliced in
half for the stewed tomatoes and add about ½ cup vegetable juice
or stock to keep the dish from getting dry. When serving, sprinkle
with feta cheese.

Combine all the ingredients into an ovenproof casserole dish. You can
freeze the dish in this form or finish it and freeze afterward. Cook for
20 minutes at 350°F.

For the Love of Lentils

Lentils deserve special recognition, and in the United States, at least three
groups focus energy on promoting this legume: The North Dakota Dry Pea and
Lentil Council, the North Dakota Dry Pea and Lentil Association, and the USA
Dry Pea and Lentil Council.

Corn Bread Stuffing

Try using precooked, drained maple bacon instead of sausage or onion-cheese bread instead of the corn bread. Proportions remain the same.

1. In a frying pan, place sausage, apples, onions, and butter; cook until tender, about 15 minutes. Move to a mixing bowl.

2. Add seasonings and bread. Slowly stir in broth until bread is well moistened.

3. Move into a greased casserole dish that is both freezer- and oven-safe. Wrap with aluminum and plastic wrap. Label and freeze.

4. Defrost before finishing; bake in 350ºF oven 25 minutes.

Everything Corn Bread
Native Americans used ground corn in baking, which is how Europeans discovered corn bread. As they traveled, they used cornmeal instead of flour. It was an inexpensive substitute and stayed fresh fairly well.

SERVES 8

INGREDIENTS

8 ounces maple-flavored pork sausage, cooked and drained

2 cups chopped, peeled apple

¾ cup chopped onion

⅓ cup butter

1 teaspoon poultry seasoning

⅛ teaspoon black pepper

¼ cup chopped fresh parsley

1 teaspoon fresh orange zest (optional)

6 cups coarsely crumbled corn bread

½ cup chicken or vegetable broth

Cheesy Sausage Casserole

SERVES 4

INGREDIENTS

2 cups marinara sauce

½ cup sweet Italian sausage, crumbled and sautéed

1 cup diced sweet onion, sautéed

2 teaspoons minced garlic, sautéed

½ teaspoon each dried basil

½ dried oregano

8 manicotti

1 cup white or Alfredo sauce

6 ounces grated Asiago or baby Munster cheese

Parmesan cheese to taste

This is a great casserole to have in the freezer for unexpected visitors. It's very tasty and filling. When you want to cook it, cover it with aluminum foil and put it in the oven at 400°F for about 60 minutes. Remove foil in the last five minutes to brown the cheese.

1. Mix marinara, sausage, onion, garlic, and spices.

2. Cook the pasta for ¾ the recommended time (it must be al dente for freezing).

3. Stuff the manicotti with the meat filling.

4. Blend white sauce with grated cheese. Pour ⅓ of this in the bottom of your ovenproof freezer dish.

5. Put the manicotti on top and pour the rest of the cheese sauce over it. Sprinkle with Parmesan to personal tastes.

6. Cover with aluminum foil, then wrap in plastic wrap. Label, date, and freeze.

Parmesan Sprouts with Prosciutto

SERVES 4 AS A SIDE DISH

INGREDIENTS
2 tablespoons butter
2 cloves garlic, minced
2 ounces thinly sliced prosciutto, slivered
1 pound Brussels sprouts, cleaned and halved
1.5 tablespoons all-purpose flour
1¼ cups cream
2 tablespoons port wine
kosher salt and ground pepper to taste
⅓ cup freshly grated Parmesan cheese

Once this dish is done, you can freeze it whole in an oven-ready dish or portion it out into individual servings. It will need to be cooked for 20 minutes at 350°F. Serve with additional freshly grated Parmesan cheese.

1. Melt butter in a large frying pan over medium-high heat.

2. Add garlic and prosciutto. Simmer for 2 minutes, stirring regularly.

3. Add sprouts. Simmer for 5 more minutes. Sprinkle flour evenly over the sprouts. Stir. Slowly add cream, followed by the port wine. Simmer about 13 minutes until the sprouts are nearly fork-tender.

4. Remove from heat, add half of the cheese, and stir well. Season with salt and pepper to taste.

5. Store in freezer-safe containers. Label and date.

Butter Blend

MAKES 1 CUP

INGREDIENTS
6 tablespoons salted butter
¼ cup olive oil

This very simple blend is perfect in cooking because the olive oil prevents it from burning. You can make herb butter by adding about 1 teaspoon of your desired herb to the spread; adjust to your personal tastes.

1. Soften the butter and mix in the olive oil until evenly distributed.

2. Place in freezer-safe container; use as butter.

INGREDIENTS

1 cup all-purpose flour

1 teaspoon baking powder

1 teaspoon granulated sugar

salt to taste

pepper to taste

¼ teaspoon dried basil

¼ teaspoon dried oregano

1 28-ounce can stewed tomatoes, drained

6 strips turkey bacon, cooked and crumbled

1 tablespoon finely minced onion

½ teaspoon Worcestershire sauce

2 large eggs

vegetable oil

Tomato Fritters

These fritters are unique in that they're savory instead of sweet. They freeze nicely in food-storage bags and may be served with any condiment that you enjoy with tomatoes. Try them with a balsamic vinaigrette reduction or a cheese sauce.

1. Mix all dry ingredients together. Add tomatoes, bacon, onion, and Worcestershire sauce to the mixing bowl and set aside.

2. Beat the eggs in another bowl. Slowly add them to the tomato-flour mix, stirring as you add them.

3. Fry the fritter batter in hot vegetable oil 1 tablespoon at a time in a pan or a deep fryer. Cook until golden brown.

4. Cool and drain on paper towels before freezing.

Turkey Bacon

Cooking with turkey bacon is one way to reduce the fat in your diet without giving up flavor. Overall, a strip of turkey bacon has 35 calories, regular bacon has 45 calories, and Canadian bacon has 60 calories. In addition, turkey bacon is not prone to the same shrinkage as regular bacon, making it economically friendly.

Citrus Peels

This is a great way to use peels. In dried form, these are excellent in canning and preserving recipes as well as for baking.

1. Shred peels; leave in a cool, dry room to dry, covered with a paper plate.

2. Use food processor or grinder to chop peels into a good size for cooking. Put in airtight container; label and store.

Citrus

Citrus fruits come to us from Southeast Asia. The word *citrus* originates from the Greek *kedros*, which was a name the Greeks used for various aromatic trees. Most of the citrus we have today are considered hybrids, and botanists are trying to determine if some trees have been overlooked in this category. Kumquats have recently been added to the citrus family.

YIELD VARIES

INGREDIENTS
citrus peels (orange, lemon, lime, tangerine, grapefruit)

Culinary Herbs

It's best to dry your herbs separately and make them into blends afterward because some dry at a different rate than others. This basic method works for drying fresh mushrooms, too.

1. Pick herbs early in the day. Strip off stem; chop finely. Reserve stems to use in aromatic potpourri; otherwise discard.

2. Place on cookie sheet with aluminum foil sprayed lightly with cooking spray. Put into a 200°F oven with door slightly ajar. Turn over with a long-handled pancake turner every 15–20 minutes for 2 hours.

3. Leave the dry herbs covered on the counter 2–3 days to make sure they're completely bone-dry.

4. Transfer into labeled jars or blend and put into jars.

MAKES 1 TEASPOON

INGREDIENTS
1 tablespoon fresh-picked herbs

Pickled Eggs

MAKES 12 EGGS

INGREDIENTS
12 hardboiled eggs
1 large red onion, sliced into rings
1½ cups white wine vinegar
½ cup white vinegar
2 cups water
½ cup sugar
1 teaspoon pickling salt
10 cloves garlic
1 tablespoon pickling spice
1 tablespoon celery seed (optional)
1 tablespoon mustard seed (optional)

This recipe is for a refrigerator pickle that will last up to 6 months if kept properly refrigerated. These can be eaten as snacks or sliced for salad topping or burger garnishes.

1. Layer eggs and onions in a 2-quart jar, leaving 1" headspace. Put remaining ingredients in a nonreactive pan; warm over medium heat until sugar dissolves.

2. Pour hot brine over eggs, leaving ¼" headspace. Seal with a sterilized lid. Refrigerate and wait about 2 weeks for the flavors to properly integrate.

Healthy Herbed Candies

MAKES 3 POUNDS

INGREDIENTS
4 cups boiling water
2 cups herb leaves with stems and blossoms
3 cups Splenda
3 cups brown sugar
½ tablespoon butter

Some good choices for this recipe include orange mint, apple mint, peppermint, lemon verbena, pineapple mint, and wintergreen.

1. Pour boiling water over the leaves and steep for 10 minutes, longer for stronger tea.

2. Meanwhile, butter a shallow pan. Set aside.

3. Strain the leaves and add the Splenda, brown sugar, and butter to the tea and bring to a boil over medium heat. Continue boiling until syrup hardens when a small amount is dropped into cold water.

4. Pour into the buttered pan. Score candy into squares before it sets or break into pieces as soon as it hardens.

5. Wrap each hardened piece in waxed paper. Store in an airtight container.

Confectioners Sugar Replacement

If you must watch your sugar intake, you can use this in any recipe that calls for powdered sugar.

Combine all ingredients in food processor or blender. Whip until well blended and store in an airtight container.

Confectioners Sugar Versus Powdered Sugar
Don't let the two names fool you. Confectioners sugar and powdered sugar are exactly the same thing. Apparently the difference in names has to do with the region in which you live. The Northern part of the United States refers to it as powdered sugar, while in the South it's known as confectioners. In England, it's icing sugar!

MAKES 3–4 CUPS

INGREDIENTS
2 cups nonfat dry milk powder
2 cups cornstarch
1 cup Splenda

Brown Sugar Replacement

This recipe replaces one cup of regular brown sugar when canning or baking. To make more than 1 cup, just multiply ingredients by the number of cups you need.

Mix ingredients together. Keep in a covered container in the refrigerator.

MAKES 1 CUP

INGREDIENTS
1 cup Splenda
¼ cup sugar-free maple syrup

Sugar- and Fat-Free Sweetened Condensed Milk

MAKES 12 OUNCES

INGREDIENTS

1⅓ cups nonfat dry milk powder

½ cup water

½ cup Splenda

This recipe needs to be stored in the refrigerator where it should chill for 2 hours before use. It has a shelf life of 2 weeks.

1. In glass measuring cup, stir together milk powder and water until they form a paste.

2. Cover and microwave on high for 45 seconds or until hot but not boiling.

3. Stir in Splenda. Cover and store.

Baking Aid

Sweetened condensed milk is often used in baking sweet treats, but its high fat content make it less than ideal. You can still get the sweet taste and creamy texture from healthy alternatives, such as this recipe. You can make it in advance and keep it in the refrigerator until you need it.

Chapter 15

Flower Power

Dandelion Honey

MAKES 1 CUP

INGREDIENTS

4 cups dandelion petals

4 cups water

½ lemon, sliced

1 teaspoons vanilla powder or extract

2⅛ cups granulated white sugar

This is delicious on pancakes, biscuits, and sweet bread.

1. Gather the flowers when they're fully open but before the full heat of the day. Remove the petals and rinse.

2. In a nonreactive pan, put the petals, water, lemon, and vanilla. Bring to a boil. Reduce heat; simmer 30 minutes. Remove from burner.

3. Let flowers steep 6 hours. Strain, pressing juice out of the flowers. Retain only the liquid; return to pan.

4. Bring the flower water to a boil, adding sugar a little at a time. Stir regularly. Reduce heat; simmer until you're happy with the consistency.

5. Pour into a hot canning jar. Cap and process 10 minutes in boiling water.

Chrysanthemum Soup

MAKES 5 PINTS

INGREDIENTS

3 whole star anise

3 cloves garlic, thinly sliced

4" fresh gingerroot, peeled and thinly sliced, divided

1 tablespoon sesame oil

3 cups water

6 cups chicken broth

1–2 tablespoons soy sauce

2½ cups diced chicken breast

½ large red onion, thinly sliced

5 cups prepared chrysanthemum

Prepare the flowers for this dish by trimming the bottoms and cutting the upper stems and leaves into 1–2" pieces.

1. Brown the anise, garlic, and half of the ginger in a soup pot with the sesame oil for 5–8 minutes.

2. Add water and remaining ginger and simmer for 15 minutes.

3. Add broth, soy sauce, chicken, and onion and simmer 15 minutes more.

4. Meanwhile, blanch chrysanthemum for 3–4 minutes. Strain and move to ice bath.

5. Add the flowers into the soup, then ladle into prepared jars.

6. Cap and seal at 11 pounds of pressure for 20 minutes for pints.

Flower Pesto

Make this pesto in late summer as your herbs begin to flower and go to seed. You can use any combination of your favorite herb flowers. This pesto is very tasty on chicken and pasta, especially when blended with a little Parmesan cheese.

1. Put all ingredients in a food processor or blender.

2. Transfer into a pan; heat through completely.

3. Put into a hot canning jar; cover and process 15 minutes in boiling water.

Sage-acity
Sage comes in more than 750 varieties and actually belongs to the mint family. Sage originated in the Mediterranean, where it traversed trade routes and reached Europe by the Middle Ages. Throughout its travels, sage was treasured as a sacred herb of various deities and one that offered healthful qualities.

MAKES 1½ CUPS

INGREDIENTS
½ cup chopped pine nuts
2 cups herb flowers
½ cup sunflower oil
2 cloves garlic, minced
2 green onions, minced
½ teaspoon canning salt
½ teaspoon freshly ground black pepper

Lavender-Peach Jam

MAKES 6½ PINTS

INGREDIENTS

⅓ cup boiling water

4 tablespoons dried lavender flowers

4 cups finely chopped peaches

¼ cup lemon juice

1 teaspoon grated lemon zest

7 cups granulated sugar

2 3-ounce pouches liquid pectin

The scent of lavender is a surprising, aromatic addition to this yummy jam.

1. In a small bowl, pour water over lavender flowers. Let steep 20 minutes. Strain; discard flowers.

2. In a large stockpot, combine peaches, lemon juice and zest, and lavender infusion. Stir in sugar until well dissolved.

3. Bring to a full rolling boil over high heat, stirring constantly. Boil hard 1 minute.

4. Remove from heat; immediately stir in pectin. Stir gently 5 minutes to prevent fruit from floating.

5. Ladle into sterilized jars, leaving ¼" headspace. Wipe rims; cap and seal.

6. Process jars 10 minutes in a water-bath canner.

Squash Flower Soup

Prepare the flowers ahead of time by rinsing them in a warm water solution consisting of 1 tablespoon salt and 2 tablespoons vinegar. The water should just cover the flowers. Drain and rinse.

1. Place the butter in a pan with onion; sauté.

2. When onion turns translucent, about 7–10 minutes, add a pinch of sugar; toss in squash flowers and garlic. Sauté 2 minutes.

3. Add chili, green onions, and broth; bring to a boil. Remove from heat.

4. Ladle hot soup into prepared jars. Cap and seal, using pressure canner at 11 pounds of pressure for 20 minutes for pints.

5. When you open and serve this soup, you can add a scrambled egg to it to thicken the stock.

Squish Squash

Cave dwellers in Mexico were eating squash as early as 6000 B.C.E. Native Americans called squash God's apple. As early as 3000 B.C.E., the Natives felt that planting squash with other crops improved the overall yield in the fields. Squash was transported to Europe by Spanish explorers.

MAKES 4 CUPS

INGREDIENTS
¼ cup butter
1 medium onion, chopped
pinch sugar
12 squash flowers
2 cloves garlic, sliced
½ teaspoon red chili flakes
3–4 green onions, chopped with tops
2 cups vegetable or chicken broth

Daylily Soup

MAKES 3–4 PINTS

INGREDIENTS

5 cups chicken broth

½ cup cooked, minced chicken

1½ tablespoons cubed salt pork

¾ cup diced potatoes

2 tablespoons minced onion

3 tablespoons minced celery

¼ teaspoon minced fresh gingerroot

¼ teaspoon salt

¼ teaspoon pepper

2 tablespoons sherry

3 teaspoons minced mushrooms

1 tablespoon soy sauce

1½ cups chopped daylilies

This is another whimsical and tasty soup. The lilies add a clove-like flavor.

1. Put all ingredients in a stockpot. Cook 20 minutes, until potatoes start to get tender.

2. Remove from heat; ladle into prepared jars.

3. Cap and process at 11 pounds of pressure for 20 minutes.

Daylily Delight
In China, daylilies have been used in food for thousands of years. The flower was so fondly regarded that the word for daylily and the concept of "forgetting one's worries" are identical.

Lavender Jelly

MAKES 4–5 PINTS

INGREDIENTS

2½ cups cold water

½ cup fresh lavender flowers or 3 tablespoons dried flowers

¼ cup fresh lemon juice

4 cups granulated sugar

1 3-ounce envelope liquid pectin

lavender food coloring (2 drops red and 2 drops blue)

This jelly comes out a very pretty color and whispers of simpler, romantic days.

1. Bring water to boil; pour over flowers. Steep 20 minutes; strain.

2. Combine infusion, lemon juice, and sugar. Bring to a full boil, stirring constantly.

3. Add pectin and boil hard 1 minute, stirring constantly. Remove from heat and add food coloring.

4. Ladle into sterilized jars. Wipe rim; cap and seal. Process in water-bath canner 10 minutes.

Rose Petal Jelly

This jelly gives you a feel for the Victorian era. The color is a lovely pink.

1. Combine rose petals, 1½ cups water, and lemon juice in a blender; blend until smooth.

2. Slowly add the sugar; blend well.

3. In a small saucepan, bring remaining 1½ cups water to a boil. Stir in pectin; boil 1 minute, stirring constantly.

4. Add hot mixture to blender; blend 1 minute.

5. Ladle into sterilized jars; remove air bubbles. Wipe rims; cap and seal.

6. Process in water-bath canner 10 minutes.

MAKES 6–7 HALF-PINTS

INGREDIENTS

2 cups edible rose petals

3 cups water, divided

juice of 2 lemons

3 cups granulated sugar

1 3-ounce package liquid pectin

Nasturtium Butter

Nasturtiums are a great addition to any foods on which you enjoy citrus peppers.

Mix ingredients together well. Refrigerate until ready to use.

MAKES ½ CUP

INGREDIENTS

½ cup unsalted butter, room temperature

2 teaspoons lemon peel, grated

1 tablespoon lime juice

3 tablespoons nasturtium blossoms, finely chopped

Marigold Butter

MAKES ½ CUP

INGREDIENTS

½ cup unsalted butter, softened

2 tablespoons minced mint

2 tablespoons minced marigold

zest of 1 lime

2 teaspoons fresh lime juice

Always nibble your marigold petals before using them in cooking. Most are spicy, but some can be very bitter. Nasturtium petals can be used as an alternative.

Soften butter; blend with remaining ingredients. Refrigerate to store; best used within 1 week.

Calendula
Another name for marigold is *calendula*. Like many other flowers, it was used medicinally in ancient times in Egypt, Greece, and India. In truth, the leaves of this plant have an antiseptic quality, and were readily used during the Civil War for treating wounds.

Sweet Pansy Pudding

MAKES 6 SERVINGS

INGREDIENTS

5 tablespoons honey

3 tablespoons finely minced pansy leaves and flowers

2 cups milk

¼ teaspoon salt

pinch ginger

pinch nutmeg

3 eggs, beaten

This pudding won't last much longer than it takes to chill. Decorate it with a fresh or candied flower.

1. In a saucepan, combine honey and pansies. Heat over medium-low heat 15 minutes, stirring constantly. Cool; put in refrigerator 2 days to infuse honey with more flavor.

2. Scald the milk; add honey mixture, salt, and spices. Stir until honey is fully dissolved.

3. Slowly whisk milk mixture into eggs. Pour into custard cups and garnish. Chill about 2 hours.

A Perfect Pansy
Historians believe the name *pansy* derives from the French *pensee*, which means "remember." Throughout Europe, the pansy quickly became a staple in gardens. Pansy tastes a little like mild wintergreen.

Banana Flower Soup

MAKES ABOUT 3 CUPS

INGREDIENTS

1 14-ounce can coconut milk

1 cup water

1 ½-inch piece ginger, peeled and grated

1 banana flower

½ teaspoon garam masala

½ teaspoon dried red chilies

1 cup raw shrimp

salt to taste

pepper to taste

oil for cooking

water

Before using banana flowers, you need to cut off the first inch of the bottom of the flower. Shred it like lettuce or chop it into smaller pieces and put it in cold water with a slice of lemon for 1 hour. Drain and add to the soup as directed.

1. Warm coconut milk, water, ½ the ginger, and banana flower together over a low heat in a nonreactive pan.

2. Meanwhile, in a frying pan use a little oil to sauté garam masala, remaining ginger, and chilies. This blend should be pasty.

3. Add shrimp; fry until cooked. Add to coconut/banana flower mix. Stir thoroughly; simmer 15 minutes.

4. Cool and transfer to freezer-safe containers. Use within 3–4 months.

Mum's Sweet Potatoes

MAKES 6 MEDIUM SWEET POTATOES

INGREDIENTS

6 medium sweet potatoes

½ cup canned crushed pineapple

¼ cup honey

2 tablespoons butter

½ teaspoon grated orange rind

¼ teaspoon vanilla

½ cup chopped chrysanthemum petals

salt to taste

pepper to taste

This is a dish you can prepare for single-serve freezing. It makes a great lunch or side dish any time. Try potatoes with a dollop of sour cream.

1. Bake the sweet potatoes with skins on at 350°F for about 50–60 minutes.

2. When tender, halve potatoes and scoop out most of inside.

3. Mix potato insides with remaining ingredients. Stuff back into skins.

4. Wrap each skin in aluminum foil; freeze.

5. Defrost and bake at 350°F for 25 minutes.

Rose Petal Drop Scones

MAKES 2 DOZEN

INGREDIENTS
2¼ cups all-purpose flour
3 teaspoons sugar
¾ teaspoon salt
2 teaspoons baking powder
½ teaspoon baking soda
pinch ginger (optional)
4 tablespoons unsalted butter
¼ cup coarsely ground nuts
¼ cup currants
1 cup heavy cream
2 tablespoons rose water
2 tablespoons rose petals, diced fine

These scones are yummy without frosting, but you can make a pink sugar glaze with rosewater to top them when you take them out of the freezer.

1. Mix together flour, sugar, salt, baking powder, baking soda, and ginger.

2. Cut in butter. Continue mixing until dough looks like crumbs.

3. Add nuts and currants; mix.

4. In a separate bowl, combine cream, rose water, and rose petals.

5. Incorporate liquid and dry ingredients. Mix to get a firm dough.

6. Place on an ungreased cookie sheet 1 heaping tablespoonful at a time.

7. Bake at 450°F for 10–12 minutes, or until golden brown.

8. Cool and place in food-storage bag in the freezer; best used within 1 month.

Lavender Crisp

The aroma of this dessert is incredible. Warm it slightly for serving and add a little sweet cream on top.

1. Mix first four ingredients together.

2. Pour into a greased 8" × 8" baking pan.

3. Combine the remaining ingredients; distribute over top of berries and flowers.

4. Bake 20 minutes at 350°F. Cool.

5. Cut into squares. Wrap in freezer wrap, then place in a food-storage bag for easy access; best used within 1 month.

MAKES 16 2" × 2" SQUARES

INGREDIENTS

3 cups blueberries

1 cup strawberries, sliced

1 teaspoon lavender flowers

¾ cup sugar

1½ cups crushed honey graham crackers

½ cup brown sugar

½ cup melted butter

½ cup diced honey-roasted peanuts

Luscious Rose-Lavender Ice Cream

This recipe is intended for an ice cream maker.

1. Mix 1½ cups sugar with rose petals to make a paste.

2. In a saucepan, mix cream, milk, and remaining sugar together. Bring to a simmer and stir until sugar dissolves. Remove from heat.

3 Whisk the egg yolks until fluffy. Add to the hot liquid very slowly, whisking constantly. Return to heat.

4. Stir in lavender and vanilla and continue heating until mixture reaches 180°F.

5. Pour into ice cream maker and follow manufacturer's directions.

6. Put in freezer-safe containers and store.

MAKES 3 CUPS

INGREDIENTS

2½ cups sugar, divided

1 cup loosely packed rose petals

1 cup heavy cream

1 cup whole milk

5 large egg yolks

½ cup lavender flowers

¼ teaspoon vanilla extract

Rose Petal Ice Cubes

12 ICE CUBES

INGREDIENTS
12 rose petals
water

These are so pretty when they are floating in a punch bowl or pitcher of iced tea or lemonade.

1. Rinse organic petals under warm water; blot dry.

2. Fill an ice cube tray ½ full with water; freeze.

3. Place a rose petal on each cube and cover with a teaspoon of water; freeze again (this secures the petal).

4. Completely fill cubes with water; freeze. Remove from trays; store in a freezer bag.

Roses Are Red

Nearly everyone knows that red roses are for romance and love, but what about other hues? Pink roses represent respect and joy. Yellow roses symbolize friendship and white roses represent purity and a new beginning. Orange roses represent zeal or passion and lavender roses mean enchantment.

Lavender Beef Jerky

You can make this jerky with roses, too.

1. Place all ingredients in a pan; warm.

2. When lavender becomes aromatic, remove from heat, about 3–5 minutes. Cool.

3. Pour everything into a food-storage bag; marinate in refrigerator 48 hours. Shake regularly.

4. Put slices in dehydrator, following manufacturer's instructions. Store in an airtight container when dried.

MAKES 2 POUNDS JERKY

INGREDIENTS
4-pound beef tenderloin, sliced thin
2 tablespoons extra-virgin olive oil
2 tablespoons white vinegar
1 cup beef stock
2 tablespoons whole black peppercorns
1½ teaspoons dried thyme
2 tablespoons dried culinary lavender flowers
2 tablespoons honey

Pickled Nasturtium

The flavor of the nasturtium is similar to capers and far less expensive. Note, however, that it's essential to use the green pods because mature pods are unsuitable for consumption.

1. Mix salt and water together with nasturtiums. Soak 3 days, making sure flowers stay beneath water's surface. Strain; put in a canning jar.

2. Mix vinegar with remaining ingredients; bring to a boil.

3. Pour over pods. Cap and seal in a hot-water bath 10 minutes.

Nasturtium's Story
This flower originated in Peru. Today, there are well over thirty varieties of nasturtium in the world. The petals have been used for hundreds of years in salads, and they're high in vitamin C. If you love birds, grow nasturtium to attract hummingbirds.

MAKES ½ CUP

INGREDIENTS
2 tablespoons pickling salt
1 cup water
½ cup green nasturtium seed pods
⅔ cup white wine vinegar
¼ cup red wine vinegar
2 teaspoons sugar
1 bay leaf
pinch thyme

Candied Angelica

YIELD VARIES

INGREDIENTS
12 ounces angelica stalks
water to cover
1 cup granulated vanilla-
scented sugar

Try this as a breath mint!

1. Cut angelica into 4-inch pieces. Cover with water; bring to a boil.

2. Drain and check for tough skin, removing it with a vegetable peeler.

3. Return to pan; add fresh water. Simmer until tender.

4. Drain and pat dry. Put in a bowl; cover with sugar and mix well. Leave 3 days, stirring periodically.

5. Simmer mixture over a low flame, slowly increasing temperature until solution boils and angelica turns translucent.

6. Drain and sprinkle with sugar.

7. Dry at 150°F for 3 hours. Wrap and store in an airtight container.

Candied Flower Petals

MAKES 1 CUP

INGREDIENTS
1 cup edible flower petals
1 cup granulated sugar
¾ cup water
powdered sugar

Use apple blossoms, plum blossoms, lilacs, geraniums, borage, or any of your other favorite edible flowers. These candied petals will keep for up to a year in an airtight container.

1. Wash edible flower petals gently and dry on paper towels. Trim away the ends; these are bitter.

2. Combine sugar and water in a saucepan and boil until it reads 234°F on a candy thermometer.

3. Pour syrup into a bowl on a bed of cracked ice. When syrup begins to crystallize, hold petals with tweezers and dip.

4. Dry petals on waxed paper and dust with powdered sugar.

Basic Flower Oil

Be careful when warming the oil for the flowers. Some flowers, like roses, are particularly sensitive to high heat and the resulting aroma is anything but pleasant.

1. Warm oil; return to bottle.

2. Add flowers to oil.

3. Cover and let blend steep 1 week.

4. Strain fresh flowers and leave oil, using it for salad, marinade, or frying.

Rose in History

There is no question that the rose is the queen of all flowers. Throughout the world, roses represent myriad things, including love and war. The flower has been around for 5,000 years and there are more than 150 species. Roses were first cultivated in China in the eighteenth century. Nearly all our modern roses can trace their heritage to this period.

INGREDIENTS
½–1 cup fresh flowers
1 quart vegetable oil

Basic Floral Liqueur

MAKES 4 CUPS

INGREDIENTS
1–2 cups flowers
4 cups vodka
1 cup sugar

Some nice blends to consider for this include roses with carnation, lemon balm, and lemon verbena or lavender with mint. If you prefer, you can use brandy instead of vodka.

1. Lightly bruise flowers so they release essential oils more readily.

2. Put flowers in the bottle with vodka.

3. Steep 2 days, then add sugar.

4. Steep 2 weeks, shaking the container daily.

5. Strain and use as desired.

Violet Vinegar

MAKES 8 OUNCES

INGREDIENTS
1 8-ounce bottle Champagne vinegar
¼ cup fragrant violet petals, rinsed

This mixture works as a salad dressing and a marinade.

1. Pour out ⅓ of vinegar into a measuring cup.

2. Place violets in the bottle; fill with vinegar. Excess vinegar can be stored elsewhere.

3. Cap and let blend steep 4 days, shaking regularly. Strain.

4. Keep in a cool, dark place. The shelf life is 1 year.

The Sacred Violet
Violets were important in various religions. Violet garlands were left at Cybele's sacred sites and rites to Attis included violets. In the Victorian era, violets were said to represent true love or truthfulness. In an odd dichotomy, they also symbolize mourning—the loss of love.

Rose Petal Syrup

Use two layers of fine cheesecloth to strain this mixture.

1. Simmer rose petals with water and sugar for 1 hour. Add drops of red food coloring until mixture reaches desired color.

2. Strain through a fine sieve.

3. Bring back to a boil and put in hot sterilized bottles. Refrigerate.

4. Keeps up to 2 weeks in the refrigerator. Can be added to sparkling water or Champagne for a delicious beverage or pour over fruit, pound cake, or pancakes.

Turkish Delight

Traditional Turkish recipes for rose petal syrup call for the inclusion of poppy petals. If you'd like to try this, add about a cup of poppy petals to the mixture, and increase the amounts of water and sugar until you get the consistency and taste you desire.

MAKES 2 CUPS

INGREDIENTS
4 cups rose petals
2 cups water
2 tablespoons sugar
red food coloring

Chapter 16

Gifts

Cinnamon Pancake Mix

MAKES 12 PANCAKES

INGREDIENTS

Pancake Mix

3 cups all-purpose flour

2 tablespoons granulated sugar or Splenda

2 tablespoons baking powder

4 teaspoons cinnamon

1¼ teaspoons fine sea salt

Ready to Bake

¾ cup milk

1 egg

2 tablespoons vegetable oil

1⅓ cups pancake mix

This mix can be bagged or put into a jar. It lasts for up to 6 months. Add a tag that provides instructions for making the pancakes.

1. Mix all ingredients together. Store in bags or jars.

2. When ready to make the pancakes, whisk together milk, egg, and oil in a bowl.

3. Add pancake mix; stir just until moist and still a bit lumpy.

4. Cook on a lightly greased griddle or in a waffle iron.

Pancake Proofing

Our Roman ancestors ate dishes that were similar to the pancakes we enjoy today. Some of the mixtures were savory and others were sweet; depending on the cooking method, the batter might come out like fritters, doughnuts, or even custard. It's traditional to consume pancakes on Shrove Tuesday before Lent begins.

Multi-Bean Soup Mix

Sixteen-ounce jars hold 2 cups of this mix. It's fun to layer the beans for visual appeal. Add a tag with instructions for making soup.

1. Combine beans and seal in separate jars.

2. To make soup, soak 2 cups of bean mix overnight in water. Drain and put in stockpot.

3. Add remaining ingredients; bring to a boil. Reduce heat; simmer 1 hour.

4. Remove bay leaf before serving.

Cheap and Healthy!

Any way you look at it, eating beans, whether dried or out of the can, is an inexpensive way to enjoy a meal—of course, opting for dried beans costs only pennies per serving, since a one-pound bag of dried beans, or about 2 cups, equals about 6 cups of cooked beans.

INGREDIENTS

Soup Mix

1 pound dried black beans

1 pound dried red beans

1 pound dried kidney beans

1 pound dried navy beans

1 pound dried great northern beans

1 pound dried baby lima beans

1 pound dried large lima beans

1 pound dried pinto beans

1 pound dried green split peas

1 pound dried yellow split peas

1 pound dried black-eyed peas

1 pound dried green lentils

1 pound dried brown lentils

Ready to Eat

2 cups bean mix

water

1 smoked ham hock

29 ounces stewed tomato

1 medium onion, chopped

1 clove garlic, minced

1 bay leaf

salt to taste

pepper to taste

¼ cup fresh parsley

1 tablespoon red wine vinegar

6 cups water

Spiced Orange Rings

MAKES 4 PINTS

INGREDIENTS
6 large oranges
cold water to cover
1½ cups granulated sugar
1½ cups white vinegar
4 2-inch cinnamon sticks
2 teaspoons whole cloves
1 teaspoon whole allspice
berries

These look beautiful in a gift basket, and they taste great, too!

1. Wash oranges. Cut into ¼-inch slices; seed.

2. Place oranges in a heavy pan; cover with cold water. Heat to boiling. Lower heat; simmer until fruit is tender, about 45 minutes. Drain in a colander.

3. Heat sugar, vinegar, cinnamon, cloves, and allspice berries until boiling. Add orange rings a few at a time; cook until rings are tender and clear, about 15 minutes.

4. Pack orange slices in sterilized pint jars, leaving ¼" headspace. Divide spices evenly between 4 jars.

5. Ladle hot syrup over orange slices, leaving ¼" headspace. Wipe rims; cap and seal.

6. Process in water-bath canner 10 minutes.

Oranges Arrive

It was 1493 when Christopher Columbus brought orange seeds to Haiti, from where they eventually made it into Florida in the early sixteenth century. The most popular oranges are sweet oranges, which come in Navel, Valencia, Persian, and Blood orange varieties.

Blueberry Chutney

Try this sweet chutney on goose, turkey, chicken, and other fowl.

1. Rinse and stem blueberries.

2. Place blueberries in a large stockpot with onion, vinegar, raisins, brown sugar, mustard seeds, gingerroot, cinnamon, salt, nutmeg, and red pepper flakes. Bring mixture to a boil.

3. Lower heat; simmer, stirring occasionally, about 45 minutes, or until chutney is thick.

4. Ladle hot chutney into sterilized jars, leaving ½" headspace. Wipe rims; cap and seal.

5. Process in water-bath canner 15 minutes. Cool.

6. Put in a cool, dark place; leave 6–8 weeks before using.

Blue Food

Blueberries carry the folk names of *hurtleberries* and *bilberries*. Unlike so many other fruits, this is one that has its roots in North America. Do not purchase underripe blueberries; they don't continue to ripen after harvesting.

MAKES 4 PINTS

INGREDIENTS

8 cups fresh blueberries, rinsed and stemmed

2 medium onions, finely chopped

3 cups red wine vinegar

1 cup golden yellow raisins

1 cup dark brown sugar, firmly packed

1 tablespoon yellow mustard seeds

2 tablespoons freshly grated gingerroot

1 teaspoon ground cinnamon

1 pinch salt

¼ teaspoon ground nutmeg

½ teaspoon dried red pepper flakes

Banana Nut Bread Conserve

MAKES 6 PINTS

INGREDIENTS

20 ripe bananas, puréed

2 tablespoons lemon juice

1½ teaspoons apple pie spice

1 1.75-ounce package powdered pectin

3 cups granulated sugar or Splenda

2 cups brown sugar or 1 cup brown sugar replacement

2 tablespoons pure walnut extract

2½ cups chopped walnuts

This tastes just like fresh banana bread. Try it warm!

1. In a large stockpot, combine puréed bananas, lemon juice, apple pie spice, and powdered pectin. Stir while bringing to a full rolling boil.

2. Add granulated sugar and brown sugar. Heat to a full rolling boil, stirring continuously. Continue to boil 1 minute.

3. Remove from heat; stir in walnut extract. Fold in chopped walnuts.

4. Ladle into sterilized jars, leaving ¼" headspace. Wipe rims; cap and seal.

5. Process in water-bath canner 10 minutes.

Go Bananas!

Bananas first appear in Buddhist texts in the year 600 B.C.E. Three hundred years later, Alexander the Great would taste banana for the first time. And like anything good, it wasn't long before merchants began taking bananas with them for trade. Bananas are recommended for people who have sensitive stomachs.

To-Die-For Hot Fudge Sauce

This hot fudge sauce is rich and creamy—truly to die for. The Kahlua adds a wonderful richness, but you may substitute pure vanilla extract.

1. In the top pan of a double-boiler, melt chocolate and butter, stirring frequently. Remove from heat and set aside. Leave double-boiler intact to remain heated while you prepare remainder of recipe.

2. In a large saucepan, combine sugar, corn syrup, and water. Over low heat, heat until sugar is dissolved thoroughly, stirring constantly.

3. Increase heat to medium-high; bring to a boil, stirring constantly to prevent scorching.

4. Reduce heat to medium-low; simmer 3 minutes, or until syrup is clear. Remove pan from heat.

5. Whisk chocolate mixture into syrup. Return pan to heat; cook until sauce becomes thick and glossy, about 10 minutes, stirring constantly.

6. Remove pan from heat; gently stir 2–3 minutes to cool sauce and release any trapped air bubbles. Stir in Kahlua or vanilla extract until well blended.

7. Ladle into sterilized half-pint jars, leaving ½" headspace. Remove air bubbles with plastic stirrer or wand. Wipe rims; cap and seal.

8. Process in water-bath canner 15 minutes. This sauce has a shelf life of about 4 months.

MAKES 6 HALF PINTS

INGREDIENTS

1 pound bittersweet cooking chocolate, chopped coarsely

1 cup unsalted butter

3 cups superfine sugar

1⅓ cups light corn syrup

1⅓ cups water

6 teaspoons Kahlua or pure vanilla extract

Caramel Maple Pecan Sauce

MAKES 3 PINTS

INGREDIENTS

1¾ cups light corn syrup

2 cups maple syrup

¾ cup water

1 cup packed brown sugar

2 cups coarsely chopped pecans, toasted

This is very tasty on top of white cakes and ice cream.

1. Combine corn syrup, maple syrup, water, and brown sugar in a stockpot. Bring to a boil over medium heat, stirring constantly. Simmer 5–8 minutes, stirring occasionally.

2. Stir in pecans; remove from heat.

3. Ladle into sterilized jars, leaving ¼" headspace. Wipe rims; cap and seal.

4. Process in water-bath canner 10 minutes.

Glazed Pineapple

MAKES 3½ CUPS

INGREDIENTS

3½ cups sliced canned pineapple

2 cups granulated sugar

⅓ cup light corn syrup

This can be eaten by itself or as a fruity topping.

1. Drain and reserve juice from canned pineapple. Dry slices with a cloth or paper towel.

2. Combine juice, sugar, and corn syrup in a large stockpot. Stir and bring to a boil.

3. Add fruit, but do not crowd it. Simmer until fruit is transparent. Lift pineapple from syrup.

4. Drain on wire cake racks until thoroughly dry. Place between waxed paper and store in a container with a tight-fitting lid.

Vidalia Onion Salad Dressing

If you like garlic and onion, try substituting minced garlic for the Herbes de Provence in this recipe.

1. In a small saucepan, stir together first seven ingredients. Add grated Vidalia onion.

2. Add the extra-virgin oil and vinegars; whisk together to blend.

3. Heat on medium 3–4 minutes, stirring constantly.

4. Ladle hot dressing into sterilized jars. Remove air bubbles. Wipe rims; cap and seal.

5. Process in water-bath canner 15 minutes.

Sweet Onion

Onions are an ancient vegetable, but the Vidalia variety has only been around for about seventy years. In 1931, a Georgia farmer named Mose Coleman discovered his onions were sweet. He took his unique onions to the farmers market during the 1940s, boosting their popularity. Now Vidalias are so popular they have their own festival.

MAKES 1 QUART

INGREDIENTS

2 cups Splenda or granulated sugar

2 teaspoons onion powder

2 teaspoons dry mustard

2 teaspoons celery seed

2 teaspoons Herbes de Provence

½ teaspoon sea salt

½ teaspoon coarsely ground black pepper

1 large Vidalia onion, grated very finely and dried

4 tablespoons extra-virgin olive oil

2 cups white vinegar

½ cup aged balsamic vinegar

Tempting Tea

MAKES 32 1-CUP
SERVINGS

INGREDIENTS
Tea Blend
1 cup lemon-flavored,
sweetened instant tea
1 teaspoon ginger
1 teaspoon allspice
1 1½-ounce package
sweetened lemonade mix
1 teaspoon dried lemon rind,
finely ground
1 cinnamon stick
Ready to Drink
1½ teaspoons tea blend
¾–1 cup hot water

You can change the iced tea flavors in this easily. For example, use raspberry iced tea and raspberry lemonade mix.

1. Combine all tea blend ingredients in a bowl; mix well. Bundle into a pretty bag and seal or tie with a ribbon, using the cinnamon stick as part of the bow.

2. To drink, put 1½ teaspoons tea blend in a cup. Add water; stir well with cinnamon stick.

Pucker Up
The first written descriptions of a lemonade-like drink are found in the writings of adventurer Nasir-i-Khusraw. He tells of Egyptian life around 1000 B.C.E. and specifically mentions the lemon juice trade.

Orange Chocolate Coffee

MAKES 16 CUPS

INGREDIENTS
Coffee Blend
⅓ cup instant coffee
½ cup cocoa powder
½ cup powdered milk
2 teaspoons dried
orange peel
2 teaspoons orange-juice
powder
Ready to Drink
1 tablespoon coffee blend
¾–1 cup boiling water
sugar to taste
chocolate sauce for garnish
whipped cream for garnish

Try this with a capful of orange or chocolate liqueur.

1. Mix all ingredients for coffee blend together. Pour into 16 pretty gift bags.

2. To make coffee, mix coffee with boiling water. Add sugar to taste. Garnish with chocolate sauce and whipped cream.

Quick Bread Coating

This is an all-purpose coating for any type of meat or vegetable.

1. Mix coating ingredients together and bag them.

2. To prepare meat or vegetables, dip meat or vegetables into egg and buttermilk.

3. Dip again in coating mix. For extra-crunchy style, repeat.

4. Deep fry or bake as desired.

MAKES 2⅔ CUPS COATING

INGREDIENTS

Coating Blend

2 cups dry bread crumbs

¼ cup flour

3 tablespoons paprika

4 teaspoons salt

2 teaspoons both onion powder and sugar

1 teaspoon basil

½ teaspoon both garlic powder and dehydrated, finely ground orange and lemon zest

Ready to Eat

1 pound meat or vegetables

1 egg

1 cup buttermilk

1 cup coating mix

Healthy Herbed Rice Mix

This is a nice recipe for using up some of the herbs and spices you've already dried. You can also add small dehydrated vegetables to this for a unique touch.

1. Mix rice blend ingredients together. Divide into bags, putting 2 cups of mix per bag.

2. To prepare rice, melt butter in a saucepan. Add rice mix; let it brown gently. Add water; bring to a full boil.

3. Reduce heat; simmer 20 minutes, covered. Let stand 5 minutes, then serve.

MAKES 10 CUPS

INGREDIENTS

Rice Blend

3 pounds long grain or brown rice

2 cups preserved celery flakes

⅔ cup preserved minced onion

½ cup preserved parsley flakes

2 tablespoons preserved chives

1 tablespoon dried tarragon

1 tablespoon garlic powder

½ tablespoon Italian seasonings (optional)

3–4 teaspoons salt

2 teaspoons pepper

Ready to Eat

2 teaspoons butter

1 cup rice blend

2 cups water

INGREDIENTS

Bread Mix

2 cups all-purpose
unbleached flour

2 teaspoons baking powder

½ teaspoon salt

½ teaspoon baking soda

2 tablespoons brown sugar

⅔ cup Parmesan cheese

4 teaspoons dried minced
onion

Baking Ingredients

1 recipe bread mix

1½ cups dark beer

INGREDIENTS

Dip Mix

2 tablespoons bacon bits

1 tablespoon instant minced
onion

1 tablespoon powdered beef
or vegetable bouillon

1 tablespoon dry minced
garlic

1 tablespoon dried dill
(optional)

Ready to Serve

2½ tablespoons dip mix

1 cup sour cream

Beer Bread

Someone once said that beer is liquid bread, so it seems natural
to put the two together!

1. To make the mix, combine first four ingredients. Put them in the
   bottom of the bag, then layer with remaining ingredients.

2. To bake, mix dry ingredients and beer. Bake in a greased loaf pan at
   375°F for 40 minutes. Cool; serve with butter or dip in cheese fondue.

Beer and Bread
The Egyptians are credited with being the first civilization to brew beer, so it's
not surprising that they also made special beer breads as early as 1000 B.C.E.
Before being served, the bread was soaked with beer foam. Beer was the
beverage for the average person, but commoners wouldn't get the most
clarified portion; that was reserved for people in authority.

Bacon Dip Mix

This is delicious with rye or pumpernickel bread. You can
substitute yogurt or cream cheese for the sour cream.

1. Combine all dip mix ingredients and put into a bag.

2. When ready to serve, combine dip mix and sour cream. Test flavor,
   adding more mix if the dip is not strong enough for your taste.

3. Chill 1 hour, and enjoy.

Healthy Creamy Cucumber Dressing

You can powder the dry cucumber by putting small pieces through a spice grinder.

1. Combine all dressing mix ingredients and put in gift container.

2. When ready to serve, add dressing mix to yogurt and lemon juice. Mix all ingredients in a blender or food processor; store in a jar in the refrigerator.

Cool as a Cucumber
Cucumbers really are cool—up to 20 degrees cooler inside than the external air! Cucumbers originally came from India. They began traveling the world around the time Greece and Rome reached their height. They arrived in France around the ninth century, England in the fourteenth century, and North America in the sixteenth century.

MAKES 1½ CUPS

INGREDIENTS

Dressing Mix

½ medium cucumber, peeled, dried, and powdered

1 clove garlic, finely minced

½ teaspoon fine sea salt

½ teaspoon ground white pepper

Ready to Serve

1 recipe dressing mix

1 cup plain nonfat yogurt

1 teaspoon lemon juice

Potato Soup Mix

This hale and hearty soup mix also makes a great foundation for scalloped potatoes and ham.

1. Combine soup mix ingredients and portion into ½-cup bags.

2. When ready to serve, place instant soup mix in a soup bowl, cup, or mug. Add water; stir until smooth.

You Say Potato
Peruvians cultivated potatoes more than 4,000 years ago. Potatoes didn't make it to Europe until the mid-sixteenth century, and when they did they were greeted with skepticism. Marie Antoinette changed all that by wearing a crown of potato blossoms in the late eighteenth century, making the potato fashionable. Today, the average American household eats more than 140 pounds of potatoes each year.

MAKES 12 SERVINGS

INGREDIENTS

Soup Mix

4 bouillon cubes, crumbled

3 cups instant mashed potato flakes, packed

2 tablespoons instant minced onions

3 tablespoons dried scallions

1 teaspoon white pepper

1 cup powdered milk

1 tablespoon onion powder

Ready to Serve

½ cup soup mix

1 cup boiling water

Healthy French Dressing Mix

MAKES 4 ¼-CUP
PACKAGES

INGREDIENTS

1 cup Splenda

4 teaspoons paprika

2 tablespoons dry yellow
mustard

2 teaspoons fine sea salt

¼ teaspoon onion powder

This dressing tastes delicious over salads, but try mixing it with beans for additional nutrition.

1. Combine all ingredients in a small bowl and stir to distribute evenly. Put in desired bags or jars; mix will keep for 6 months. Affix the following instructions for use.

2. Combine ¼ cup French dressing mix with ¾ cup extra-virgin olive oil, 6 tablespoons sugar-free ketchup, and ¼ cup vinegar.

3. Shake until well blended. Chill before serving. Makes about 1¼ cups French dressing.

Healthy Salad Dressing

Salads are a natural addition to a healthy diet. The vegetables in salad contain valuable nutrients, and they fill you up so you don't have room for dessert at the end of a meal. However, unhealthy salad dressings add unnecessary fat and calories. Olive oil is the perfect base for a salad dressing; it is known to decrease levels of bad cholesterol.

Cream of Mushroom Soup Mix

Canned soups are high in sodium, but this cream of mushroom soup mix packs just as much flavor.

1. Blend dry ingredients together, then evenly divide into five boxes, bags, or jars. Affix the following instructions.

2. Place 1 cup soup mix into 1 pint of boiling water, stirring constantly until smooth and thickened. Cover and cook over very low heat 20 to 30 minutes.

MAKES ABOUT 5 CUPS MIX

INGREDIENTS

2 cups home-dried mushrooms, chopped

2 tablespoons home-dried onion flakes

1 teaspoon home-dried grated lemon rind

1 tablespoon Greek seasoning

6 tablespoons cornstarch

1½ teaspoons fine sea salt

¼ teaspoon ground white pepper

2 cups powdered milk

Onion Soup Mix

5 tablespoons of the mix equals 1 ¼-ounce package of commercial dry onion soup mix.

Mix the dry goods together and portion out in packages.

MAKES 3½ CUPS MIX

INGREDIENTS

2¼ cups minced onion flakes

1 cup beef flavored instant bouillon

¼ cup onion powder

1 teaspoon celery salt (or celery seed)

1 teaspoon sugar or Splenda

½ teaspoon white pepper

Mexican Fiesta Dip Mix

MAKES 2 CUPS

INGREDIENTS

Mix Ingredients

½ cup dried parsley

⅓ cup minced onion

¼ cup dried chives

⅓ cup chili powder

¼ cup ground cumin

¼ cup salt

Ready to Serve

3 tablespoons Mexican Fiesta dip mix

1 cup mayonnaise

1 cup sour cream or low-fat yogurt

Serve this dip with tortilla chips or fresh vegetables.

1. Combine the spices and divide evenly into gift containers. Affix the following instructions for use.

2. Combine 3 tablespoons Mexican fiesta dip mix, 1 cup mayonnaise, and 1 cup sour cream or low-fat yogurt. Whisk until smooth.

3. Refrigerate 2 to 4 hours.

Concentrating on Cumin

Cumin is a very common herb in Mexican and Mediterranean cooking. Its flavor is somewhat bitter and hot. It grows easily in a variety of environments, but for some reason it never became very popular in Europe except during the medieval era.

Trail Mix

MAKES 4 CUPS

INGREDIENTS

1 cup Rice Chex cereal

1 cup small pretzel twists

½ cup honey roasted peanuts

⅔ cup sweetened dried fruit

1 cup M&Ms

½ cup sesame sticks

Trail mix is great to take out on the road, but remember to keep the container tightly sealed to prevent it from going stale.

Layer this mix in a gift container.

Packaging and Shipping Notes

If you're sending your gifts, you must be careful to keep things from breaking. If you're shipping internationally, you'll need to review your ingredients to make sure the products won't be confiscated. Certain seeds in food won't make it past inspection points. If you do your research, you'll be able to provide a detailed ingredient list for customs so nothing gets left behind.

Shipping within your own state or country is easier, but still take the time to package carefully. Get bubble wrap, packing peanuts, Styrofoam, and other packaging materials. Wrap each item separately and make sure there's a layer of packing material between the gift items and the wall of the box. Boxes of homemade goods, especially jars, get heavy. Make sure the box you've chosen can handle the weight you put in it, and use good packing tape to seal it.

Don't forget to clearly mark the box with the correct destination address and a return address. Additionally, put a sheet inside each box with the recipient's name and address. Include a packing list and a list of ingredients in case anyone has allergies. If a recipient gets a box that has been messed with, these materials will help you establish an insurance claim.

Check online to find a shipper. Every service lets you preprice items. This way you can determine which service offers you the best pricing and service for your goods. Get insurance, especially if you are shipping glass, and always keep your receipt until you hear the package has arrived.

If a box arrives damaged, tell your recipient to keep the box. This is essential. Many mailing services will not honor insurance coverage if they cannot see the original box and its contents, no matter how messy.

If you follow these basic guidelines, your packages should arrive safely; if they don't, you'll be able to recoup your loss.

Appendix A

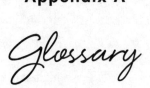

Glossary

alum
Until recently, a common ingredient in pickling recipes. It has been found to cause stomach problems.

antioxidant
Keeps food from browning. Examples include lemon and lime juice.

bacteria
Organisms that may be harmful if not destroyed properly. Any low-acid recipes must be processed in pressure canners to 240°F for a specific length of time.

blanch
A fast bath in boiling water, usually followed by an ice or cold-water bath. Prepares many fruits and vegetables for preserving.

boiling-water canning
Process requiring jars be completely immersed in boiling water for a set length of time in order to bring the food to 212°F and create a vacuum seal on the lids.

botulism
A toxin that may grow in foods that haven't been properly processed (allowing bacteria to reproduce). Canning and preserving methods strive to eliminate these toxins by removing air and the use of acids and high temperatures that kill spores.

brine
A mixture consisting primarily of salt and water, used in pickling.

candying
Encrusting with sugar, often through the use of boiling syrup. A common method of preserving fruit rinds and ginger for baking purposes.

canning salt
A fine salt with no iodine or anticaking ingredients that can discolor vegetables.

cheesecloth
A cloth used to strain pulp or juice, especially for jelly making. It's also useful in pickling for holding spices unwanted in final jars.

chutney
A slow-cooked blend of fruit, vegetables, spices, and/or vinegar.

cold pack
A canning process in which fruits and vegetables go into the jar raw. Afterward, some type of canning liquid is added (usually hot) and the jars processed.

conserve
Jam-like spread, often using two or more fruits, and possibly including nuts.

crisping agent
Sometimes called Pickle Crisp. A commercial product used to keep pickles fresh in lieu of alum.

dial gauge
Part of pressure canner that shows what pressure level the canner has reached.

fermentation
A method of preserving food by introducing yeasts. Unanticipated fermentation can indicate other micro-organisms that can cause sickness.

gelling point
A temperature of 220°F brings various liquids to gel.

headspace
Amount of room left between the top of the food and the lid in a canning jar. This room is necessary to create a vacuum seal.

high-acid food
Food with a pH value of 4.6 or less, like tomatoes and many fruit juices. Can be processed using boiling-water methods.

hot pack
A form of canning where food goes into the jars hot to be processed.

jam
Crushed fruit and sugar (sometimes nuts) processed together into a spread.

jelly
A firm spread made from juice and sugar to which pectin may be added.

low-acid food
Foods with a pH higher than 4.6. Examples include most seafood, meat, and vegetables. These foods must be pressure canned, heated to 240°F.

marmalade
A spread that includes fruit and peel pieces mingled into a jelly base.

pectin
A fruit and vegetable carbohydrate frequently used to make jelly, jam, and other spreads.

pickling
A preservation process that uses vinegar with spices and water. Foods are processed in hot-water canners.

preserves
A spread that preserves fruit in sugar syrup. The fruit retains its shape.

pressure canning
A process used on low-acid foods that cooks them to 240°F throughout, killing bacteria.

processing
Heating canning jars to specific temperatures for a specific amount of time to kill bacteria, mold, and yeast. Also creates the vacuum seal on canned foods.

raw pack
Filling jars with unheated meat or fish prior to processing.

relish
A blend of diced vegetables or fruits in a seasoned vinegar solution.

reprocessing
Removing and reheating the lid, cleaning and reheating the jar, and reheating the food inside the jar according to the recipe, followed by processing again, to try to save food when the jar doesn't seal properly.

smoke curing
A way of preserving food by smoking it. Also adds flavor to the preserved item.

syrup
A blend of sugar and other liquids used to cover ingredients in a jar before processing.

venting
Heating of canning jars to force the air out.

weighted gauge
A gauge on pressure canners consisting of weights, normally for 5, 10, and 15 pounds of pressure, which go on top of a valve. When the weight rocks, the right pressure has been achieved.

Appendix B

Conversion Tables

Metric Conversions	
⅕ teaspoon	1 milliliter
1 teaspoon	5 milliliters
1 tablespoon	15 milliliters
1 fluid ounce	30 milliliters
⅕ cup	50 milliliters
1 cup	240 milliliters
2 cups (1 pint)	470 milliliters
4 cups (1 quart)	.95 liters
4 quarts (1 gal.)	3.8 liters
34 fluid ounces	1 liter
4.2 dry cups	1 liter
2.1 pints or 1.06 quarts	1 liter
1 ounce	28 grams
3.5 ounces	100 grams
1 pound	454 grams
2.2 pounds (or 35 ounces)	1 kilogram
Temperature	
Fahrenheit	***Celsius***
225°F	110°C
250°F	130°C
300°F	150°C
350°F	180°C
400°F	200°C

U.S. Measurement Equivalents	
1 pound	2 cups
48 teaspoons	1 cup
16 tablespoons	1 cup
12 tablespoons	¾ cup
10 tablespoons + 2 teaspoons	⅔ cup
8 tablespoons	½ cup
6 tablespoons	⅜ cup
5 tablespoons + 1 teaspoon	⅓ cup
4 tablespoons	¼ cup
2 tablespoons	⅛ cup
2 tablespoons + 2 teaspoons	⅙ cup
1 tablespoon	1/16 cup or 3 teaspoons
2 cups	1 pint (16 ounces)
2 pints	1 quart
1 ounce	2 tablespoons
6 teaspoons	⅛ cup
1 teaspoon	⅓ tablespoon

Index

THE EVERYTHING SERIES!

BUSINESS & PERSONAL FINANCE

Everything® Accounting Book
Everything® Budgeting Book, 2nd Ed.
Everything® Business Planning Book
Everything® Coaching and Mentoring Book, 2nd Ed.
Everything® Fundraising Book
Everything® Get Out of Debt Book
Everything® Grant Writing Book, 2nd Ed.
Everything® Guide to Buying Foreclosures
Everything® Guide to Fundraising, $15.95
Everything® Guide to Mortgages
Everything® Guide to Personal Finance for Single Mothers
Everything® Home-Based Business Book, 2nd Ed.
Everything® Homebuying Book, 3rd Ed., $15.95
Everything® Homeselling Book, 2nd Ed.
Everything® Human Resource Management Book
Everything® Improve Your Credit Book
Everything® Investing Book, 2nd Ed.
Everything® Landlording Book
Everything® Leadership Book, 2nd Ed.
Everything® Managing People Book, 2nd Ed.
Everything® Negotiating Book
Everything® Online Auctions Book
Everything® Online Business Book
Everything® Personal Finance Book
Everything® Personal Finance in Your 20s & 30s Book, 2nd Ed.
Everything® Personal Finance in Your 40s & 50s Book, $15.95
Everything® Project Management Book, 2nd Ed.
Everything® Real Estate Investing Book
Everything® Retirement Planning Book
Everything® Robert's Rules Book, $7.95
Everything® Selling Book
Everything® Start Your Own Business Book, 2nd Ed.
Everything® Wills & Estate Planning Book

COOKING

Everything® Barbecue Cookbook
Everything® Bartender's Book, 2nd Ed., $9.95
Everything® Calorie Counting Cookbook
Everything® Cheese Book
Everything® Chinese Cookbook
Everything® Classic Recipes Book
Everything® Cocktail Parties & Drinks Book
Everything® College Cookbook
Everything® Cooking for Baby and Toddler Book
Everything® Diabetes Cookbook
Everything® Easy Gourmet Cookbook
Everything® Fondue Cookbook
Everything® Food Allergy Cookbook, $15.95
Everything® Fondue Party Book
Everything® Gluten-Free Cookbook
Everything® Glycemic Index Cookbook
Everything® Grilling Cookbook
Everything® Healthy Cooking for Parties Book, $15.95
Everything® Holiday Cookbook
Everything® Indian Cookbook
Everything® Lactose-Free Cookbook
Everything® Low-Cholesterol Cookbook

Everything® Low-Fat High-Flavor Cookbook, 2nd Ed., $15.95
Everything® Low-Salt Cookbook
Everything® Meals for a Month Cookbook
Everything® Meals on a Budget Cookbook
Everything® Mediterranean Cookbook
Everything® Mexican Cookbook
Everything® No Trans Fat Cookbook
Everything® One-Pot Cookbook, 2nd Ed., $15.95
Everything® Organic Cooking for Baby & Toddler Book, $15.95
Everything® Pizza Cookbook
Everything® Quick Meals Cookbook, 2nd Ed., $15.95
Everything® Slow Cooker Cookbook
Everything® Slow Cooking for a Crowd Cookbook
Everything® Soup Cookbook
Everything® Stir-Fry Cookbook
Everything® Sugar-Free Cookbook
Everything® Tapas and Small Plates Cookbook
Everything® Tex-Mex Cookbook
Everything® Thai Cookbook
Everything® Vegetarian Cookbook
Everything® Whole-Grain, High-Fiber Cookbook
Everything® Wild Game Cookbook
Everything® Wine Book, 2nd Ed.

GAMES

Everything® 15-Minute Sudoku Book, $9.95
Everything® 30-Minute Sudoku Book, $9.95
Everything® Bible Crosswords Book, $9.95
Everything® Blackjack Strategy Book
Everything® Brain Strain Book, $9.95
Everything® Bridge Book
Everything® Card Games Book
Everything® Card Tricks Book, $9.95
Everything® Casino Gambling Book, 2nd Ed.
Everything® Chess Basics Book
Everything® Christmas Crosswords Book, $9.95
Everything® Craps Strategy Book
Everything® Crossword and Puzzle Book
Everything® Crosswords and Puzzles for Quote Lovers Book, $9.95
Everything® Crossword Challenge Book
Everything® Crosswords for the Beach Book, $9.95
Everything® Cryptic Crosswords Book, $9.95
Everything® Cryptograms Book, $9.95
Everything® Easy Crosswords Book
Everything® Easy Kakuro Book, $9.95
Everything® Easy Large-Print Crosswords Book
Everything® Games Book, 2nd Ed.
Everything® Giant Book of Crosswords
Everything® Giant Sudoku Book, $9.95
Everything® Giant Word Search Book
Everything® Kakuro Challenge Book, $9.95
Everything® Large-Print Crossword Challenge Book
Everything® Large-Print Crosswords Book
Everything® Large-Print Travel Crosswords Book
Everything® Lateral Thinking Puzzles Book, $9.95
Everything® Literary Crosswords Book, $9.95
Everything® Mazes Book
Everything® Memory Booster Puzzles Book, $9.95

Everything® Movie Crosswords Book, $9.95
Everything® Music Crosswords Book, $9.95
Everything® Online Poker Book
Everything® Pencil Puzzles Book, $9.95
Everything® Poker Strategy Book
Everything® Pool & Billiards Book
Everything® Puzzles for Commuters Book, $9.95
Everything® Puzzles for Dog Lovers Book, $9.95
Everything® Sports Crosswords Book, $9.95
Everything® Test Your IQ Book, $9.95
Everything® Texas Hold 'Em Book, $9.95
Everything® Travel Crosswords Book, $9.95
Everything® Travel Mazes Book, $9.95
Everything® Travel Word Search Book, $9.95
Everything® TV Crosswords Book, $9.95
Everything® Word Games Challenge Book
Everything® Word Scramble Book
Everything® Word Search Book

HEALTH

Everything® Alzheimer's Book
Everything® Diabetes Book
Everything® First Aid Book, $9.95
Everything® Green Living Book
Everything® Health Guide to Addiction and Recovery
Everything® Health Guide to Adult Bipolar Disorder
Everything® Health Guide to Arthritis
Everything® Health Guide to Controlling Anxiety
Everything® Health Guide to Depression
Everything® Health Guide to Diabetes, 2nd Ed.
Everything® Health Guide to Fibromyalgia
Everything® Health Guide to Menopause, 2nd Ed.
Everything® Health Guide to Migraines
Everything® Health Guide to Multiple Sclerosis
Everything® Health Guide to OCD
Everything® Health Guide to PMS
Everything® Health Guide to Postpartum Care
Everything® Health Guide to Thyroid Disease
Everything® Hypnosis Book
Everything® Low Cholesterol Book
Everything® Menopause Book
Everything® Nutrition Book
Everything® Reflexology Book
Everything® Stress Management Book
Everything® Superfoods Book, $15.95

HISTORY

Everything® American Government Book
Everything® American History Book, 2nd Ed.
Everything® American Revolution Book, $15.95
Everything® Civil War Book
Everything® Freemasons Book
Everything® Irish History & Heritage Book
Everything® World War II Book, 2nd Ed.

HOBBIES

Everything® Candlemaking Book
Everything® Cartooning Book
Everything® Coin Collecting Book
Everything® Digital Photography Book, 2nd Ed.

Everything® Drawing Book
Everything® Family Tree Book, 2nd Ed.
Everything® Guide to Online Genealogy, $15.95
Everything® Knitting Book
Everything® Knots Book
Everything® Photography Book
Everything® Quilting Book
Everything® Sewing Book
Everything® Soapmaking Book, 2nd Ed.
Everything® Woodworking Book

HOME IMPROVEMENT

Everything® Feng Shui Book
Everything® Feng Shui Decluttering Book, $9.95
Everything® Fix-It Book
Everything® Green Living Book
Everything® Home Decorating Book
Everything® Home Storage Solutions Book
Everything® Homebuilding Book
Everything® Organize Your Home Book, 2nd Ed.

KIDS' BOOKS

All titles are $7.95
Everything® Fairy Tales Book, $14.95
Everything® Kids' Animal Puzzle & Activity Book
Everything® Kids' Astronomy Book
Everything® Kids' Baseball Book, 5th Ed.
Everything® Kids' Bible Trivia Book
Everything® Kids' Bugs Book
Everything® Kids' Cars and Trucks Puzzle and Activity Book
Everything® Kids' Christmas Puzzle & Activity Book
Everything® Kids' Connect the Dots
	Puzzle and Activity Book
Everything® Kids' Cookbook, 2nd Ed.
Everything® Kids' Crazy Puzzles Book
Everything® Kids' Dinosaurs Book
Everything® Kids' Dragons Puzzle and Activity Book
Everything® Kids' Environment Book $7.95
Everything® Kids' Fairies Puzzle and Activity Book
Everything® Kids' First Spanish Puzzle and Activity Book
Everything® Kids' Football Book
Everything® Kids' Geography Book
Everything® Kids' Gross Cookbook
Everything® Kids' Gross Hidden Pictures Book
Everything® Kids' Gross Jokes Book
Everything® Kids' Gross Mazes Book
Everything® Kids' Gross Puzzle & Activity Book
Everything® Kids' Halloween Puzzle & Activity Book
Everything® Kids' Hanukkah Puzzle and Activity Book
Everything® Kids' Hidden Pictures Book
Everything® Kids' Horses Book
Everything® Kids' Joke Book
Everything® Kids' Knock Knock Book
Everything® Kids' Learning French Book
Everything® Kids' Learning Spanish Book
Everything® Kids' Magical Science Experiments Book
Everything® Kids' Math Puzzles Book
Everything® Kids' Mazes Book
Everything® Kids' Money Book, 2nd Ed.
Everything® Kids' Mummies, Pharaoh's, and Pyramids
	Puzzle and Activity Book
Everything® Kids' Nature Book
Everything® Kids' Pirates Puzzle and Activity Book
Everything® Kids' Presidents Book
Everything® Kids' Princess Puzzle and Activity Book
Everything® Kids' Puzzle Book

Everything® Kids' Racecars Puzzle and Activity Book
Everything® Kids' Riddles & Brain Teasers Book
Everything® Kids' Science Experiments Book
Everything® Kids' Sharks Book
Everything® Kids' Soccer Book
Everything® Kids' Spelling Book
Everything® Kids' Spies Puzzle and Activity Book
Everything® Kids' States Book
Everything® Kids' Travel Activity Book
Everything® Kids' Word Search Puzzle and Activity Book

LANGUAGE

Everything® Conversational Japanese Book with CD, $19.95
Everything® French Grammar Book
Everything® French Phrase Book, $9.95
Everything® French Verb Book, $9.95
Everything® German Phrase Book, $9.95
Everything® German Practice Book with CD, $19.95
Everything® Inglés Book
Everything® Intermediate Spanish Book with CD, $19.95
Everything® Italian Phrase Book, $9.95
Everything® Italian Practice Book with CD, $19.95
Everything® Learning Brazilian Portuguese Book with CD, $19.95
Everything® Learning French Book with CD, 2nd Ed., $19.95
Everything® Learning German Book
Everything® Learning Italian Book
Everything® Learning Latin Book
Everything® Learning Russian Book with CD, $19.95
Everything® Learning Spanish Book
Everything® Learning Spanish Book with CD, 2nd Ed., $19.95
Everything® Russian Practice Book with CD, $19.95
Everything® Sign Language Book, $15.95
Everything® Spanish Grammar Book
Everything® Spanish Phrase Book, $9.95
Everything® Spanish Practice Book with CD, $19.95
Everything® Spanish Verb Book, $9.95
Everything® Speaking Mandarin Chinese Book with CD, $19.95

MUSIC

Everything® Bass Guitar Book with CD, $19.95
Everything® Drums Book with CD, $19.95
Everything® Guitar Book with CD, 2nd Ed., $19.95
Everything® Guitar Chords Book with CD, $19.95
Everything® Guitar Scales Book with CD, $19.95
Everything® Harmonica Book with CD, $15.95
Everything® Home Recording Book
Everything® Music Theory Book with CD, $19.95
Everything® Reading Music Book with CD, $19.95
Everything® Rock & Blues Guitar Book with CD, $19.95
Everything® Rock & Blues Piano Book with CD, $19.95
Everything® Rock Drums Book with CD, $19.95
Everything® Singing Book with CD, $19.95
Everything® Songwriting Book

NEW AGE

Everything® Astrology Book, 2nd Ed.
Everything® Birthday Personology Book
Everything® Celtic Wisdom Book, $15.95
Everything® Dreams Book, 2nd Ed.
Everything® Law of Attraction Book, $15.95
Everything® Love Signs Book, $9.95
Everything® Love Spells Book, $9.95
Everything® Palmistry Book
Everything® Psychic Book
Everything® Reiki Book

Everything® Sex Signs Book, $9.95
Everything® Spells & Charms Book, 2nd Ed.
Everything® Tarot Book, 2nd Ed.
Everything® Toltec Wisdom Book
Everything® Wicca & Witchcraft Book, 2nd Ed.

PARENTING

Everything® Baby Names Book, 2nd Ed.
Everything® Baby Shower Book, 2nd Ed.
Everything® Baby Sign Language Book with DVD
Everything® Baby's First Year Book
Everything® Birthing Book
Everything® Breastfeeding Book
Everything® Father-to-Be Book
Everything® Father's First Year Book
Everything® Get Ready for Baby Book, 2nd Ed.
Everything® Get Your Baby to Sleep Book, $9.95
Everything® Getting Pregnant Book
Everything® Guide to Pregnancy Over 35
Everything® Guide to Raising a One-Year-Old
Everything® Guide to Raising a Two-Year-Old
Everything® Guide to Raising Adolescent Boys
Everything® Guide to Raising Adolescent Girls
Everything® Mother's First Year Book
Everything® Parent's Guide to Childhood Illnesses
Everything® Parent's Guide to Children and Divorce
Everything® Parent's Guide to Children with ADD/ADHD
Everything® Parent's Guide to Children with Asperger's
	Syndrome
Everything® Parent's Guide to Children with Anxiety
Everything® Parent's Guide to Children with Asthma
Everything® Parent's Guide to Children with Autism
Everything® Parent's Guide to Children with Bipolar Disorder
Everything® Parent's Guide to Children with Depression
Everything® Parent's Guide to Children with Dyslexia
Everything® Parent's Guide to Children with Juvenile Diabetes
Everything® Parent's Guide to Children with OCD
Everything® Parent's Guide to Positive Discipline
Everything® Parent's Guide to Raising Boys
Everything® Parent's Guide to Raising Girls
Everything® Parent's Guide to Raising Siblings
Everything® Parent's Guide to Raising Your
	Adopted Child
Everything® Parent's Guide to Sensory Integration Disorder
Everything® Parent's Guide to Tantrums
Everything® Parent's Guide to the Strong-Willed Child
Everything® Parenting a Teenager Book
Everything® Potty Training Book, $9.95
Everything® Pregnancy Book, 3rd Ed.
Everything® Pregnancy Fitness Book
Everything® Pregnancy Nutrition Book
Everything® Pregnancy Organizer, 2nd Ed., $16.95
Everything® Toddler Activities Book
Everything® Toddler Book
Everything® Tween Book
Everything® Twins, Triplets, and More Book

PETS

Everything® Aquarium Book
Everything® Boxer Book
Everything® Cat Book, 2nd Ed.
Everything® Chihuahua Book
Everything® Cooking for Dogs Book
Everything® Dachshund Book
Everything® Dog Book, 2nd Ed.
Everything® Dog Grooming Book

Everything® Dog Obedience Book
Everything® Dog Owner's Organizer, $16.95
Everything® Dog Training and Tricks Book
Everything® German Shepherd Book
Everything® Golden Retriever Book
Everything® Horse Book, 2nd Ed., $15.95
Everything® Horse Care Book
Everything® Horseback Riding Book
Everything® Labrador Retriever Book
Everything® Poodle Book
Everything® Pug Book
Everything® Puppy Book
Everything® Small Dogs Book
Everything® Tropical Fish Book
Everything® Yorkshire Terrier Book

REFERENCE

Everything® American Presidents Book
Everything® Blogging Book
Everything® Build Your Vocabulary Book, $9.95
Everything® Car Care Book
Everything® Classical Mythology Book
Everything® Da Vinci Book
Everything® Einstein Book
Everything® Enneagram Book
Everything® Etiquette Book, 2nd Ed.
Everything® Family Christmas Book, $15.95
Everything® Guide to C. S. Lewis & Narnia
Everything® Guide to Divorce, 2nd Ed., $15.95
Everything® Guide to Edgar Allan Poe
Everything® Guide to Understanding Philosophy
Everything® Inventions and Patents Book
Everything® Jacqueline Kennedy Onassis Book
Everything® John F. Kennedy Book
Everything® Mafia Book
Everything® Martin Luther King Jr. Book
Everything® Pirates Book
Everything® Private Investigation Book
Everything® Psychology Book
Everything® Public Speaking Book, $9.95
Everything® Shakespeare Book, 2nd Ed.

RELIGION

Everything® Angels Book
Everything® Bible Book
Everything® Bible Study Book with CD, $19.95
Everything® Buddhism Book
Everything® Catholicism Book
Everything® Christianity Book
Everything® Gnostic Gospels Book
Everything® Hinduism Book, $15.95
Everything® History of the Bible Book
Everything® Jesus Book
Everything® Jewish History & Heritage Book
Everything® Judaism Book
Everything® Kabbalah Book
Everything® Koran Book
Everything® Mary Book
Everything® Mary Magdalene Book
Everything® Prayer Book

Everything® Saints Book, 2nd Ed.
Everything® Torah Book
Everything® Understanding Islam Book
Everything® Women of the Bible Book
Everything® World's Religions Book

SCHOOL & CAREERS

Everything® Career Tests Book
Everything® College Major Test Book
Everything® College Survival Book, 2nd Ed.
Everything® Cover Letter Book, 2nd Ed.
Everything® Filmmaking Book
Everything® Get-a-Job Book, 2nd Ed.
Everything® Guide to Being a Paralegal
Everything® Guide to Being a Personal Trainer
Everything® Guide to Being a Real Estate Agent
Everything® Guide to Being a Sales Rep
Everything® Guide to Being an Event Planner
Everything® Guide to Careers in Health Care
Everything® Guide to Careers in Law Enforcement
Everything® Guide to Government Jobs
Everything® Guide to Starting and Running a Catering
    Business
Everything® Guide to Starting and Running a Restaurant
**Everything® Guide to Starting and Running
    a Retail Store**
Everything® Job Interview Book, 2nd Ed.
Everything® New Nurse Book
Everything® New Teacher Book
Everything® Paying for College Book
Everything® Practice Interview Book
Everything® Resume Book, 3rd Ed.
Everything® Study Book

SELF-HELP

Everything® Body Language Book
Everything® Dating Book, 2nd Ed.
Everything® Great Sex Book
**Everything® Guide to Caring for Aging Parents,
    $15.95**
Everything® Self-Esteem Book
Everything® Self-Hypnosis Book, $9.95
Everything® Tantric Sex Book

SPORTS & FITNESS

Everything® Easy Fitness Book
Everything® Fishing Book
Everything® Guide to Weight Training, $15.95
Everything® Krav Maga for Fitness Book
Everything® Running Book, 2nd Ed.
Everything® Triathlon Training Book, $15.95

TRAVEL

Everything® Family Guide to Coastal Florida
Everything® Family Guide to Cruise Vacations
Everything® Family Guide to Hawaii
Everything® Family Guide to Las Vegas, 2nd Ed.
Everything® Family Guide to Mexico
Everything® Family Guide to New England, 2nd Ed.

Everything® Family Guide to New York City, 3rd Ed.
**Everything® Family Guide to Northern California
    and Lake Tahoe**
Everything® Family Guide to RV Travel & Campgrounds
Everything® Family Guide to the Caribbean
Everything® Family Guide to the Disneyland® Resort, California
    Adventure®, Universal Studios®, and the Anaheim
    Area, 2nd Ed.
Everything® Family Guide to the Walt Disney World Resort®,
    Universal Studios®, and Greater Orlando, 5th Ed.
Everything® Family Guide to Timeshares
Everything® Family Guide to Washington D.C., 2nd Ed.

WEDDINGS

Everything® Bachelorette Party Book, $9.95
Everything® Bridesmaid Book, $9.95
Everything® Destination Wedding Book
Everything® Father of the Bride Book, $9.95
Everything® Green Wedding Book, $15.95
Everything® Groom Book, $9.95
Everything® Jewish Wedding Book, 2nd Ed., $15.95
Everything® Mother of the Bride Book, $9.95
Everything® Outdoor Wedding Book
Everything® Wedding Book, 3rd Ed.
Everything® Wedding Checklist, $9.95
Everything® Wedding Etiquette Book, $9.95
Everything® Wedding Organizer, 2nd Ed., $16.95
Everything® Wedding Shower Book, $9.95
Everything® Wedding Vows Book, 3rd Ed., $9.95
Everything® Wedding Workout Book
Everything® Weddings on a Budget Book, 2nd Ed., $9.95

WRITING

Everything® Creative Writing Book
Everything® Get Published Book, 2nd Ed.
Everything® Grammar and Style Book, 2nd Ed.
Everything® Guide to Magazine Writing
Everything® Guide to Writing a Book Proposal
Everything® Guide to Writing a Novel
Everything® Guide to Writing Children's Books
Everything® Guide to Writing Copy
Everything® Guide to Writing Graphic Novels
Everything® Guide to Writing Research Papers
Everything® Guide to Writing a Romance Novel, $15.95
Everything® Improve Your Writing Book, 2nd Ed.
Everything® Writing Poetry Book